FOUNDATION

NOIR CITY®

OFFICIAL MAGAZINE OF THE FILM NOIR FOUNDATION

ANNUAL TWELVE

The Best of **NOIR CITY** e-magazine

2019

PUBLISHED BY THE FILM NOIR FOUNDATION
San Francisco | Los Angeles | New York

NOIR CITY ANNUAL 12: The Best of NOIR CITY 2019

All proceeds from the sale of this book go directly to the non-profit Film Noir Foundation's mission to find and preserve *films noir* in danger of deterioration, damage or loss, and to ensure that high quality prints of these classic films remain in circulation for, we hope, theatrical exhibition to future generations.

Interested in contributing to *NOIR CITY e-magazine*? Contact us at mailbox@filmnoirfoundation.org. Accepted submissions are published with the permission of the authors and the Film Noir Foundation claims no exclusive rights to the material.

FIRST EDITION

Cover art and book design by Michael Kronenberg

ISBN 978-0-578-61783-1

FRONT COVER: Gene Tierney in *Leave Her to Heaven* (1945), art by Michael Kronenberg

FRONTISPIECE: Burt Lancaster in *The Killers* (1946)

BACK COVER: *The Lady from Shanghai* (1947), lobby card

INTRODUCTION

WHO OWNS NOIR?

The Film Noir Foundation enjoyed another productive and exciting year in 2019, despite a sense of growing unease in the culture at large about the fate, not just of noir, but of classic (re: "old") movies. I wish everyone felt the way Martin Scorsese does—"There are no 'old' films, they're just movies you haven't seen yet." Truthfully, the unease I'm referring to doesn't really exist in the culture "at large." It exists within an ever-expanding group of savvy and sophisticated cinephiles that is, paradoxically, perceived as increasingly marginal by the massive corporations that own classic cinema.

As anyone who has searched for a classic film on Netflix or Amazon knows, their idea of "classic" extends all the way back to 1990. When AT&T acquired TimeWarner Media—after assuring Congress the massive merger would give consumers more options and competitive pricing in its entertainment choices, the telecom giant's first major move was to pull the plug on FilmStruck, an eclectic on-line cinema service created through a partnership of Turner Classic Movies (now in the AT&T fold) and The Criterion Collection[1]. A backlash erupted, led by some of the world's most prominent filmmakers. It accomplished little. AT&T quelled the controversy by alleging classic films would be part of a new "three-tiered" streaming service it was devising. That service is called HBO Max—a major tip-off as to AT&T's priorities. There is no indication yet how—or if—classic films will be part of the service.

As the dust from FilmStruck's demise was settling, another *major* merger happened: The Disney Company acquired 20th Century–Fox. The deal included, of course, the entire Fox film library. Within weeks I heard from repertory theater programmers around the country that Disney was shutting the Fox vaults; prints of Fox titles would, with rare exceptions, no longer be available for theatrical screening. As of this writing, we have yet to see the impact this will have on entities like TCM, which has licensed Fox films as part of its repertoire for 25 years. One startling aspect of the Disney decision is now coming to light—Fox classics are being shopped to contemporary filmmakers as fodder for remakes: a new version of *Laura* is in development, and Guillermo del Toro is remaking *Nightmare Alley*. I personally know other filmmakers who have been given the Fox film catalog for the express purpose of culling remake material.

What's infuriating isn't the notion of remakes—that's always happened. It's the prospect of mega-companies electing to deep-six the originals. I'm not being an alarmist. There is precedent. When a film like MGM's *Rogue Cop* (1954) or RKO's *The Devil Thumbs a Ride* (1947) goes AWOL, it's not really missing, it's just held hostage, typically by studios that don't want to pay the legal fees involved in clearing up issues with copyright or underlying literary rights. Quite simply, it would cost more to pay lawyers to resolve such issues than they'd ever see in receipts from Blu-ray sales or streaming licenses. Or so they think. So the films are abandoned.

As Netflix, Disney, AT&T, Amazon, Comcast, and a few others jockey to dominate a future where streaming is the public's preferred viewing method, the numbers will never add up for "old movies."

---

1 Criterion has soldiered on alone, drawing largely on its own catalog of international and art house titles. The Criterion Channel is indispensable for adventurous cinephiles.

In a world where on-line "hits" determine what is available for viewing, there is no way *Mildred Pierce* can compete with the latest Twitter-driven media darling—and those darlings are all these companies really care about.

This wouldn't be a dire situation if the market was rational, and there was a safe haven where movie lovers could find older films as conveniently as they call up *anything* from the last ten years on Netflix or Amazon. (I hope that TCM maintains that role, but we'll have to see …)

And this brings up the biggest issue of all, one largely unreported in the media (it's had a few other issues to obsess over). For all intents and purposes, the companies I've been talking about are now today's version of the "Golden Age" studios—they aren't merely distributing "content" to your home theater (re: computer), they are *making* the content as well. In other words, *vertical integration*—control of the manufacture, distribution, and exhibition of films. What Columbia boss Harry Cohn once called "the world's biggest racket."

Vertical integration *was* a racket; that's why the U.S. government outlawed it in the landmark 1948 "Paramount Decree," which prohibited studios from monopolizing the market by owning the content, distribution channel, and exhibition venue—precisely what's happening today. And wouldn't you know it—the U.S. Justice Department under the current administration is overturning the Paramount Decree, claiming modern technology has rendered it obsolete. In truth, such antitrust legislation is more essential than ever, given that at no time has America's cinematic legacy been controlled by so few entities, none of which have exhibited any concern for its cultural significance, only its profit potential.

The Film Noir Foundation can't fight the government, or the corporations that own our film history. They can snuff out that history, gradually or suddenly, if that's what they want to do—because that's how the game is being rigged. But *we* will continue our mission: educating, inspiring, edifying and, most gloriously, restoring films that would otherwise be lost. The latest resurrections, both from Argentina, *The Beast Must Die* (1952, *La bestia debe morir*) and *The Black Vampire* (1953, *El vampiro negro*) were the most dramatic rescues yet—each was only months from decaying beyond reclamation. Now they are completely restored, almost good as new, and ready to be discovered by that ever-expanding group of savvy and sophisticated cinephiles who care about the art of noir enough to donate to its salvation—unlike some mega-corporations I could mention.

—*Eddie Muller*

El vampiro negro (1953), a dazzling reimagining of Fritz Lang's *M*, is one of two restorations of Argentine noir classics debuting in 2020. Shown are Nelly Panizza and Nathán Pinzón, a popular comedic actor daringly cast against type as the killer. Román Viñoly Barreto directed both this and the FNF's other new restoration, *La bestia debe morir* (*The Beast Must Die*, 1952)

SHAMUS DUST

HARD WINTER   COLD WAR   COOL MURDER

JANET ROGER

"Janet Roger doesn't better Chandler, but she runs him pretty damn close with a taut and poetic style that never fails to shimmer..."
Fully Booked

BEVERLY HILLS
BOOK AWARDS™
WINNER
Crime Fiction 2019

janetroger.com

HOW THE F.B.I. TOOK A CHA

Pickup

with MURVY
WILLIS B.

starring RICHARD WIDMARK · JEA

CE ON A B-GIRL...AND WON!

ON SOUTH STREET

20th CENTURY-FOX

RICHARD KILEY
Y · MILBURN STONE · PRODUCED BY JULES SCHERMER · DIRECTED BY SAMUEL FULLER · SCREEN PLAY BY SAMUEL FULLER · FROM A STORY BY DWIGHT TAYLOR

PETERS · THELMA RITTER

Robert De Niro in
Taxi Driver (1976)

TABLE OF CONTENTS

ESSAYS

66

182

226

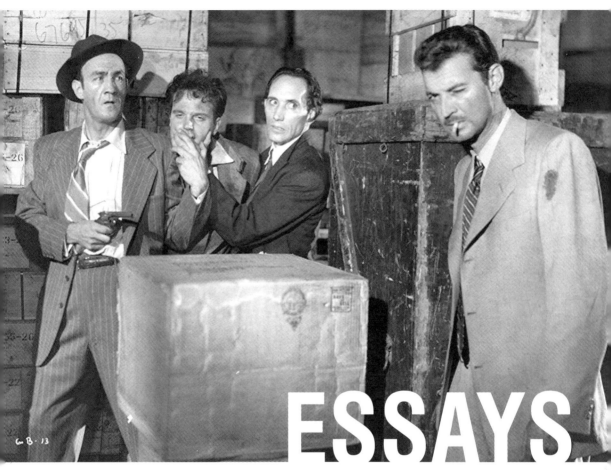

ESSAYS

SECTION ONE

Booze and Blackouts in Film Noir

HUNGOVER

Jake Hinkson

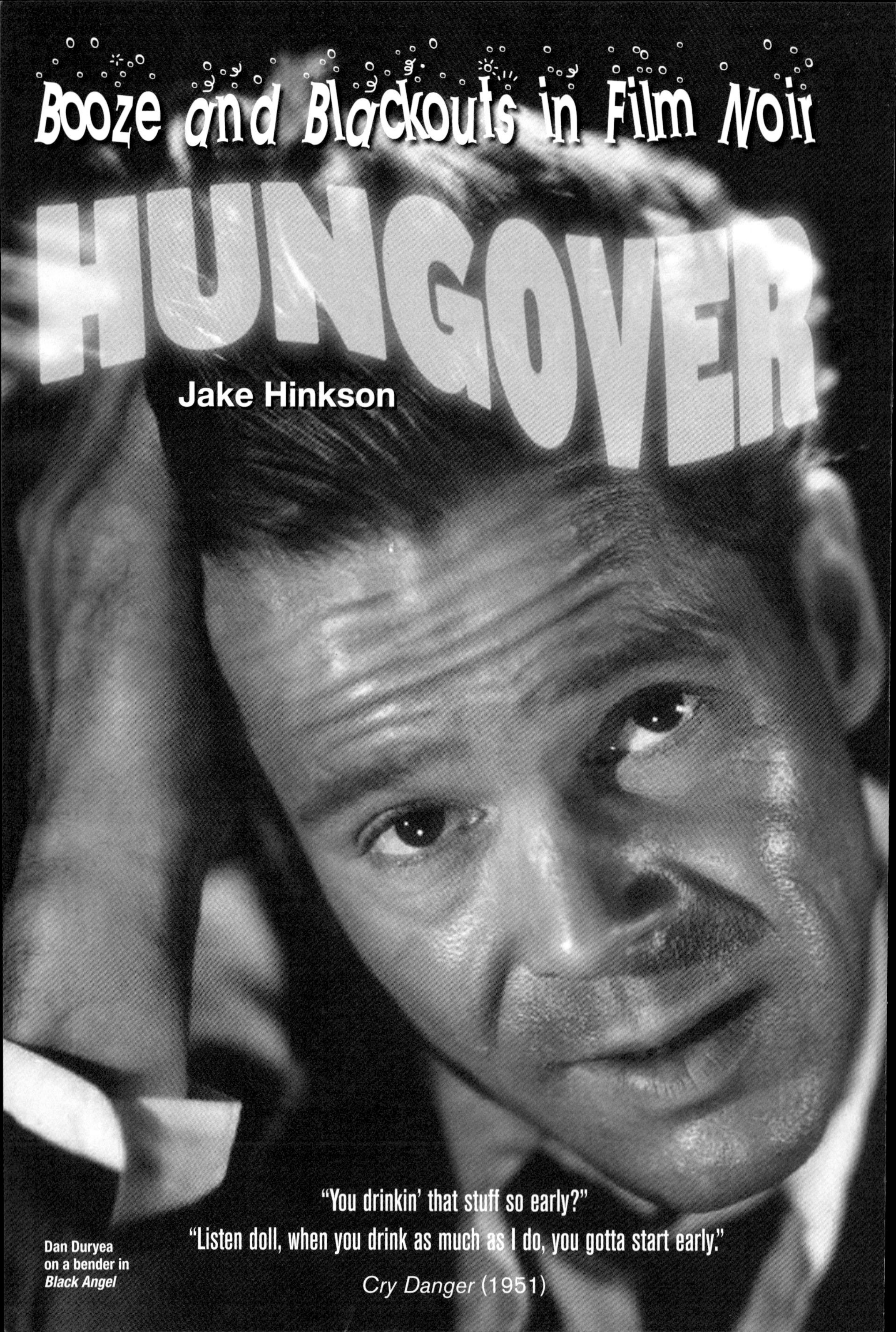

Dan Duryea
on a bender in
Black Angel

"You drinkin' that stuff so early?"
"Listen doll, when you drink as much as I do, you gotta start early."

Cry Danger (1951)

Recall, if you will, the 1949 mystery *D.O.A.* It has one of noir's juiciest setups: after a hard night of drinking, an accountant played by Edmond O'Brien wakes up to discover that someone has slipped him a fatal poison. "I don't think you understand," explains a doctor with zero bedside manner—"You've been murdered." With such a gonzo plot, it's easy to overlook the importance of *D.O.A.*'s boozy first act, which follows O'Brien as he goes on a boisterous bar crawl looking for sex with a group of smashed out-of-town salespeople. These opening scenes set up an edgy world of free-flowing liquor and the dangerous temptations that accompany it. This is the place where many noirs begin, and while O'Brien's situation may be extreme, he's far from the only guy in a film noir who ever woke up wondering what the hell happened the night before.

In fact, because alcohol is as elemental to noir as chiaroscuro and cigarettes, this is a fairly common occurrence. Characters drink when they're doing everything from making love to hatching bank heists. They drink when they're happy and they drink when they're sad. Usually, the drinking itself is not seen in a negative light. It's just something people do. Occasionally, though, all this drinking carries a real cost.

Take, for instance, the familiar figure of the boozer. Always in his cups, and usually lost in some dream of long-faded glory, the boozer helps establish an atmosphere of weakness and doom. Think of Robert Warwick's drunk thespian spouting off slurred pronouncements in *In a Lonely Place* (1950), or Jay Novello's disgraced alkie doctor cradling his dogs in *Crime Wave* (1954), or Ian Keith's drunken circus-show clairvoyant drinking his way to his doom in *Nightmare Alley* (1947). All these guys, and many more like them, establish the noir universe as a place where actions have consequences. A movie doesn't have to preach many sermons against alcohol with these living wrecks staggering around.

On the distaff side, no one portrayed gin-soaked women quite as convincingly as Esther Howard, memorable as Jessie Florian in *Murder, My Sweet*

The boozer queen was undoubtedly Esther Howard. An accomplished comedienne (she was a near-constant presence in the comedies of Preston Sturges throughout the 1940s), in the dark world of noir she's best remembered for playing drunks like the tricky Jessie Florian in *Murder, My Sweet* (1944) and *Born to Kill*'s (1947) boozy boardinghouse owner, Mrs. Kraft. Howard's gift in these brief roles is to be both broadly funny and yet somehow touching at the same time, bringing pathos to something that could have been played merely for cheap laughs. With her wasted stare and marbled voice, Howard always seems tethered to some ancient hurt. We know she's drinking to forget something. Or someone.

Of course, it wasn't all so dark. The glorious Elsa Lanchester steals *Mystery Street* (1950) away from stars Ricardo Montalban and Sally Forrest as Mrs. Smerrling, the boozy boardinghouse owner turned blackmailer who disrupts the best-laid plans of both the police and the killer they're pursuing. Stashing her liquor bottles in drawers and snooping around in the lives of her tenants, she supplies this otherwise stolid procedural with a wickedly funny heart. While the film was designed as an early progenitor of the CSI-based mystery, Mrs. Smerrling unleashes a chaotic galaxy of tipsy eccentricity every time she shows up on-screen, supplying wit and energy to balance out all the deadly talk of fibers and bone fractures.

Hands down the funniest drunk in film noir is Delong, the one-legged ex-Marine played with dry martini wit by Richard Erdman in *Cry Danger* (1951). The bleary-eyed Delong tags along with freshly sprung ex-con Rocky Mulloy (Dick Powell) because he's hoping to get a piece of some missing loot, and also because he needs something to do between binges. Screenwriter William Bowers gives Mulloy and Delong enough snappy dialogue to fill two movies:

Mulloy: You're a pint ahead of schedule.
Delong: Only the blind can really see.
Mulloy: Well, you're only half blind.
Delong: I'll fix that.
Mulloy: You know, I had another friend once who had trouble with that stuff. He found a way to get off of it.
Delong: How?
Mulloy: He quit.
Delong: Thank you, Billy Sunday.

While noir storytellers didn't deliver a lot of temperance lectures, they did love repeating a winning formula, and they knew they'd found one in what we might call the blackout noir. In these films,

Regis Toomey and Dick Powell consider the astounding alcohol consumption of Richard Erdman in *Cry Danger*. Erdman's bourbon-fueled character was a self-parody of the film's screenwriter, William Bowers, who preferred working with adult libations at hand

the boozer takes center stage and their troubled drinking drives the plot. Here, sweaty, disheveled drunks are forced to wrestle with the demon in the bottle, and booze isn't just a sexy prop in a seduction scene—it's the poison at the center of the protagonist's life.

The key blackout noir is 1946's *Black Angel*. We meet alcoholic songwriter Marty Blair (Dan Duryea) as he's trying to get into the apartment building of his duplicitous ex-wife Mavis (Constance Dowling). Bounced by a vigilant doorman, he hits the bars and gets blasted out of his mind. Later that night, Mavis is murdered. Her married boyfriend, Kirk Bennett (John Phillips), is convicted of the crime, but Bennett's forgiving wife Catherine (June Vincent) sets out to find the real killer. She enlists the aid of boozy Marty, who tries to help her but ends up falling in love with her. When Catherine rejects Marty's declaration of love, he does what he does best—he goes out and gets hammered. This time, however, the binge *triggers* his memories, and in a gripping flashback it is revealed Marty is the one who murdered Mavis.

The predominant theme of the blackout noir is guilt. The guy coming out of his blackout is tormented by the creeping suspicion that he did something wrong, a powerful feeling even when it turns out to be baseless. *Black Angel* is notable because it's one of the few blackout noirs where this guilt is earned. Directed by Roy William Neill from a screenplay by Roy Chanslor, the film marked a departure for star Dan Duryea, who had just been thrust to fame playing unrepentant sleazes for Fritz Lang in *The Woman in the Window* (1944) and *Scarlet Street* (1945). Here, he's haunted, though he can't say why until it's too late. The sexy Dangerous Dan spark is gone, replaced by a heavier kind of charisma—the palpable aura of doom.[1]

If we had to trace the blackout noir back to the psychosis (and drinking) of one man, it would be writer Cornell Woolrich. Alcoholic and deeply self-loathing, Woolrich was the source of the plot for *Black Angel* (based on his novel), as well as *Fall Guy* ((1947) based on his story "C-Jag") about another drink-and-drug-fueled blackout. Importantly, though, he also practically invented the subgenre of amnesia noir (*Street of Chance* [1942], *Fear in the Night* [1947], and *Nightmare* [1956] where all made from his work). The plots of those films operate like metaphorical blackouts, the same sense of bewildered guilt covering everything like a fog. Men wake up covered in blood or haunted by visions

---

1   Duryea would give one of his best performances as another tortured alcoholic in *Chicago Calling* (1951).

June Vincent and Dan Duryea in the Cornell Woolrich penned thriller *Black Angel*

Novelist Cornell Woolrich, himself a prodigious drinker, wrote a plethora of stories in which booze, guilt, and memory loss spurred the suspenseful plots

of violence, always wondering the same thing, "What did I do last night? What did I do?"

One of the most important figures in the development of noir, Woolrich had a worldview more despondent and disturbed than any crime writer of his era. After a disastrous marriage when he was young (it ended when he went missing for a few days and his wife discovered a diary in which he detailed his sexual encounters with other men), he took up permanent residence in a ratty hotel and churned out nightmare after nightmare, a decades-long avalanche of neurotic fiction. An obsessive writer, fixated on certain reoccurring themes rather than intricacies of plot, he seemed compelled to tell one particular story over and over again: a man awakens in a daze, unable to remember what happened the night before but plagued by a sick suspicion he has done something terrible.

How much of Woolrich's obsession with this nightmare scenario traced back to his own binge drinking and shadowy sexual life is anyone's guess, but the stories of his benders and disappearances are legendary. After Woolrich's death, the writer and editor Donald Yates would remember, "Back in the fifties … he had this habit of disappearing from his hotel for months at a time. Few people had any notion where he went. When he came back, it was evident he hadn't escaped anything." Eventually, his capacity to write was washed away by the near-constant river of booze running through him. A slow, painful decline followed, and Woolrich fell into his final restful sleep in 1968.[2]

2   Starting in 2009, the blackout plot Woolrich pioneered served as the basis for the dark comedy *The Hangover* and its highly successful sequels. A trilogy about three friends who get hammered and wake up in progressively more horrific situations, the series grossed $1.4 billion worldwide. One wonders what Woolrich would have made of this turn of events. Of all the variations of this plot he put into print, it never occurred to him to make it funny. Maybe that's because he didn't have a sense of humor (which he didn't), or maybe it's because in the Woolrich universe, you always wake up alone.

Zachary Scott shed his high-toned manners and sartorial splendor to play drunken dick Max Thursday in *Guilty Bystander*

Of course, Woolrich wasn't the only writer who took a crack at the blackout noir. Screenwriter and novelist (*Detour*) Martin Goldsmith wrote *Blind Spot* (1947), which tells the story of Jeffrey Andrews (Chester Morris), the boozy author of much-respected but little-bought "psychological novels." When his publisher suggests he write a mystery to increase sales, Andrews boasts that he'd never write such tripe. Before he storms out of the office, though, just to prove that he could write pop fiction if he wanted to, he improvises a locked-room mystery in which a publisher is found murdered inside his locked office. Satisfied he's made his point, Andrews saunters out and drinks himself into a blackout. The next morning, he awakens to the news that his publisher has been murdered exactly as he described. The driving force of Goldsmith's blackout plot isn't guilt as much as resentment, in particular the resentment of a working writer in Hollywood. *You have no idea*, the movie seems to be saying. *You'd drink, too.*

A much heavier work of booze and consequences is *Guilty Bystander* (1950) made by the husband-and-wife team of director Joseph Lerner and editor Geraldine Lerner. The film follows an alcoholic ex-cop named Max Thursday (Zachary Scott) as he searches for his missing child. *Guilty Bystander* must surely rank as one of the darkest noirs ever made. It's a cheap affair, tossed together on a small budget in New York, but it has real bite, mostly because it refuses to see Thursday's drinking as anything other than a plague on himself and his family.

The first stop on Max's search to find his child leads to a creepy doctor. The doctor offers him a drink. At first, Max refuses. Then he has one. Then two. Then three. Then the next thing we know, he's coming to in a jail cell. Fifteen minutes into his quest to find his missing child, our hero has gotten blackout drunk. This shame finally forces Max to clean up and get serious. Here, the blackout represents rock bottom, and the desperation of these scenes helps make *Guilty Bystander* one of noir's grittier looks at alcoholism.

Realism aside, the blackout plot serves two main functions. First, it sets up a mystery to be solved. In *Crossfire* (1947), a young soldier goes out drinking with his buddies on shore leave and blacks out. He awakens to find that a civilian has been murdered and all evidence points to him. In *Night without Sleep* (1952), a famous composer gone to seed on drink wakes up from a blackout with the unsettled feeling that he murdered a woman the night before. In *Blackout* (1954), an American ex-serviceman in London is getting blitzed one night when a pretty girl offers him 500 pounds to get married. Next thing he knows, he's waking up with blood on his clothes.

In each of these movies, the blackout is the plot device that moves the mystery into place. What's interesting, though, is the second function the blackout performs, which is thematic. Because the protagonist doesn't know what he's done (or hasn't done), the mystery is one of fraught self-discovery. Not only can't he trust the world around him, he can't even trust himself. And isn't that what noir is all about?

Even more than most films from the classic era, the blackout noir tends to be male-centric. One important exception to this drunken hegemony is *The Blue Gardenia* (1953). Depressed because she's just received a kiss-off letter from her fiancé stationed overseas, Norah Larkin (Anne Baxter) agrees to go on a date with creepy commercial artist Harry Prebble (Raymond Burr). First, Prebble gets her drunk, telling her that the fruity Polynesian Pearl Divers he keeps buying her are "mostly ice and pineapple." Then he takes her back to his place for a "party" with some "friends" supposedly on their way. By this point, when Norah is almost blacking out, Prebble sexually assaults her. She grabs a fireplace poker, lashes out at him, then loses consciousness. Sometime later, she stumbles out of the apartment in the rain, makes it home, and passes out. In the morning, Prebble's body is found, and a search begins for the woman who was with him.

Based on the excellent short story "The Gardenia" by Vera Caspary (*Laura*), *The Blue Gardenia* is a #MeToo movie before its time, a pointed look at sexual violence and gendered double standards. Caspary, a feminist who ended her 1979 autobiography *The Secrets of Grown Ups* with the hope, "In another generation, perhaps the next, equality will be taken for granted," might be surprised (or might not) to know how much her story and the film made from it feels like a headline from 2019. As the search for Prebble's killer splashes onto the front pages, Norah lives in a world of silent guilt, hiding what happened from her cheery roommates, racked with self-doubt. Was she responsible for what happened? What *did* happen? Will anyone believe her?

After a thematically satisfying conclusion, director Fritz Lang and his screenwriter Charles Hoffman fumble the epilogue with a clanking return to gender norms, cheerfully reestablishing the same lopsided order that has always enabled the Harry Prebbles of the world, both in Hollywood and beyond. Yet feminist critics and noirphiles have largely embraced the film for the way it takes the well-worn blackout murder trope and does something visceral and complex with it. Norah and her friends may be smiling at the end, but the film's unsettling vision lingers.

Ultimately, it's easy to see why so many intriguing noir plots have been based around drinking. The loosening of inhibitions is, after all, the place where most noir begins. The blackout plot, in particular, takes this notion a step further, asking what people are capable of once they lose all control. Untethered from whatever code of ethics we consciously adhere to, these films argue, the average person is capable of anything.

Have fun reflecting on these issues tonight over cocktails. Just be sure to drink responsibly and tip your bartender. ■

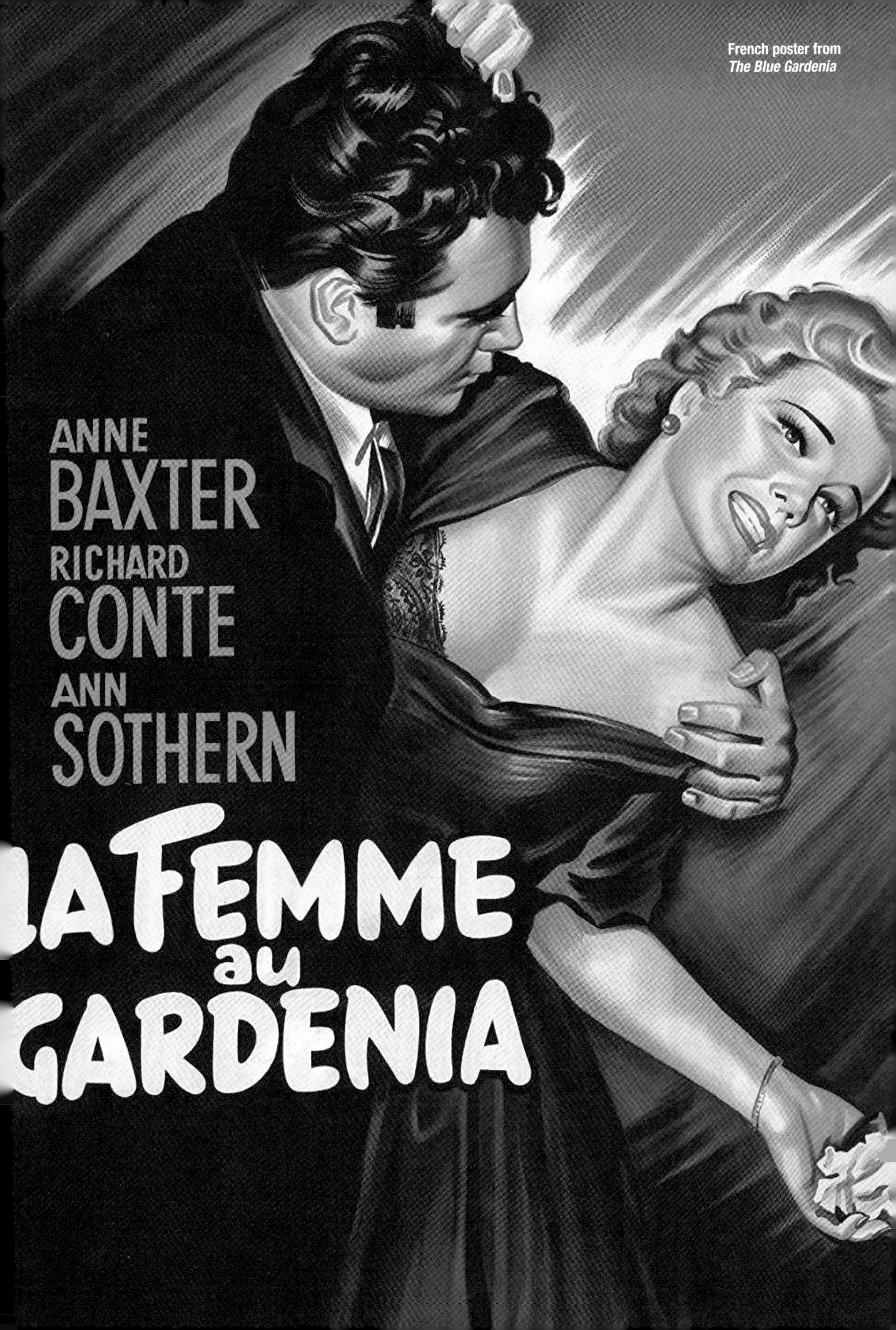

ANNE
BAXTER
RICHARD
CONTE
ANN
SOTHERN
LA FEMME
au
GARDENIA

French poster from
The Blue Gardenia

THE
CHICAGO
WAY

Alan K. Rode

How the Mob and the movie
studios sold out the Hollywood
labor movement and set the
stage for the Blacklist

In the early 1930s, Hollywood created an indelible image of the urban gangster. It is a pungent irony that, less than a decade later, the film industry would struggle to escape the vise-like grip of actual gangsters who threatened to bring the movie studios under its sinister control.

Criminal fiefdoms, created by an unholy trinity of Prohibition-era gangsters, ward-heeling politicians, and crooked law enforcement, infected numerous American metropolises —but Chicago was singularly venal. Everything and everybody in the Windy City was seemingly for sale. Al Capone's 1931 federal tax case conviction may have ended his reign as "Mr. Big," but his Outfit continued to grow, exerting its dominion over various trade unions. Mobsters siphoned off workers' dues, set up their cohorts with no-show jobs, and shook down businesses to maintain labor peace. Resistance by union officials was futile and sometimes fatal. At least 13 prominent Chicago labor leaders were killed; and not a single conviction for any criminals involved. Willie Bioff and George Browne were ambitious wannabes who vied for a place at the union trough. Russian-born Bioff was a thug who served the mob as a union slugger, pimp, and whorehouse operator. The hard-drinking Browne was vice president of the Local 2 Stagehands Union, operated under the umbrella of IATSE (The International Alliance of Theatrical Stage Employees, Moving Picture Technicians, Artists and Allied Crafts, hereafter referred to as the IA). He had run unsuccessfully for the IA presidency in 1932. Bioff and Browne recognized in each other a kindred spirit; they partnered up for a big score.

The Outfit powerhouses Frank "The Enforcer" Nitti (above) and Paul "The Waiter" Ricca (pictured right center in an unaccustomed police lineup)

Their gravy train would arrive when Local 2's contract with Paramount's Balaban-Katz theater chain expired. The contract had included a temporary Depression-induced salary reduction, but wages were to be restored under a new agreement. Barney Balaban bridled at any such hike, claiming it would open the floodgates for raises to other employees. As he was already bribing the head of the corrupt Projectionist's Union, Balaban offered a similar deal to Browne, putting him on the company's payroll. Bioff then told the theater magnate it would cost $50,000 to guarantee no raises and labor peace. Balaban, who became president of Paramount Pictures in 1936, negotiated them down to $20,000 and paid with a company check recorded as a donation to the Stagehand Union's soup kitchen.

Bioff and Browne boasted about their extortion coup during an evening of drinking and gambling at Club 100, a popular Chicago nightspot that Al Capone's cousin Nick Circella ran for the Outfit. Circella informed his superiors. Two days later, Browne and Bioff were frog-marched to a meeting with a pair of the Outfit's key leaders: Frank "The Enforcer" Nitti and Paul "the Waiter" Ricca.

Nitti asked if Browne intended to run for the IA presidency again in 1934. Getting a "Yes," Nitti made the mob's prototypical offer, the one that couldn't be refused:

"In this world, if I scratch your back, I expect you to scratch mine. If you can win by yourself, you don't need us. But if you want our help, we'll expect you to cooperate. Fair enough?"

Browne and Bioff bought in and the Outfit's plan to subvert the movie business was underway.

The motion picture industry had always deployed a "divide and conquer" strategy to counter the emerging union movement. In 1927, the studios formed a company-sponsored union, the Academy of Motion Picture Arts and Sciences (AMPAS), specifically to curb the spread of unionism from technical crafts to the ranks of actors, writers, and other "creatives." The Studio Basic Agreement (SBA) set salaries for craft workers. Each studio controlled seniority among its own employees making it difficult for unions to recruit new members. Many rank and file workers had dual memberships in the IA and the International Brotherhood of Electrical Workers (IBEW) or the Carpenters Union.

The July 1933 strike by Sound Local 695 against Columbia Pictures was a disaster for the IA. When Columbia mogul Harry Cohn wouldn't budge, the other Hollywood IA locals walked out in support. The studios responded by locking out the strikers, dropping the IA from the Basic Studio Agreement and hiring IBEW and Carpenters Union members. The strike was crushed and membership in the IA plummeted.

The Outfit got a briefing on the movie capital's labor travails from Johnny Roselli, a Capone aide who'd relocated to Los Angeles in the mid-1920s. "Handsome Johnny" seamlessly insinuated himself into the realm of the Hollywood elite and the L.A. underworld. Roselli reported that the Hollywood trade unions were down, but not out. Studios remained susceptible to a strong union because of their dependence on specialized technical workers—and the vulnerability of their far-flung theater chains.

Reporters were barred from the 1934 IA Convention in Knoxville, Tennessee, where inside the hall a Who's Who of organized crime was meeting: Meyer Lansky, Bugsy Siegel, Lucky Luciano, and Abner "Longie" Zwillman mixed with the delegates. Louis "Lepke" Buchalter, who controlled IA Local 306 in New York, was George Browne's floor manager. Overt intimidation was unnecessary as the sitting IA president had resigned in the wake of the Columbia strike fiasco. Elected by acclamation, Browne named Bioff as his deputy. The newly minted officials were immediately assigned "minders" by the Outfit. Nick Circella kept an eye on Browne, and he introduced Bioff to Roselli, who was in New York taking a periodic rest cure for his tuberculosis.

The new IA leadership quickly consolidated its position: the Outfit took over the Projectionists and the Theater Janitors unions after the leaders of both those unions were killed in two more unsolved gangland assassinations. Nick Circella was appointed president of Projectionists Local 110. A strike by projectionists against Paramount theaters cowed all the studios into restoring the IA to the Studio Basic Agreement. In no time, membership in Hollywood's IA locals began to recover.

Browne and Bioff held their coming out party on July 15, 1935, when they called a strike against the RKO theater circuit. The company handed over $87,000 so their theaters could reopen. Next up was the Loew's chain, parent company of MGM, of which Nick Schenck was the top man. The fifth richest man in America, Schenck and his older brother Joseph were Russian-born Jews who, like most of the other movie moguls, had risen from poverty through a rough-and-tumble world. Joe had co-founded 20th Century–Fox with Darryl F. Zanuck less than two months earlier. To the Schenck brothers, cutting backroom deals with gangsters was just another part of the business. Following the recently passed National Labor Relations Act, what studio bosses *really* feared was the rise of unionism in the motion picture business. Nick Schenck paid Bioff and Browne $143,500. Other studios that owned theater chains weighed in with more payoffs: Paramount anted up $138,000 and Warner Bros. forked over $91,000. All these machinations were cloaked by a phony projectionist strike in New York against Paramount staged on November 30, 1935. An "emergency meeting" of union leaders and studio negotiators was held the next day as a smokescreen for the press. The money changed hands; the meeting concluded with the announcement that the IA had been granted the first-ever closed shop agreement in the industry's history. Unannounced was the part of the deal in which the IA guaranteed there'd be no strikes at the studios. Wages of rank and file workers were immediately cut by 35¢ an hour. Later estimates placed the savings in labor costs, just for Loew's and RKO, at over $3 million in the first year of the IA deal.

Browne placed Bioff in charge of the IA's Hollywood operations with authority to assume control

20th Century-Fox chairman Joseph Schenck (center) is flanked by cinema legends (left to right) Mary Pickford, Charlie Chaplin, Darryl F. Zanuck, Samuel Goldwyn, and Douglas Fairbanks Sr.

of any local. A member of Local 37—the industry's largest local of backlot craft workers—recalled Bioff striding through the meeting hall, flanked by thugs toting violin cases, to declare that the IA was taking over and would be appointing new officers.

The duo's insatiable greed almost got the better of them after Browne levied a 2% surcharge on all IA members' paychecks. Instead of kicking back the usual 50% to Chicago, they prepared a second set of books and pocketed the money. The Outfit discovered the double cross and an enraged Nitti confronted a cowering George Browne who later testified, "I thought he was going to push me out the window." Nitti decreed the Outfit would, from then on, get two-thirds of the lucre rather than the previous 50-50 split. The illegal union surcharge was eventually overturned by the courts, but not before workers had been cheated out of several million dollars. For studio bosses, the worm turned in April 1936. Browne, Bioff, and Circella appeared in Nick Schenck's New York office and declared they'd close down every Loew's theatre in the country unless they were paid $2,000,000. After conferring with Robert Kent at Fox, Schenck reconvened the meeting and said there was no way he could raise that amount. "Okay, I'll take one million," Bioff said. "With a hundred grand upfront." The payment schedule: $50,000 per year from Fox, Warner Bros., MGM, and Paramount; $25,000 from RKO, Columbia, and the lesser studios. Three days later, in a room at the Waldorf Astoria, Kent and Schenck delivered $50,000 apiece in $100 dollar bills and watched while the three gangsters counted the cash on adjoining twin beds.

Only Columbia was immune to the shakedown. Harry Cohn (who had secretly obtained an underworld loan from Longie Zwillman to purchase his controlling shares of Columbia stock) appealed to his close friend Johnny Roselli, who interceded on his behalf. Bioff protested that he had Nitti's okay to extort Columbia, but Roselli, accompanied by L.A. mob boss Jack Dragna, paid a visit one

Under the leadership of Guild president Robert Montgomery (second from right), SAG successfully resisted pressure and physical threats from the IATSE and the studios; the 1937 SAG negotiating committee (left to right): Franchot Tone, Aubrey Blair, Montgomery, and Kenneth Thomson

evening to Bioff's home. Columbia never had another problem with the IA. The incident revealed that the Outfit's true power didn't reside with Frank Nitti; it was Paul Ricca and Anthony "Joe Batters" Accardo (nicknamed by Capone for his enforcement skill with a baseball bat) calling the shots from Chicago.

What started as an extortion racket became a partnership. Albert Warner told the FBI that in the spring of '36, he'd received a call from Nick Schenck saying an agreement had been made to pay Willie Bioff as a way of preventing labor difficulties at the studios. These payments, from 1937 to 1941, were disguised as commissions for raw film stock. According to the FBI, Joe Schenck told Louis B. Mayer, "He [Bioff] is all right and he is here and can do favors. It is just as well to have someone friendly." Mayer confirmed the conversation, saying that Schenck advised "to keep him [Bioff] friendly, life would be easier to operate the plant [studio]." The moguls became downright affable towards the former pimp and whorehouse manager. Joe Schenck paid for ocean cruises and a tour of Europe for Bioff and his wife. At a gala send-off (paid for by the moguls), Harry Warner and his wife gave the Bioffs a floral arrangement accompanied by a telegram: "Sorry we are not on the boat with you. … Take it easy and have a good time."

Dissidents in Local 37 sued the IA over the 2% wage surcharge and won reelection. In retaliation, the IA dissolved Local 37 and created five smaller locals comprising individual crafts. The progressives responded by forming a new union, the United Studio Technicians Guild (USTG) and petitioned the newly constituted National Labor Relations Board (NLRB) for a representation election. Bioff portrayed the USTG as a putsch led by the Congress of Industrial Organizations (CIO) while George Browne made speeches condemning the progressives in the IA as Communists. Red-baiting would become a tactic repeatedly used to condemn so-called "subversives" in the union ranks.

With connivance from the studios, Bioff announced the negotiation of substantial raises for the IA's unions. The USTG lost the election. Activists were banned from rejoining their unions unless they dropped their lawsuit and signed a humiliating apology to Bioff and Browne. Studios blackballed any members who wouldn't sign the pre-printed IA apology.

After the courts upheld the constitutionality of the 1935 Wagner Act, the Federated Motion Picture Crafts (FMPC) organized some trades that were among the lowest-paid and hardest-working at the studios. Utility workers, for instance, were being paid 62¢ an hour with no minimum hours and no overtime. When the studios refused to recognize these workers, the FMPC struck. Bioff and Roselli imported Chicago Outfit muscle and forced IA members to cross FMPC picket lines. The strike became a bloody free-for-all when the FMPC enlisted San Pedro longshoremen and members of locally based CIO unions to battle the IA goons.

To prevent the Screen Actors Guild from aligning with the FMPC, the IA threatened a projectionists' strike—unless the studios recognized SAG and began negotiations. The combined efforts of the IA, the movie studios, and SAG effectively put down the strike. With the exception of the painters, the other trades returned to work at the same pay level. The Los Angeles Labor Council passed a resolution branding the IA as "a company union and a scab-herding agency."

Although SAG finally won recognition from the studios (it took four years), its president, Robert Montgomery, warned actors not to trust the IA. His instincts were confirmed when Bioff launched a campaign to bring SAG into his fiefdom. When Montgomery resisted, Chicago-style organizing followed: SAG executive board members received death threats. Board member George Murphy was told his children would have acid thrown in their faces. A bomb was found in another board member's car. Montgomery refused to be cowed. In public, he and other SAG officials were protected by a posse of movie stuntmen. Carey McWilliams, attorney for the Local 37 dissidents, and syndicated columnist Westbrook Pegler eventually took the lead on exposing the IA's criminality to the public, but Robert Montgomery was the difference maker. He hired private investigators to probe Bioff's past, uncovering a $100,000 loan that helped Bioff finance a 70-acre estate in Reseda. The mobster at that time lacked legitimate assets to purchase the property. He'd asked Joe Schenck to create a phony paper loan that he secretly paid back. This seemingly minor transgression resulted in Bioff's downfall.

Previous investigations of the IA by Los Angeles DA Buron Fitts (he called complaints about Bioff's conduct a "misunderstanding") and the California State Assembly (key congressional officials were bribed) had gone nowhere. Montgomery had SAG's investigative file on Bioff personally delivered to U.S. Treasury Secretary Henry Morgenthau on July 1, 1938. The actor reasoned that since the U.S. Treasury took down Al Capone, they could deal with a wannabe like Willie Bioff.

But when Treasury sent a criminal referral to the Justice Department, Charles Carr, the assigned prosecutor, claimed "the government was on a hopeless fishing trip," infuriating Treasury and FBI agents who'd been actively investigating the Outfit's influence in Hollywood. It was later alleged that Carr had been offered the U.S. Attorney's position in Los Angeles in return for not pursuing the case against Bioff.

The matter would have continued to languish if not for Westbrook Pegler's columns on IA corruption, which he renewed in November 1939. Sifting through old Chicago police records, the columnist discovered that Bioff had an outstanding 1922 pandering conviction and had skipped out on his six-month sentence. A warrant was issued for Bioff's arrest, and the story made headlines coast-to-coast. U.S. Secretary Morgenthau demanded that Robert Montgomery's investigative file be retrieved and reviewed by a different prosecutor. Pegler won a Pulitzer Prize for breaking the sensational scoop. Bioff returned to Chicago to serve his four-month sentence in the city lockup. By the time he returned to Hollywood, events had overtaken him. On January 10, 1940, Bioff was indicted for income tax evasion based on the $100,000 "loan" from Joseph Schenck. George Browne made more speeches accusing Communists inside the IA of conspiring to take over the union, while depicting Bioff as a selfless labor leader who was "the victim of a merciless series of scurrilous attacks." In addition to the Red-baiting broadsides, Browne invited Congressman Martin Dies, Jr. (D-Texas) to probe "subversion" in the movie industry. Although Dies' most memorable achievement to that point was listing 10-year old Shirley Temple as a possible Communist dupe, his investigative committee was reconfigured in 1938 as the permanent House Committee on Un-American Activities (HUAC).

In a plea bargain, Joe Schenck copped to a reduced sentence for perjury in exchange for testifying against Bioff, Browne, and Circella. Schenck was convinced that if the extent of his dealings with the IA's gangsters was revealed, he might spend the rest of his life behind bars. Fortunately for his brother and the other producers, the prosecutors were solely focused on nailing Bioff and Browne. The crimi-

Left: Lawyer Sidney Korshak, fixer extraordinaire, functioned as the Outfit's hidden hand in Hollywood and Las Vegas for a half century. Right: Frank Nitti (center with mustache) couldn't cope with the prospect of hard time after his 1943 indictment so he opted for an Outfit-influenced retirement plan: suicide

nal pair were indicted on federal tax evasion and racketeering charges on May 23, 1941.

Attorney Sidney Korshak was assigned as Bioff's attorney. Korshak was the Outfit's undercover front in Hollywood. He was a renowned fixer whose unprecedented power over studio bosses, union heads, and everybody else who mattered became the stuff of Tinseltown legends. Korshak instructed Bioff that he would admit to taking Schenck's money, stay off the witness stand, and "do your time as a man." Browne received the same marching orders. Nick Circella went on the lam.

Obedience was never one of Bioff's strong points. On the stand, he accused studio bosses of bribing him to maintain labor peace—while remaining mute about the Outfit's orchestration of the scheme. It didn't work. It took the jury only two hours to return guilty verdicts. Bioff got ten years, Browne eight. On December 1, 1941, Nick Circella was arrested in Chicago. He kept his mouth shut, pleaded guilty, and was sentenced to prison.

The case might have ended there but for a startling bit of testimony from Harry Warner. The eldest Warner brother had been one of a parade of movie executives testifying to the Bioff-Browne shakedowns. Under oath, Warner recalled Bioff's explanation for an increase in payments from the studios: "The boys in Chicago insist on more money." The heat came down on Bioff, Browne, and Circella to rat out their bosses.

A hideous murder in Chicago flipped the case. Police responding to reports of smoke from an Addison Street apartment on February 2, 1943, discovered the mutilated corpse of nightclub hostess Estelle Carey—Nick Circella's girlfriend. She had been beaten, stabbed repeatedly, then doused with gasoline and set on fire. Circella, who had been flirting with prosecutors about cooperating, clammed up permanently. George Browne's wife received an anonymous call threatening her with dismemberment if her husband testified. The volatile Bioff reacted in a typically contrarian manner. The doting husband and father was enraged by the Outfit's intimidation tactics. He went straight to the prosecu-

Above: While a senator, Harry S. Truman (left) intervened to get cushy treatment for his imprisoned mentor, Kansas City political boss Thomas J. Pendergast (right); Left: Roy Brewer (left) and Ronald Reagan purged suspected Communists from the IATSE and SAG and established the anti-Communist Labor League of Hollywood Voters

tor and asked: "What do you want to know?"

As a result, Roselli, Nitti, Ricca, and five other Outfit members were indicted for extortion and conspiracy on March 18, 1943. Roselli, who had wrangled himself a military enlistment to take the heat off, was brought into court in an Army private's uniform. The Outfit's inner circle turned on Nitti, who had initiated the scheme that now threatened to bring them down. An irate Paul Ricca reportedly insisted that Nitti needed to take the fall for the organization as Capone had done previously ... or else. Nitti was already in poor health; he'd served a previous prison stretch with difficulty. On March 19, a man clutching a whiskey bottle and a revolver was reported weaving back and forth on the tracks of the Illinois Central Railroad. It took three shots to the head for Frank Nitti to cash in his Outfit retirement plan.

Bioff ended up recanting much of his previous testimony about the studio extortion racket. He revealed the shenanigans of the studio heads, including a $200,000 bribe from Nick Schenck to head off a federal investigation of the IA. He also declared Sidney Korshak to be "our man in Hollywood." A terrified George Browne corroborated enough of Bioff's testimony. On December 31, 1943, the Outfit's leaders were found guilty. They all received ten-year sentences and $10,000 fines.

The aftermath was not leavened with compensating moral values. The convicted mobsters were

Willie Bioff meets his Maker: the pint-sized ex-union boss was blown to bits after starting his vehicle outside his Phoenix home in 1955; Bioff's inability to maintain a low profile made it easy for the Outfit to square accounts with him

shipped to a medieval hellhole, the Federal Penitentiary in Atlanta. The convicts kept their heads down while renowned Outfit fixer Murray "Curly" Humphreys went to work.

Humphreys reached out to Paul Dillon, a Kansas City attorney whose ties with local political boss Thomas J. Pendergast extended to the White House. The Pendergast machine had held sway in Missouri for more than two decades. One of Pendergast's political appointees was a former WWI Army officer and family friend—Harry S. Truman. After being appointed a county judge in 1922, Truman looked the other way as Pendergast and his cronies stole everything in Kansas City that wasn't nailed down. In 1934, Truman became a Senator in an election marred by voter fraud. Senator Truman tried to block a federal investigation into Pendergast's activities, and he later intervened with prison officials to get favorable treatment for his mentor after Pendergast was convicted and sentenced for income tax evasion in 1939. "Give 'em Hell Harry" always pledged undying loyalty to his friends—a character trait the Outfit understood.

The Outfit cons (less Roselli) were soon transferred from Atlanta to the friendlier confines of Leavenworth Penitentiary. Renowned trial lawyer Maury Hughes, a longtime friend of Attorney General Tom Clark, was hired by the Outfit to lobby for its imprisoned leaders. Clark was the same AG who inexplicably disbanded the FBI's Capone-Outfit squad and blocked a Federal investigation into Kansas City voter fraud. On August 5, 1947, Hughes met with the head of the federal parole board (of which three members were appointed by Clark). Less than a week later, paroles for Ricca, Roselli, and all the others were granted over the vociferous objections of the prosecutors who'd put them away. The press cried foul, and Republicans launched a series of investigations that were stonewalled by Clark—who would soon be elevated to the Supreme Court by President Truman. Another outrage soon followed: Truman personally pardoned Joe Schenck after the mogul had served only four months of his year-and-a-day sentence for income tax evasion.

After several years of relative labor calm in Hollywood during the war, battle flared between the IA and the Conference of Studio Unions (CSU), a breakaway organization comprised of USTG leftovers, the Painters Union, and IA progressives. Led by Herbert Sorrell, the CSU fought the IA and the studios from 1945-47, the most violent phase of Hollywood's long-running labor strife. On October 5, 1945, a riot erupted when IA strike-breakers tried to storm through 800 CSU picketers outside the Warner Bros. front gate in Burbank. Autos were overturned and 50 people were injured as studio police deployed tear gas and high-pressure fire hoses. Jack Warner and his retinue observed the fray from the safety of a soundstage roof. Burbank police waded in and Sorrell and other CSU leaders were beaten and arrested. The IA had divested itself of its gangster overseers, like a snake shedding its skin, but its methods remained the same.

Roy Brewer became the IA's new Hollywood representative and partnered with the studios and SAG (now led by Ronald Reagan) to eliminate the CSU. Brewer stuck with the Browne-Bioff play-book, claiming the rival union was rife with Communists bent on subverting the labor movement. Having crushed the strike and purged the disloyal, Brewer established (with Ronald Reagan) the anti-Communist Labor League of Hollywood Voters and later succeeded John Wayne as president of the Motion Picture Alliance for the Preservation of American Ideals. Testifying before HUAC, Brewer named 13 actors, directors, and screenwriters as Communists. He quickly expanded his power by acting as a clearinghouse for blacklisted artists and crafts people: Brewer allowed people to work in the movie business provided they proved their allegiance by naming suspected Communists. It was a perverse brand of trade unionism, ironically more reminiscent of Joseph Stalin than Al Capone.

Other than Joe Schenck, no studio executives who used publicly held company funds to pay off gangsters were charged with a crime. Johnny Roselli was hired by his pal Bryan Foy as a producer at Eagle-Lion Studios, where he imbued *He Walked by Night* (1948) and *Canon City* (1949) with an innate sense of criminal realism. Paul Ricca returned to Chicago to continue running the Outfit with Joe Batters. The mob's profile in Hollywood became lower, but still prominent. Labor advisor Sidney Korshak kept the town's unions and movie studios dancing to the mob's tune. After taking control of the Teamsters Union and accessing its pension fund as their personal piggy bank, the Outfit really opened up the throttle in Las Vegas, using Roselli and other front-people to skim untold millions from the casinos. Life was harder for other principals. George Browne went into hiding, finally drinking himself to death. Nick Circella served his time in prison, then fled to South America and was never seen again.

On November 4, 1955, "Al" Nelson, a close friend of Arizona Senator Barry Goldwater, walked out of his house in Phoenix and started his truck. A titanic blast adorned Nelson's neighborhood with debris and body parts. William "Al" Nelson was posthumously identified as Willie Bioff. He'd been hiding for more than a decade in Arizona, until he foolishly ventured into Las Vegas working under his new name as entertainment director of the Riviera. Paul Ricca and Joe Batters didn't like loose ends. This was their finale to the mob's Hollywood story—scripted The Chicago Way. ■

HANDSOM

A Dashing Gangster. The "Keeper of the Bs."

Son of the Catholic Censor-in-Chief.

How did this unholy trinity create a trio

of film noir classics? Read on . . .

By John Wranovics

TAKES TI

E JOHNNY

Handsome Johnny, the Hollywood Kid, was above the fold once more. In April 2017, President Trump ordered the release of 19,045 previously classified files on the JFK assassination—and the klieg lights shined once again on that Golden Era gangster *de luxe*, Johnny Roselli. The National Archives is still holding an estimated 30,000 relevant documents close to its vest (until at least October 26, 2021), but these latest offerings held some new details on organized crime's role in various attempts by the CIA to kill Fidel Castro. As a result, many of the old Roselli tales were exhumed once more: How young Italian immigrant Filippo Sacco (born in Esperia, Italy, in 1905), busted for robbery in Boston, hightailed it to Chicago and charmed his way into Capone's inner circle. How in 1923, now sporting the handle Roselli, he was sent to Los Angeles as an advance scout for the Chicago mob and quickly fell in with vice kingpin Jack Dragna working the floating casinos anchored three miles offshore. Later, he was given oversight of the mob's interest in publisher Moses Annenberg's horseracing wire—a service relied upon by bookies nationwide.

SELTOWN

Johnny Roselli, seen here in mugshots from 1925, had been sent to Los Angeles in 1923 to represent the Capone gang's interests

Over the years, Roselli became notorious in Hollywood and Las Vegas, the stuff of legend. Some believe he popped out of a storm drain in Dealey Plaza, rifle in hand, on November 22, 1963. He ran guns and trained Cuban exiles in support of the CIA's ill-fated Bay of Pigs mission. The "horse head in the bed" scene in *The Godfather*? Reputedly a riff on Handsome Johnny's strong-arming of Columbia chief Harry Cohn into casting Frank Sinatra in *From Here to Eternity*.

But we're not here to consider those tales. Our focus is on how it happened that in 1947 Handsome Johnny, only days out of the Federal pen in Atlanta, having served three years of a ten-year stretch for his role in the mob's extortion of Hollywood studios and unions, immediately became an associate producer at Eagle-Lion studio. That's where, over the next couple of years, Roselli had a hand in (and a share of the profits from) three film noir classics: *T-Men* (1947), *He Walked by Night* (1948), and *Canon City* (1948).

A CAREER IN MOVIEMAKING seemed unlikely for Johnny Roselli back on March 4, 1943. That's when he was indicted for his role in the mob-sponsored shakedown of Hollywood studios and unions. His escape ploy—enlisting in the Army—failed: he was nabbed, still in uniform, at Camp Forrest, Tennessee, and hauled to New York for arraignment. The authorities produced records showing that, since 1925, "Roselli was picked up by police four times on suspicion that he had been in robberies, once on suspicion of grand larceny, once was charged with possessing concealed weapons and that each time he was picked up revolvers, sawed-off shotguns or knives were found on his person, in his automobile or rooms."

Roselli was convicted and shipped to Atlanta Federal Penitentiary on April 4, 1944. Purportedly due to the lobbying of mob fixer Murray "The Hump" Humphreys, Roselli was granted parole on August 13, 1947. Two days later, he was back in Los Angeles. The FBI succinctly described what happened next: "Roselli was provided immediately with employment by Bryan Foy, a motion picture producer, as an assistant purchasing agent for Eagle-Lion in Hollywood, California. Roselli remained

Movie producer Bryan (Brynie) Foy, "The Keeper of the Bs," established himself in the 1930s as a renegade with sensational, exploitive, and controversial features

with that company until Foy took employment with Warner [Bros.] Studios in about 1950."

In October 1950, Roselli testified at the headline-grabbing Kefauver crime commission hearings:

Mr. Halley: *Since 1947, what have you been doing?*

Mr. Roselli: *Since 1947, I have been in the picture business. I came home and worked as an assistant purchasing agent at Eagle-Lion studio. I later was assistant producer to Bryan Foy and associate producer with Robert T. Cain productions. ... I was an associate producer of two pictures which I helped finance and produce.*

A year and a half before his Kefauver appearance, Roselli had been re-arrested in Los Angeles for parole violations, specifically "associating with unsavory characters and failing to register with police upon entering the city." He fought parole revocation in federal court and lost. His lawyers took the case to the Federal Parole Board in Washington, D.C., where they prevailed. Handsome Johnny was freed in November. Newspapers reported: "Until the revocation of his parole, Roselli had been working as an associate producer with several film studios and a technical adviser on crime pictures. He said that he plans to immediately return to his film work in Hollywood."

Mr. Halley. *What are the circumstances of your being unemployed? Are you simply retired?*

Mr. Roselli. *No. The circumstance, I think, is that two years ago when my parole was revoked I was in the process of making these two pictures, and they were later released. Since then, I just haven't been able to get any employment anywhere since Mr. Foy went to Warner Bros.*

HOW DOES A NOTORIOUS MOBSTER and felon go directly from a federal prison cell into a film studio office? The answer lies in careful consideration of the career of Bryan Foy (born Bryan Fitzgerald in 1896), who, during the period in question, served as Eagle-Lion's head of production. In Roselli's voluminous FBI file, an anonymous informant noted, "Foy has a reputation within the industry for hiring ex-convicts and hoodlums who come out to Hollywood in search of work."

So, what kind of man was Bryan Foy?

Known by some as "The Keeper of the Bs" for his storied career cranking out bottom-of-the-bill fodder, Bryan Foy ("Brynie" to his close friends) was the eldest of the Seven Little Foys, the most famous family act in vaudeville. The children sang, danced, and joked in support of the paterfamilias, Eddie Foy (born Eddie Fitzgerald), a veteran singer and comic whose lengthy career included an appearance in Tombstone, Arizona, that coincided with the shootout at the OK Corral (October 26, 1881). Eddie was known to quip, "Sure took me a long time to get this act together."

In 1915, young Bryan got his first taste of filmmaking when Mack Sennett starred the Foy troupe in a short subject. Asked what specific talent he brought to the act, Bryan Foy would reply, "I'm the tallest one." Three years later, Foy flew the coop enlisting in the U.S. Navy. Two weeks later, his mother died and he soon developed severe anxiety issues ("Patient is nervous and easily excitable at which times condition is aggravated and seriously interferes with his duties.") He was given an honorable discharge.

Having written novelty tunes for the family's act, Foy tried songwriting partnering with fellow vaudeville veteran Charles "Chuck" Riesner. For the comic duo Gallagher and Shean (the latter an uncle to the Marx Brothers), Foy wrote the hit which made its subjects stars of the Ziegfeld Follies. Some claim the tune was the last great success of the sheet music business before the advent of radio. Unfortunately, Foy had sold the lyrics for $100 and a gold cigarette case, and so he earned no royalties.

In 1920, Foy married and briefly toiled as a stockbroker, but he soon rejoined Riesner writing comedy bits for the movies. At Fox Studios in 1922, he was assigned to direct comedy shorts. Still bitter from not sharing in the success of "Mr. Gallagher and Mr. Shean," he sued the eponymous duo—and the song publisher Jack Mills, Inc. (Mills Music, Inc.) for a cut of the music roll and recording profits. He lost badly and publicly. According to family members, "Bryan was upset about the outcome for a long time."

Though rancorous and twitchy (25 years later, in 1938, his nervous tics still merited mention in a profile piece), Foy nevertheless found his niche in the film world. In 1923, he formed an independent outfit to supply Universal with "Hysterical History" comedy shorts, parodying subjects like Rip Van Winkle, Rembrandt, and Nero. In 1927, he co-wrote Buster Keaton's feature *College*. In the meantime, Riesner worked with Charlie Chaplin as assistant director on films such as *The Pilgrim*, *The Kid*, and *The Gold Rush*. Foy and Riesner reunited at Warner Bros.—the former as a writer, the latter a director—on *The Fortune Hunter* (1927) for Chaplin's brother, Syd.

Warner then sent Foy to Brooklyn to oversee production of its Vitaphone shorts, which synchronized recorded discs with silent films. He produced 400 "Vitaphone Varieties" over the next three years, most featuring vaudevillians and popular singers. Ignoring his superiors, Foy expanded an intended two-reel talkie, *Lights of New York*, into history's first all-talking full-length feature, released in July 1928. Foy's insubordination resulted in this low-budget ($75,000) gangster picture (unimpressive in acting and plot) earning Warner Bros. $1,200,000. It also introduced to the culture the immortal gangster line, "Take him for a ride."

Returning to Hollywood, Foy formed his own company, Bryan Foy Productions. An early release, *Myrt and Marge* (1933), featured Ted Healy and his Three Stooges. Foy then decided to swim against the mainstream: he cranked out sensational, exploitive, and controversial features such as *Elysia (Valley of the Nude)*, filmed in a nudist camp; *What Price Innocence*, about the dangers of unmarried sex; *Tomorrow's Children*, a "study" of eugenics (aka test-tube babies), and *High School Girl*, offering more warnings of under-age sex.[1] Foy's reputation as a renegade was now established. A Motion Picture Producers and Distributors Association interoffice memo from April 1934, regarding

---

1   The latter two were scripted by Wallace Thurman, a leading Harlem Renaissance literary figure. Foy made 27 films over three decades with Crane Wilbur, director of the two Thurman-scripted films. Intriguing to consider the continued alliance of these three men had Thurman not died in 1934, aged 32, from tuberculosis. Wilbur worked on two of the three Roselli Eagle-Lion projects; he was screenwriter on *He Walked by Night* and he wrote and directed *Canon City*.

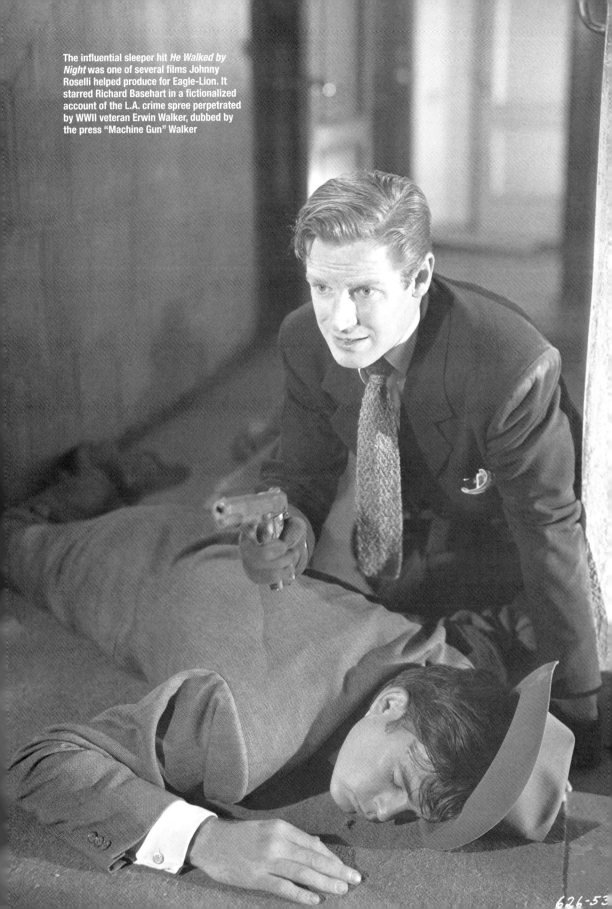

The influential sleeper hit *He Walked by Night* was one of several films Johnny Roselli helped produce for Eagle-Lion. It starred Richard Basehart in a fictionalized account of the L.A. crime spree perpetrated by WWII veteran Erwin Walker, dubbed by the press "Machine Gun" Walker

626-53

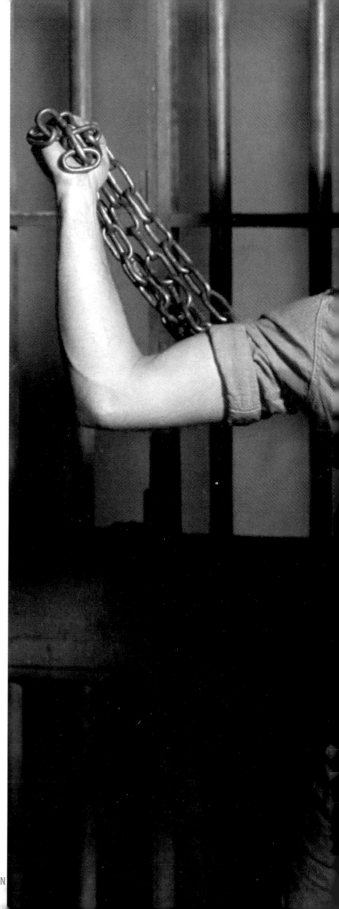

Tomorrow's Children, warned that Foy was "certain to be increasingly troublesome as time goes on. He is avowedly out to make pictures off the beaten track, with the idea that in this way he may be able to make a good living. He has gone on the record, repeatedly, as of the opinion that he cannot compete with other companies making the usual type of pictures and that he must resort to the sensation, the shocking and the lurid."

But by 1935, now 39-years old, Bryan Foy was back at Warner Bros. in charge of its B-film production. He had oversight of almost half the studio's annual output, producing 125 films over the next six years. Foy was notorious for remaking the same film. Vincent Sherman, recalling what it was like to work for Foy at the time, said that after his first draft of *Crime School* was rejected, Foy instructed him to graft the first half of the script for *The Mayor of Hell* with the second half of *San Quentin*. Others found Foy an inspiration: legendary screenwriter Dalton Trumbo, beginning his career in the Warner trenches, credited Bryan Foy for teaching him how to write screenplays tersely and efficiently, with an emphasis on action and pace.

When Warner Bros. shut down its B-picture division in 1941, Foy decamped to 20th Century–Fox.

ON APRIL FOOLS DAY 1940, Johnny Roselli married movie actress June Lang (born Winifred Vlasek). The marriage, which put an immediate end to June's girl-next-door image, ended in divorce court by early 1943, with Lang declaring that Roselli "not only objected to my continuing career, he refused to explain why he would go away for two weeks at a time."

It's not known how or when Foy and Roselli met each other, whether it was socially or professionally. They likely crossed paths in the 1930s when Handsome Johnny provided mob muscle to the film industry in the form of strike-breakers. It could have been as early as 1933 when IATSE and Pat

Inside the Walls of Folsom Prison (1951), starring Steve Cochran and David Brian, was another Crane Wilbur prison yarn produced by Foy with the help of Joseph Breen, Jr.

Shown here with her first husband, actor William Campbell, Judith Campbell Exner became well known for her associations with John F. Kennedy and Chicago mob boss Sam Giancana when she testified in 1975 before the U.S. Senate's Church Committee investigating CIA assassination attempts on Fidel Castro

Casey, the Producer Association's labor representative, failed to block a strike by the Sound Men's Union. Newspapers cited eleven studios likely to be affected, and included Bryan Foy Productions in with majors like Warner Bros., MGM, Paramount, and Fox. Roselli was on Casey's payroll at the time, as well as being a "labor consultant" for IATSE.

It's possible the two connected when Foy produced a film about Roger Touhy, a Chicago rival of Roselli's patron, Al Capone. One historian has written that "years before his incarcertion, Roselli allegedly worked with his boss at Eagle-Lion, Brynie Foy, in producing the B movie *Roger Touhy, Gangster*, which was released by 20th Century–Fox in 1944." Touhy had been convicted (possibly framed) for the kidnapping of con man Jack "Jake the Barber" Factor, younger half-brother of makeup legend Max Factor. He broke out of prison on October 9, 1942. Only days later, October 13, 1942, the *New York Times* reported that, "'Prison Break,' a photo play to be based on the life of Roger Touhy, who escaped last week from Joliet Prison, was added to the production schedule of Bryan Foy." Recaptured, Touhy was back in Stateville prison by New Year's Eve.

Could Johnny Roselli have been involved *sub rosa* or otherwise? Pre-production on the film reportedly began in January 1943. Roselli had been in the Army since December 2, 1942, and then arrested in the IATSE extortion case on March 19, 1943, which would have left only a couple of months for any possible interaction with Foy.

BRYAN FOY LEFT 20TH CENTURY–FOX in April 1946 to become production chief at upstart Eagle-Lion Pictures. Aubrey Schenck, nephew of Fox production exec Joe Schenck, signed on as E-L's executive producer. Coming into the fold as a consultant was Elmer Lincoln Irey, retired chief coordinator of the U.S. Treasury Department's police units—the guy credited with nailing Capone on tax-evasions charges in 1931. A trade report of July 20, 1948, noted that Irey "went to Hollywood last spring when (Eagle-Lion) intended to make a picture version of the Al Capone case. ... Mr. Irey was ready to cooperate in the venture but the Johnston Office vetoed it."

Under the guidance of new chief Eric Johnston, the MPAA (renamed from MPPDA) was on the warpath against films such as *Dillinger* and *Roger Touhy, Gangster*, which "celebrated" notorious criminals—*especially* Al Capone. On December 4, 1947, the Johnston office banned 14 films as "unsuitable for re-release or re-reissue," including Foy's *Roger Touhy, Gangster*. And for the fourth time in five years, the MPAA rejected a proposed film about Capone.

Switching gears, Foy scrapped the Capone pic and gave the green light to *T-Men*, featuring a production crew comprising not only the U.S. Treasury agent who actually brought down Capone—but an ex-con who'd learned the ropes of racketeering straight from "Scarface."

With Handsome Johnny on staff at Eagle-Lion, he and Foy became inseparable. Roselli was quickly promoted out of the purchasing department. He helped produce *Canon City*—like *Roger Touhy, Gangster*, another "ripped from the headlines" prison-break tale. According to an FBI informant, Roselli was promoted to producer status "because this would be an easy way for Bryan Foy to raise his salary."

Mr. Roselli: *Mr. Foy thought that I had the ability to become a producer. I was in the process of getting a story down on paper when a prison break broke out in Colorado at that time, and after that Mr. Foy and I were always together. I say always, maybe ninety percent of the time. We developed an idea to do this picture. He was the head of the studio at the time.*

We put a writer to work on this. He first submitted the idea to the studios, to the president of the company. They were in no position or didn't like the idea of the picture. They said if we could get an outside interest to produce this, they would be glad to go along, he and his brother, that is. Mr. Foy said that you and my brother, Charlie, can possibly finance this thing, and if you haven't the money, I will lend you some, or whatever you can do. I said, "How much money would it take?" He said, "It wouldn't take too much. Maybe we can get it and organize a firm." So we organized this firm and brought in a man by the name of Robert T. Cain.

The Chairman: *How much interest did you have in the company?*

Mr. Roselli: *Twelve percent, I think. Oh, no. It figured around eleven percent of the total picture.*

One explanation for Foy's affinity with the so-called "Italian underworld," given his promoted Irish ethnicity, is that he was actually half Italian; his mother, Madeline Morando, was a native of Torino. According to Foy's niece, Uncle Brynie and Roselli "were like the Rover Boys; they went everywhere together." In the popular juvenile book series, there were three Rover brothers. Foy and Roselli's third wheel was Allen Smiley (born Aaron Smehoff)—Bugsy Siegel's right-hand man.

Smiley, like Roselli, was a charmer. An illegal immigrant from Russia, he landed at the Preston youth prison in California's Gold Country in 1926 after robbing a drug store in San Francisco. In stir, he made the fortuitous acquaintance of famed filmmaker Cecil B. DeMille, there doing research for *The Godless Girl* (1929). Freed a year later, Smiley hitchhiked to Hollywood where DeMille put him to work at Paramount. Flummoxed by his ambiguous functions, the trade press typically described Smiley as a "sportsman."

Smiley's daughter, Luellen, writing in her memoir *Cradle of Crime*, shared fond memories of Bryan Foy: "I called him 'Brynie' and he was a close friend of Dad and Mom. He taught me to water-ski in San Diego." When Foy lived in Encino, he would often drive to the studio with his friend Al Smiley. Allen Smiley and Bugsy Siegel had been busted for bookmaking in 1944. Columnist and producer Mark Hellinger, who had contacts in the movies and the *demi monde*, appeared in court as a character witness for Siegel. Hellinger had also worked with Bryan Foy, first in 1938 as screenwriter on *Comet Over Broadway*, and again in 1939 when they co-produced *Hell's Kitchen*.

On the night of June 20, 1947, while Handsome Johnny was still warehoused in Atlanta, Smiley and Siegel were loafing on the davenport at the home of Bugsy's girlfriend, Virginia Hill. As Smiley later told police, "I ducked to the floor when I heard the shots and shattering glass. I don't know how many shots were fired, but when I looked up at Siegel, I could see he had taken most of them." Nine shots in total, the first one blowing out Bugsy's right eye. Smiley escaped unscathed.

Mr. Halley: *Do you know Smiley?*

Mr. Roselli: *Yes. I knew him since he worked at Paramount as assistant director, and after that.*

Much later, in the 1970s, when Smiley and Roselli would pal around together at the Friars Club and other hot spots, they became known as the "Silver Foxes" thanks to their lush, elegantly coiffed manes.

ANOTHER CRUCIAL FIGURE in Roselli's and Foy's partnership was Joseph Breen, Jr., son of Production Code Administration (PCA) chief Joseph I. Breen. Shrewdly brought aboard at Eagle-Lion to help skirt censorship problems, Breen Jr. was working for Foy as early as the spring of 1947 when he submitted the script for *Railroaded* (then called *Tomorrow You Die*) to his dad for approval. According to Max Alvarez's book *The Crime Films of Anthony Mann*, Breen Jr. often conferred with his father on Eagle-Lion's behalf seeking script approvals for Foy projects that included *T-Men*, *Raw Deal*, and *He Walked by Night*. Before Anthony Mann moved from Eagle-Lion to MGM, taking the film *Border Incident* (and cameraman John Alton) with him, Breen Jr. also sought PCA approval for that script, then called "T-Men on the Border."

Post Eagle-Lion, the Bryan Foy–Crane Wilbur–Joe Breen, Jr. team was back in action at Warner Bros. Foy produced the war film *Breakthrough* (1950) in an effort to recapture his and director Lewis Seiler's earlier success with *Guadalcanal Diary* (1943). *Breakthrough* was written by Breen Jr. based on his experiences as an Army captain in France during World War II. Another Foy project, *Inside the Walls of Folsom Prison* (1951), had Crane Wilbur yet again as director and screenwriter, with Breen Jr. serving as dialogue director. Actor William Campbell, who appeared in both films, was at the time married to the former Judith Immoor. Roselli met the alluring woman while socializing with Foy and Campbell; he later introduced her to Frank Sinatra, who in turn introduced her to President John F. Kennedy and Chicago mob boss Sam Giancana. Judith Campbell Exner (she divorced her actor husband in 1958) later testified before the U.S. Senate's Church Committee in 1975 to having affairs with both Kennedy and Giancana. Meanwhile, Roselli's filmmaking ambitions continued apace. According to U.S. Probation records, Handsome Johnny was in 1952 working with Poverty Row studios Monogram and Mutual Pictures. At Monogram (what was left of it), he co-produced the low-budget Red Scare picture *Invasion, U.S.A.* (1952). Roselli and Bryan Foy were both virulent anti-Communists. In November 1947, after Congress held the Hollywood Ten in contempt, Foy was the lone studio head willing to go on record about firing or suspending left-wing writers. "I agree with the decision one hundred percent," Foy said. "And if I find any pinkos that I don't know on my lot I'll get rid of them if I can. They don't have to be Communists. I'll try to clean out any leftists." In 1951, he and Crane Wilbur teamed once again to make the feature *I Was a Communist for the F.B.I.*

Foy then shocked the industry by turning religious. A 1952 *Los Angeles Times* article titled "Bryan Foy Evolution Described as Amazing" told of the producer's pivot from prison, war, and crime genres to "pictures that have a spiritual purpose." With Crane Wilbur at the helm, Foy produced the hit *The Miracle of Our Lady of Fatima* (1952). His next project, *The Four Chaplains*, was based on a true WWII story of four fledgling chaplains who, after their ship was torpedoed, gave their life jackets and lifeboat seats to others, choosing to drown holding hands and singing hymns. Joe Breen, Jr., was announced as screenwriter. The film never got made. Foy's sudden Catholic bent wasn't a complete surprise; in 1946, he had wanted Irene Dunne to star in an Eagle-Lion biopic of Mother Cabrini.

Writer Bernard Gordon, who worked on *Crime Wave* (1953) for Foy at Warner Bros., remembered "Brynie" as "pleasant and easy enough to work for," but added that he "sounded like a man who had never gotten past grade school, maybe never even into it." He also recalled Breen Jr. claiming to have been about to enter seminary when the war started. According to Gordon, Breen Jr. "couldn't be mistaken for anything but a priest, or a priest manqué."

Yet, here were the Jesuitical Joe Breen, Jr., and Johnny Roselli sharing a close friendship and

Bryan Foy produced *The City Is Dark* in 1952 from an original treatment by Crane Wilbur. Warner Bros. sat on the André de Toth-directed feature for two years before releasing it as *Crime Wave*

strange business association. *The Hollywood Reporter* of October 3, 1951, reported that Roselli and Lewis Seiler had purchased from Breen the rights to *At the End of the Santa Fe Trail* and that "the two would make the film as an independent venture, with Seiler directing and Roselli producing." The book, by Sister Blandina Seagale, was a memoir of the Italian nun's adventures in the Old West where she nursed and counseled outlaw Billy the Kid.

Mr. Robinson: *Do you have any possibility of employment?*

Mr. Roselli: *Yes. I have just purchased a story—not employment, but of doing some work on a picture. I just purchased the published book called* End of the Santa Fe Trail *to develop a story and script possibly to make a motion picture out of it.*

Six years later, in 1957, Seiler found himself in a legal dispute with Samuel G. Engel and 20th Century–Fox over who actually owned the rights to Seagale's book. Neither party ever filmed the story.

While making these religious pictures, Joe Breen, Jr., was serving on the boards of several Las Vegas enterprises the FBI associated with Roselli; the suspicion was that Breen was acting as a front for the felon (and, by extension, the mob). In April 1958, it was announced that nightclub impresario Monte Proser had consummated the "biggest deal in club entertainment history" when he signed with Hilton Hotels to produce all of its shows.[2] Articles of Incorporation for Monte Proser Productions, Inc. (filed Sept. 5, 1957) include Joseph I. Breen as one of the corporation's directors. The FBI also investigated Roselli's involvement in a company called Nevada Concessions. According to FBI files, Roselli was forced to give up concessions at the Tropicana because the Gaming Control Board wouldn't grant the casino a license if he were connected to it. Handsome Johnny, files noted, "relinquished his interest in

2   Proser owned the famed Copacabana nightclub in New York City with his silent partner, mobster Frank Costello.

Handsome Johnny as an older man. Right: Johnny Roselli's remains found in a floating oil drum - Dumfoundling Bay, FL, part of the Intracoastal Waterway, 1976

the gift shop. … He did not mention who purchased the gift shop concession." Articles of Incorporation for Nevada Concessions list Joseph Breen, Jr., as President. Likewise, news reports stated that in 1967 Breen wanted to acquire the gift shop concession at the Frontier Hotel, but had been turned down. According to Breen Jr., "Johnny walked to a telephone, made a call, then came back and told me the concession was mine." The article claims that, "in gratitude, Mr. Breen made Mr. Roselli a partner."

Handsome Johnny's high life came to end sometime in August 1976. It was the last time he'd make a splash in the papers. Three months after his second and final testimony before the U.S. Senate's Church Committee, empaneled to investigate CIA assassination plots, Roselli suffered a grim fate. The official report of the Dade County, Florida, medical examiner tells it best: "Received in the morgue is a standard two-ribbed, rusted drum with numerous slit-like perforations cut with a cutting torch. … Drum has a diameter of 22 inches and a height of 36 inches. The drum is stenciled with 'Toulene 55 gal.' It has had its lid cut off, apparently with a cutting torch. A lid is affixed to the drum by chains held together with bolts." Chains, in fact, were wrapped around the drum top to bottom. "The drum emits [the] stench of decomposition. Fatty solidified foul-smelling debris is adherent to the drum."

Inside were the remains of one John Roselli, aged 71. The makeshift sarcophagus had been found floating in the Intracoastal Waterway. The coroner determined that the victim had been wearing a pink polyester Prince Igor Burma shirt and a pair of Jockey Life Slim Guy underwear, size 36. No mention of Roselli's pants; his legs had been sawed off, not completely but just enough to allow them to be, as the report put it, "fractured terminally." A terrycloth gag was taped around Roselli's head, covering his mouth and nose. Cause of death: asphyxiation. Some argue whether his "sleeping with the fishes" finale stemmed from injudicious skimming of Las Vegas casino profits or from Handsome Johnny's telling the Feds that he believed Fidel Castro had killed JFK.

Whatever the motive, Johnny was silenced forever.

After Roselli's remains were found, Bryan Foy gave a statement to the *New York Times*: "We never saw the gangster side of him. … Half the people in this town were his friends. No one who ever had a drink or dinner with Johnny ever picked up the check." Similarly, they quoted Breen Jr. saying, "In all the time I knew him, John never asked me to do anything illegal, or even immoral."

And with that, we'll give Brynie Foy the last word: "The only B picture is a bad picture." ■

of the Past

Collecting Film Noir Posters

Brian Light

Growing up in New York City in the 1960s, films like *The Maltese Falcon*, *Laura*, *Double Indemnity*, *Sunset Boulevard*, and *Cry of the City*, among others, made quite an impression on me. But it wasn't until the late '70s, when I came across Paul Schrader's essay "Notes on Film Noir" in a back issue of *Film Comment*, that I began to recognize the stylistic and thematic elements that connected these films. I sought out theaters where I could see them on the big screen. In the 1970s and '80s, Manhattan boasted some great revival theaters: The Little Carnegie, in the basement of Carnegie Hall; The Bleeker Street Cinema; Theater 80 on St. Marks Place; and the Thalia, up on 95th Street & Broadway.

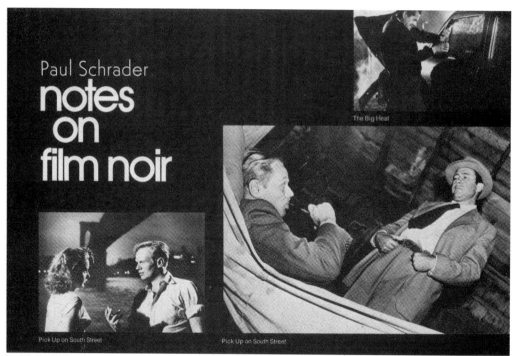

Paul Schrader's seminal essay in *Film Comment*

All manner of foreign, independent, and genre films were screened in these cozy venues. *The Village Voice* was the go-to calendar guide, and when it told me the Thalia was rolling out an ambitious film noir retrospective, screening a triple-feature every mid-week afternoon—I knew how I'd be spending my Wednesdays. First up was a program devoted to Fritz Lang. The first film, *The Big Heat*, *was* a stiff jab to the solar plexus. *The Blue Gardenia* didn't have quite the same edge, but was intriguing nonetheless. I was on the fence about staying for the third feature, *Scarlet Street*, although it did star Eddie Robinson. I decided to give it twenty minutes. Fifteen minutes in, I was stapled to my seat. When Robinson grabbed that handy ice pick—there was no going back for me. On the way out, poleaxed, I lingered to feast my eyes on some vintage movie posters displayed in the lobby expressly for the festival.

I was no neophyte regarding movie posters. I'd been collecting since the mid-'70s, a time when paper (a collector's term for posters) could be had for a song. The material was out there—it was only a question of personal preference. My focus was on two favorite directors: Alfred Hitchcock and Preston Sturges. I had accumulated posters in varying sizes on some of their key titles, many of which command respectable prices in today's market. What appealed to me was how the best of them captured the spirit of the films— graphic designs that expressed precisely what you loved about the movie. That afternoon in the lobby of the Thalia was a turning point for me. I realized how well the visual elements of noir were transmuted into the poster designs—broken men and scheming women elbow-deep in crime and betrayal, struggling and often failing to find a way out. It's perversely invigorating to watch these sordid stories unfold in the darkness of a movie theater—and the posters conveyed the same feeling. I decided then and there to trade all my posters (well, except for *Shadow of a Doubt* and *Strangers on a Train*) and go all-in on film noir.

Back then, there were plenty of options to feed the paper habit. New York hosted several annual trade shows at the Sheraton Hotel in Times Square. A monthly show, smaller in scale, was organized by the Gallagher brothers in Saint Anne's church basement on West 19th Street, where you'd be likely to rub elbows with talk-show legend Joe Franklin, digging through a pile of movie stills. There

The author's office. Anchored in the corner by a rare insert for *The Maltese Falcon*, a black-and-white "full bleed" one-sheet for *Kiss of Death* and a *Double Indemnity* one-sheet from Barbara Stanwyck's personal collection

were assorted shops around town specializing in movie memorabilia: Mark Ricci's Memory Shop on "Book Row," Cinemabilia (a few blocks east; one of François Truffaut's haunts when in Manhattan), and Jerry Ohlinger's Movie Material Store in Greenwich Village were my favorite stamping grounds. Long-time New Jersey collector Steve Sally and his son had a hole-in-the-wall storefront off 8th Avenue in the Theater District, and there was Movie Star News on West 14th Street, where legendary smut purveyor Irving Klaw plied his trade in the 1950s. Irving died in 1966, but his sister Paula presided over the second-floor shop until rent increases forced her to relocate to West 18th Street in the early 1980s.

Hunting expeditions often led to oddball interactions, and for those The Memory Shop topped the list. Homeless people occasionally swept the three steps leading down to the shop, and Mark— whom Leonard Maltin said reminded him of Pancho Villa (in more ways than one)—was stationed behind the splintered and worn wooden counter. He sported a dusty gray toupée that resembled a deconstructed bird's nest, and he never failed to look distant and disinterested. Every title I inquired about elicited the same response: "That's been weeded out, but come back next week and I'll see what I can dig up." Then, he would disengage, and that was my cue to drift. My return trips often yielded choice pieces: one-sheets for *The Palm Beach Story* and *Vertigo*, a style "B" half-sheet for *Notorious*, to name just a few. After my noir epiphany, Mark surprised me with not one, but *two* complete lobby card sets for *Detour* in the original brown distribution envelopes, a style "B" half-sheet for *Brute Force*, and one-sheets for *The Big Combo* and *The Big Heat*.

Joe Burtis, a long-time private collector and Director of Client Services at The Motion Picture Arts Gallery in New Jersey, traversed the same terrain:

When I was 15, my father would shuttle me in on the train from New Jersey to visit three shops all within a few blocks of each other. Cinemabilia, the most user-friendly, had books and magazines displayed neatly on wooden shelves, and there were bins of cardboard-backed photos.

Cigar-chomping Jerry Ohlinger, New York's "last man standing" in the movie memorabilia trade, at one of four incarnations of his famed shop

Customer service, however, was not on the menu. The proprietor, Ernest Burns, was an imposing character and his manner was like Clifton Webb on a bad day. The Memory Shop was easily the shabbiest of the bunch and Movie Star News was by far my favorite, and the reason I initially collected photos more than anything else. I would patiently pull out and sort through manila folders for *711 Ocean Drive*, *Thieves' Highway* or whatever other movies I had recently seen. My father, who was an advertising executive and a very proper old-school WASP would sit patiently making small talk with Paula Klaw, which was a sight in and of itself.

As I made the rounds year in and year out, I formulated a theory on four general types of collectors:

• Those who buy as an investment and are motivated to sell high or trade up when the opportunity arises;
• Those who collect movie posters that feature particular stars, like William Powell, Marilyn Monroe, or Charlie Chaplin;
• Those enthusiasts driven by a personal connection to a specific movie, i.e. *Casablanca*, *King Kong*, *Citizen Kane*, *This Gun for Hire*, or genre style, i.e. silent films, horror films, screwball comedies, film noir, and
• Those who collect for the graphic design—the exotic, erotic, or novelty content. It's not necessary for them to have seen the movies represented in their collections, they simply take pleasure in the poster itself.

Naturally, there is crossover between each type of collector. Joe and I happen to fall into the third category; Steve Olson, a private collector and proprietor of AAA Vintage Movie Posters, is in the fourth group:

I collect posters more for the art than the movie, and each era and country seem to have their own aesthetic. Polish posters have the most intense, unique, and frequently macabre posters, while the Italian posters of the '40s and '50s usually have a high level of artistry and design. A favorite type of mine are the party posters that came out of the roaring '20s and early '30s, with everyone having the most fun imaginable and titles like *Down to Their Last Yacht* and *Hips... Hips... Hooray*.

When my poster passion moved permanently to Dark City, I strove to be a completist, an admittedly unattainable goal, but I had the proverbial dog-on-a-bone tenacity. The mission led me to formulate my own grading system for posters, breaking them into three categories:

- A great movie, but an average poster design *(Force of Evil)*
- An average movie, but a great poster design *(Somewhere in the Night)*
- A great movie *and* a great poster design *(T-Men)*

These categories are entirely subjective—one man's Picasso is another man's Pollock—but they have helped me establish the criteria by which I built my collection.

Anyone new to poster collecting should familiarize themselves with the various sizes and formats that were produced for American advertising campaigns (pre-1980s). The 27" x 41" one-sheet (portrait format) provides the general dimensions that all other poster sizes correspond with, give or take a few inches in height or width.

Other sizes include:
- **Half-sheet** (landscape format, 22" x 28")
- **Insert** (portrait format, 14" x 36")
- **Lobby Card** (landscape format, 11" x 14")
- **Window Card** (portrait format, 14" x 22")
- **Two-sheet** (portrait or landscape format, 41" x 54")
- **Three-sheet** (portrait format, 41" x 81")
- **Six-sheet** – (square format, 81" x 81")
- **Twenty-four-sheet** (billboard format, 246" x 108")

Two other posters sizes—30" x 40" and 40" x 60", both on card stock—are far less common.

Since the late 19th century, most posters were stone lithographs, meaning they were printed in individual color stages using limestone plates (eventually replaced with zinc plates), a process similar to woodblock and linocut prints. By the early '50s, stone lithography was gradually replaced by offset photolithography, a less expensive and labor-intensive process by which the original artwork is photographed and a printing plate is made from the film. Original stone/zinc lithos of one-sheets and three-sheets are prized by serious poster collectors.

From 1940 to the early 1980s, most movie posters were printed by regional National Screen Service (NSS) branches and typically distributed through independent movie poster exchanges to participating theaters. These posters were never intended to be distributed to the general public. Lobby cards were issued in sets of eight—a title card and seven scene cards—except for Paramount films, which did not issue title cards. Depending on the studio, one-sheets, half-sheets, and inserts were issued in multiple styles with different artwork or inset photos designated by "A" or "B" in the lower left corner. Some studios even produced one-sheets in more than two styles—the 1931 *Dracula* poster was, for example, produced in as many as six styles. The last two digits of the original release date can be found in the lower right corner along with the NSS print number, i.e. 48/245 indicating

The author's office. A gallery of Humphrey Bogart title lobby cards and two style "A" half-sheets for *Out of the Past* and *Gun Crazy*

the release date of 1948, and the 245th movie released that year. If a movie was rereleased at a later date, the artwork may contain a slight variation in graphic design and the new release date will be preceded by an "R." Initially, the posters were "rented" with the film print and returned. Eventually, the nominal rental fee became a purchase fee, and only the film print would be returned. With the exception of lobby cards, most posters were machine folded, and often refolded multiple times to facilitate mailing. This accounts for the creases seen in most posters from that period. They were occasionally rolled or stored flat and never folded, but that's rare. Half-sheets, inserts, lobby cards, and window cards are printed on card stock; one-sheets, three-sheets, six-sheets, and twenty-four-sheets were printed on paper stock.

There are several things to look for when considering the purchase of a poster: paper separation (generally along the fold lines), toning (age-related darkening), and brittle texture (dried-out paper). All these condition issues can be repaired by a qualified restorer. However, paper loss—in which portions are missing from the poster—requires not only a skilled restorer, but a true artist to paint or airbrush in the missing areas after the poster has been mounted on linen or Japanese rice paper to stabilize it.

Mario Cueva, the force behind Lumiere Poster Restoration, applies a near-forensic approach to his work:

Each poster is unique in its requirements, but the most difficult repair is when a poster has completely dissected at the fold lines and has many areas of paper loss. Often just putting it all back together is a challenge. All the pieces must harmoniously align, from that point forward, all measurements must match to the original poster size, then we must research high resolution images to recreate missing areas, and match colors.

Having an excellent restorer at your disposal gives you greater buying power. Over the years, I've

TERRIFIC . . . and True!

THE RAW, SAVAGE, SCREEN-SEARING STORY OF THE TREASURY'S TOUGH GUYS!

T-MEN

Presented by
EDWARD SMALL

STARRING
DENNIS O'KEEFE

WITH MARY MEADE · ALFRED RYDER · WALLY FORD
JUNE LOCKHART · CHARLES McGRAW

Produced by   Directed by
AUBREY SCHENCK · ANTHONY MANN

Written by John C. Higgins · Suggested by a Story by Virginia Kellogg
AN EAGLE LION FILMS RELEASE

Country of Origin: U.S.A.   48/663

acquired a number of choice posters that most collectors passed on due to condition issues. After my restoration artist—and he is an artist—worked his magic, they look as good as they did when first released. The price I paid, combined with the restoration fees, were often well below the poster's current market value. A reputable dealer or auction house should provide a detailed condition report, including ALL the restoration (if any) done to the piece. If one has the opportunity to view a poster in person, holding it to a light source will reveal any portions that were missing prior to restoration. And always look at the piece "off axis" (from different angles) to detect the over-application of paint. Some collectors prefer unrestored posters regardless of condition (more common in Europe) because they feel signs of age lend "character" to the piece. If one elects to have a piece restored, it is advisable to choose a qualified expert with a solid reputation. Ask to see examples of their restoration work, such as before-and-after high resolution images. A great restoration job will not only make the poster look better, it will also preserve and add value to the piece. A poor restoration job—improper mounting, applying of too much paint, or over air-brushing—will devalue the piece and could require further restoration down the road.

If you plan to frame your poster(s), it's also advisable to use a professional, reliable framer. As with the linen and Japanese paper used to mount and restore the poster, all the framing materials should be archival (acid free.) Never have a poster mounted on foamcore board and never use glass which can stick to the poster over time. Plexiglass with a UV, non-glare filter (which prevents fading and eliminates reflections) is the best option. Once the piece is framed, the back is usually sealed with brown Kraft paper to prevent dust and/or silver fish from affecting the piece. Because of this, it's hard to see what materials were used. This is where the reliability of the framer comes into play. As I moved around New York, and later to Los Angeles, I often evaluated a new apartment or house not by how much natural light filled the spaces, but by how much "wall-estate" there was. Having essentially maxed out my current space, I tend to rotate posters; in the process, I discovered that one framer—whom I no longer use—relied on low-grade commercial cardboard to shore up the rear of the poster inside the frame, forming an acidic environment for the poster. Needless to say, that's a major no-no.

Collecting is a financial investment and an emotional one, as well. I recommend collecting posters related to the films you feel most passionate about, those films you would like to take home and surround yourself with, be it in your living room, dining room, office, or bedroom. For me, they are all old friends that keep me company as I marshal through the daily grind. Robert Mitchum, Gene Tierney, Burt Lancaster, Barbara Stanwyck, Eddie Robinson, Liz Scott, Robert Ryan, and Gloria Grahame all live on, not only on celluloid and Blu-ray…they continue to reside right here with me in my home. ■

This page - Ava Gardner in *Singapore* (1947)
Above right - Joan Crawford in *Rain* (1932)

Asian Exotica

THE FAR EAST IN FILM NOIR

Lisa Lieberman

Asia was prime territory for dark, disturbing tales well before the noir era. Some of the best-known films set in the East originated in the 1920s or earlier as risqué melodramas on the Broadway stage or the silent screen. Remade in the '40s and '50s—in censored versions—they still have the power to unsettle.

"Darling, it's those little inconveniences that make the Orient so interesting," the American tourist played by Spring Byington tells her husband in *Singapore* (1947). She's the acquisitive sort of tourist who gives Americans abroad a bad name. Rickshaw rides, frenetic sightseeing excursions, antique vases to show off to the folks back home in Minneapolis. Mrs. Bellows proves that exotic travel need not be mind expanding, but she's hardly typical of Westerners in this film. Amid the secret gambling dens that can only be reached by boat, the shady White Russians trafficking in precious gems, Matt Gordon (Fred MacMurray) is perfectly at home. Granted, it's hard to believe he's a smuggler. Not when he's falling in love with Ava Gardner's character, Linda. We're never told what brought Linda to Singapore on the eve of World War II. Wanderlust, perhaps, or boredom. She's wealthy, with a life to go back to in New York, but after a week spent drinking gin slings with Matt, she's ready to abandon it all. Nor is she put off when she encounters one of his light-fingered associates rifling their hotel room. Learning that the exquisite pearl necklace Matt gave her is contraband, she lies to the police about how she got it, and she lies easily. The couple seem destined for a life of piracy, but the Japanese attack on Singapore derails their love affair. Five years later, after a stint in the Navy, Matt returns to retrieve the stash of pearls he'd hidden in his suite. He believes Linda is dead, but then he glimpses her on the dance floor in the arms of another man: her husband. She's calling herself Ann, and claims she doesn't recognize him. The old Matt, the pirate, would have stolen her away, but the war has changed him, made him noble, like Humphrey Bogart in *Casablanca*.

Even at his worst, MacMurray's a boy scout compared to Gene Tierney's character in *The Shanghai Gesture* (1941). Poppy has come to China straight from finishing school looking for excitement, and the casino run by Mother Gin Sling (Ona Munson in yellowface) has it all. Shanghai, "a speck . . . torn away from the mystery of China," we are informed at the end of the title sequence, "grew into a refuge for people who wished to live between the lines of laws and customs—a modern Tower of Babel." Indeed, our first glimpse of Mother Gin Sling's establishment, a high-angle shot of the circular gaming room, shows a dizzying scene of greed and confusion, like something out of Hieronymus Bosch—with the addition of Marcel Dalio (pre-*Casablanca*) presiding over the roulette table. "It smells so incredibly evil," says Poppy, settling in at the bar. "I didn't think such a place existed except in my own imagination. Anything could happen here." At Mother Gin Sling's prompting, the Fez-wearing gigolo played by Victor Mature draws Poppy into depravity and she is soon adrift, utterly lost, just as she wanted.

That impulse, the willful plunge into the abyss, was endorsed by 19th-century Romantics. Better to succumb to a destructive, all-consuming obsession than to live without passion. Some, like Thomas Coleridge, used opium to reach this place. His famous poem, "Kubla Khan," composed in 1797 while under the influence, was replete with sensuous images of the Mongol emperor's "pleasure dome:" lush gardens filled with fragrant, incense-bearing trees; a deep, romantic chasm haunted by a woman "wailing for her demon-lover;" the fertile earth, trembling and panting; a sacred river flowing into a sunless sea; a spouting fountain.

You get the point. Asia carried an erotic charge that fit with the Romantic sensibility. The hero of Alphonse de Lamartine's *Raphaël* luxuriated in his suffering, describing death as "a voluptuous surrender into infinity," a fatalistic outlook that Lamartine apparently acquired in the 1830s during his travels throughout the Orient (a term that encompassed the Middle East, India, China, Japan, Korea, the Philippines, and Southeast Asia). Artistic pilgrimages to far-off lands—actual travel, as opposed to opium-fueled fantasies—grew increasingly common as the 19th century progressed. The East was seen as a site of forbidden pleasures, and audiences were keen to indulge vicariously in the illicit activities described in the creative works these journeys inspired.

After seeing the Tahiti exhibit at the 1889 Universal Exposition in Paris, Paul Gaugin set off for the South Seas in quest of "a more natural, more primitive, and above all, less spoiled life," as he expressed it in a letter to Vincent van Gogh, a life he chronicled in a memoir of the nine years he spent on Tahiti, *Noa Noa*, and in the paintings of the half-naked island girls he slept with. Pierre Loti's semi-autobiographical novel about a Japanese geisha abandoned and betrayed by the French naval officer who purchased her as his temporary bride while stationed in Nagasaki, *Madame Chrysanthème* (1888), was another titillating account from this period. Reworked into the short story "Madame Butterfly" (1898) by the American writer John Luther Long, it was subsequently adapted for the stage becoming the inspiration for Puccini's famous opera, which premiered at La Scala in 1910. Numerous silent film versions followed, the most notable being the 1915 adaptation with Mary Pickford as the geisha and *The Toll of the Sea* (1922), a rare technicolor feature starring Chinese-American actress Anna May Wong as the abandoned bride.

Rivaling the passive, sexually available Asian woman was the fascinating figure of the evil genius, Dr. Fu Manchu, with his plans for world domination and his lust for white women. British author Sax

Gene Tierney in *The Shanghai Gesture* (1941)

Rohmer claimed he knew nothing about China, but that wasn't quite true. By the time he began the series in 1912, he had plenty of material to work with, most of it made up. Gambling, opium dens, white slavery, and perverse sexual acts were attributed to the Chinese, fueling the anti-immigration sentiment that resulted in quotas and restrictive laws in America such as the Chinese Exclusion Act of 1882. In England, Rudyard Kipling wrote of his wanderings in Limehouse, the Chinese quarter in London's East End, with revulsion. "I hated the Chinaman before; I hated him doubly as I choked for breath in his seething streets." The weekly *Girl's Own Paper*, a Christian publication founded in 1880 and aimed at the moral improvement of women and children, complained about "the readiness of the Chinese to settle in the midst of other nations," raising concern over racial mingling.

Publicly, audiences may have been averse to the depiction of interracial romances between whites and Asians, but the frisson of such unions was undeniable. Japanese actor Sessue Hayakawa, the first Asian to play an Asian character on-screen, was a matinee idol well before Valentino. Best known today for his performance as the sadistic Colonel Saito in *The Bridge on the River Kwai* (1957), he first gained notice in the role of a Japanese ivory dealer who brands the shoulder of the white woman he lusts after in Cecil B. DeMille's *The Cheat* (1915), an act that seemed only to enhance his allure in much the same way that Valentino's rape of the dancing girl would a decade later in *Son of the Sheik* (1926). "My crientele is women. They rike me to be strong and violent," Hayakawa allegedly told a reporter.

The film versions of Rohmer's stories pandered to moviegoers' prurient interests. Made before the Hays Code, *The Mask of Fu Manchu* (1932) packs quite a fetishistic kick. There's a little something for everyone here: scenes of the evil doctor (Boris Karloff in yellowface) preparing to torture the handsome fiancé of the blonde heroine, stroking his victim's naked chest with his long fingernails before injecting him with a serum that will turn him into a slave. A kinky sequence where the young man is whipped by two semi-naked black minions of Fu Manchu's daughter (Myrna Loy in yellowface). Loy's character is clearly enjoying the spectacle, but her heart still belongs to Daddy.

An early Frank Capra film, *The Bitter Tea of General Yen* (1933), features an interracial romance between a white missionary played by Barbara Stanwyck and a Chinese warlord (Swedish heartthrob Nils Asther in yellowface). Stanwyck's character is captured by the warlord and she has an erotic dream about him, imagining him as a brutal and passionate lover, although he turns out to be a gentleman and, in a departure from the novel upon which the film was based, their mutual attraction remains chaste. *General Yen* was yanked eight days into its run, the sight of "a Chinaman attempting to romance with a pretty and supposedly decent young American white woman," as Sam Shain put it in *Variety*, deemed too shocking for audiences at the time. Nevertheless, the film was selected as the first film to be screened at Radio City Music Hall.

Leaving miscegenation aside, adulterous liaisons were the norm in Hollywood films produced during the Golden Age and set in exotic Asian locales. *Sadie Thompson*, a 1928 silent, has Gloria Swanson as a former prostitute ravished by a stern—and married—missionary (Lionel Barrymore) in Pago Pago; the 1932 version of the story, *Rain*, starred Joan Crawford and Walter Huston; there was even a 1953 3D musical adaptation with Rita Hayworth. The frustrated overseer of a rubber plantation in French Indochina (Clark Gable) initiates an affair with his engineer's wife (Mary Astor) in *Red Dust* (1932), but relinquishes her and allows himself to finally be consoled by the good-time girl played by Jean Harlow. The action moves to Africa in the 1953 remake, *Mogambo*, but Gable remains, with Ava Gardner in the Harlow role and Grace Kelly as the adulterous wife. (Kelly and Gable reputedly had a thing going during the production.) Greta Garbo, meanwhile, forgets her saintly husband (Herbert Marshall) and succumbs to the advances of a married diplomatic attaché in cholera-ridden China in *The Painted Veil* (1934). This film was remade twice, as *The Seventh Sin* (1957), with Eleanor Parker and directed by Ronald Neame, and with an all-star cast in 2006 including Naomi Watts and Liev Schreiber.

The Letter was only remade once, but the second (1940) version, directed by William Wyler and

Barbara Stanwyck in *The Bitter Tea of General Yen* (1933)

Bette Davis in *The Letter* (1940)

starring Bette Davis, is the epitome of Asian noir.[1] The 1929 version had Jeanne Eagels as the wife of an English rubber plantation owner in Malaysia who shoots her lover (Herbert Marshall) when she learns that he is leaving her for his Chinese mistress, then tries to convince the colonial authorities that she acted in self-defense. It earned Eagels an Oscar nomination, but the pairing of William Wyler and Bette Davis, like that of Josef von Sternberg and Marlene Dietrich, was pure magic. Maybe Davis was right when she claimed that an affair between a star and her director produces electricity that the audience feels. She called Wyler the love of her life, and her performances in the three films they made together during their tempestuous relationship—the other two were *Jezebel* (1938) and *The Little Foxes* (1941)—were magnificent.

"Every time I met him, I hated myself, and yet I lived for the moment when I'd see him again," Davis's character confesses in *The Letter*, and we believe her. The isolation of the Malay plantation, the sultry climate, the strangeness of the country has unmoored her, and when we meet her lover's Chinese "wife" (Gale Sondergaard in yellowface), we are brought up against that unnerving strangeness. Davis' character had written a letter summoning her lover to the plantation on the evening when she shot him. If this evidence comes to light, she will no longer be able to maintain her story—that he surprised her while her husband (Herbert Marshall) was away and would have violated her—had she not seized a gun and impulsively shot him. Sondergaard's character has the letter and threatens to turn it over to the prosecution unless Davis agrees to meet her. A gong sounds. The beaded curtain at one end of the room where Davis has been waiting parts and the dragon lady emerges, her face impassive. Coldly, she accepts the money that Davis' lawyer has brought in exchange for the incriminating letter, which she drops on the floor for Davis to pick up. In his *New York Times* review of the film, Bosley Crowther remarked upon "the enigmatic menace of the native woman," while *Variety* called Sondergaard "the perfect mask-like threat." The Dragon Lady (a term coined by cartoonist Milt Caniff in 1936 for a character in his strip *Terry and the Pirates*) seemed the perfect embodiment of the East's most threatening, yet enticing, aspects.

Good stories make good movies. The author of "Miss Thompson," *The Painted Veil*, and *The Letter* was a master storyteller who reveled in the strangeness he discovered in Asia, not only because it provided material for stories, but

1   The story was filmed a third time, but it was moved stateside in David Goodis' reimagining of Somerset Maugham's classic, retitled *The Unfaithful* (1947).

Jane Russell in *Macao* (1952)

because he found it liberating. W. Somerset Maugham was born during the height of the Victorian era. Orphaned at a young age, he was sent to live with his uncle, a vicar, and placed in boarding school at the age of eleven. Early on, he was attracted to men, but with Oscar Wilde (whose writing he admired) convicted and sentenced to two years hard labor for homosexuality just as Maugham was coming of age, he found it prudent to pursue his romantic adventures on the continent, in places known to be more tolerant than England. In Paris, Maugham saw an exhibit of Gauguin's Tahitian paintings, and once he was earning enough income from his literary career to permit him to travel further afield, he sailed to Polynesia with a male companion, Gerald Haxton, leaving his wife and daughter behind. There he began *The Moon and Sixpence*, a novel inspired by the life of Gauguin, and also wrote the story "Miss Thompson," which his protégé John Colton would adapt for the stage as *Rain*. A second expedition took Maugham and Haxton to China, Shanghai being the high point of their journey. "Here," as Selina Hastings writes in her biography, *The Secret Lives of Somerset Maugham*, "every kind of sexual delicacy was provided, the famous boy brothels in particular popular with Europeans." *The Painted Veil* was inspired by this trip, *The Letter* by a later voyage to Singapore.

Maugham specialized in tales of frustrated passion among expatriate missionaries, businessmen, diplomatic personnel, administrative functionaries and their wives in Britain's colonial outposts. Hastings suggests that his bad women were not truly bad because he fully inhabited anyone who suffered for love, having experienced such loneliness firsthand. The films made from Maugham's stories get under the skin because his characters' torments feel authentic, and much more could be conveyed explicitly before the Hays Code. *The Shanghai Gesture*, written by his protégé John Colton, had this quality as well, which helps to explain why Josef von Sternberg was so eager to direct it. "The pain that fascinates and the pleasure that kills," as decadent poet Charles Baudelaire put it, was always his subject.

In contrast, *Singapore* and *Calcutta* (1947), lack depth. In the latter film, Alan Ladd falls in love with the fiancée of his murdered friend, a fellow pilot who'd stumbled upon a smuggling ring in the Indian city. The fiancée (Gail Russell), a seemingly innocent young American woman, turns out to be allied with the smugglers. Ladd is not as astute as Humphrey Bogart in *The Maltese Falcon* and has to slap her around to get the truth out of her, but otherwise he's a straight arrow. The city of Calcutta harbors an interesting mix of characters of various nationalities—many of them criminal, but none of them sinister. Ladd was in no real danger of losing his bearings there.

Robert Mitchum and Jane Russell are two lost souls, both of them hiding their vulnerability behind wise-cracking facades in *Macao* (1952), a film with a troubled history of its own. Josef von Sternberg was hired by Howard Hughes to direct the picture, which was intended to showcase Russell's talents, but he treated the actress so atrociously that Hughes fired him and brought in Nicholas Ray to complete the project. The tension on the set probably accounts for the edgy performances of the two stars. Mitchum's character, Nick, rescues Julie (Russell) from a lecherous fellow passenger on the steamer that is taking them to Macao. In return, she picks his pocket, takes the cash, and drops his passport and wallet overboard, but despite the inauspicious beginning to their relationship, they seek refuge in one another. "I'm so tired of running," she tells him. "What else can we do?" Nick replies. He's had his own run-ins with the law, as he explains to the crooked casino boss, Halloran (Brad Dexter), who suspects him of being an undercover police detective. Everyone in Halloran's orbit is tainted, from his Japanese henchman (Korean-American actor Philip Ahn) to the corrupt Portuguese police lieutenant (Thomas Gomez) and his insecure mistress, the croupier played by Gloria Grahame. Even the real undercover detective (William Bendix) who is trying to take Halloran down uses Nick as a decoy to get what he wants. By the time we get to the stunning chase scene on the docks, dangling fishnets and long shadows shot in von Sternberg's trademark style, we don't know who to trust.

Asia is more than a colorful backdrop in *Macao*. Dangerous, disorienting, and exhilarating, the best of the noir films set in the East demonstrate that no matter how far you travel for an exotic adventure, you cannot escape your demons. ∎

FALLOUT

WHEN RED SPIES CRISS-CROSSED WITH FILM NOIR

The True Story of Vladimir Pozner, Irving Lerner, and Ben Maddow

By John Wranovics

Not long after the bombing of Japan in early August 1945 hastened the end of World War II, Congress began investigating Soviet spy rings within the United States that were hunting for atomic secrets. The probe gave rise to the Red Scare and was the first signpost on the road to the Cold War. The American public's mood, a mix of fear and paranoia, imbued new themes of existential dread in postwar film noir. Soon, movies like *Walk a Crooked Mile* (1948), *The Atomic City* (1952), *Split Second* (1953), *Kiss Me Deadly* (1955), and *City of Fear* (1959), among many others, gave nuclear radiation a starring role.

Beyond the cinematic references, there was a real-world intersection of noir and the bomb. The surprising story shines a light on how closely the activities of leftist screenwriters and directors Vladimir Pozner (*The Conspirators* [1944], *The Dark Mirror* [1946]), Irving Lerner (*Murder by Contract* [1958], *City of Fear* [1959]), and Ben Maddow (*Framed* [1947], *Intruder in the Dust* [1949], *The Asphalt Jungle* [1950]), overlapped with Soviet espionage efforts to steal A-bomb secrets from scientists at the University of California in 1943 and 1944.

In 1943 and 1944, as scientists at the University of California developed the first atom bomb, left-wing filmmakers (clockwise, top left) Ben Maddow, Vladimir Pozner, and Irving Lerner all found their way to Berkeley and surprising proximity to atomic secrets

In fact, noir and the bomb were linked from the start. In 1942, J. Robert Oppenheimer, then overseeing development of the atom bomb, first at UC Berkeley and later in Los Alamos, New Mexico, recruited physicist Robert Serber to work on the Manhattan Project. Serber, who chose the code names for the first devices, later recalled, "At Los Alamos I had given the bombs names descriptive of their shapes; the gun assembly was 'The Thin Man,' taken from the title of the Dashiell Hammett detective novel. … 'The Fat Man,' for the implosion bomb, then followed naturally, after Sidney Greenstreet's role in *The Maltese Falcon*."

Another criss-crossing of noir and the bomb is found almost a year after the war ended, in July 1946, when the US government conducted "Operation Crossroads" tests in the Marshall Islands. On the Bikini Atoll, the first A-bomb since Nagasaki, a 23-kiloton device, was detonated. It was named "Gilda" after Rita Hayworth's character in Charles Vidor's 1946 classic. The bomb's casing was adorned with the actress's image. On the night of the test, June 30, 1946, Orson Welles, then married to Hayworth, spoke on ABC radio:

Her face is not on the atom bomb by her own choosing, but by election of the fliers who will drop the bomb. … I want my daughter to be able to tell her daughter that grandmother's picture was on the *last* atom bomb ever to explode.

A month later the FBI filed a classified report entitled "Soviet Activities in the United States."[1] In the "Atom Bomb Espionage" section, the report states:

---

1   Held in the Clark Clifford papers at the Harry S. Truman Library, Independence, Missouri.

The first overt attempt of Soviet Espionage Agents to obtain information regarding the atom bomb was made at the Radiation Laboratory of the University of California, Berkeley, California. At the solicitation of Peter Ivanov, Secretary of the Soviet Consulate in San Francisco, California, George Charles Eltenton, a British scientist who had worked in the Soviet Union, requested Haakon Maurice Chevalier, a Professor of Languages at the University of California, to approach scientists working on the atom bomb project for information to be transmitted to the Soviet Union through consulate channels. Chevalier tried unsuccessfully to obtain data from Professor J. R. Oppenheimer in the early spring of 1943.

The report also describes a second incident at the university:

During the winter of 1944 Irving Lerner, then employed in the Motion Picture Division of the Office of War Information, attempted to make motion pictures of the cyclotron at the University of California in Berkeley. These scheduled motion pictures were completely unauthorized and Lerner acted without the knowledge of the Office of War Information or the Office of Censorship. Lerner was a contact of both (Arthur) Adams and (Eric) Bernay, above mentioned, and subsequently resigned from the Office of War Information to take employment at Keynote Recordings, Inc. Adams disappeared from New York January 23, 1945 and is believed to have returned to Moscow, USSR where his wife resides.

J. Robert Oppenheimer (called "Opje" or "Oppie" by acquaintances) and Haakon Chevalier were for many years inseparable friends, but their relationship would end in betrayal after the physicist informed the government about Chevalier's conversational suggestion of sharing atomic secrets with the Russians. His initial convoluted attempts to shield Chevalier's name from federal investigators ultimately led to Oppenheimer being stripped of his security clearance in 1954.

Chevalier was a popular young professor at UC Berkeley. A renowned translator of French literature, he introduced to American readers many major writers, including Anatole France, André Malraux, and Louis Aragon. Another of these writers was Vladimir Solomonovich Pozner— "Voldoya" to friends. A Parisian of Russian descent, Pozner spent his youth in St. Petersburg before returning to France, where he studied at the Sorbonne and joined the French Communist Party.

Pozner first befriended Oppenheimer when he stopped in Berkeley to stay with Chevalier during a road trip across the United States in 1938. Three years later, with the war blazing, Pozner left France again and made his way to the Bay Area for a longer stay. He and his family moved to 272 Coventry Road in Berkeley, a four-minute drive from Oppenheimer's house at 1 Eagle Hill Road in the neighboring town of Kensington. Soon after, Pozner found work as a shipwright and checker at Permanente Metals's Kaiser Shipyard No. 2 in Richmond, helping to build Victory and Liberty ships for the war effort.

Pozner's most recent novel, *Deuil 24 heures*, a fictional account of his year serving in the French army, was translated by Chevalier and published to critical acclaim in the United States as *The Edge of the Sword* in 1942. It also caught the attention of Dashiell Hammett and Lillian Hellman. Herman Shumlin, Hellman's regular producer, took an option on the book, hoping Hellman could turn it into a play. Hammett composed a glowing endorsement for the book's publisher: "Vladimir Pozner's *The Edge of the Sword* is by far the best novel that has come out of this war so far—and not many better novels have come out of any war."

During their two-and-half-year stay in Berkeley, the Pozners' relationship with the Chevaliers and Oppenheimers grew stronger. What knitted them together was their shared interest in leftist politics and literature. Pozner later remembered that Oppenheimer "had read and knew well the works of Marx and Lenin, all their works." The three families socialized regularly from the time the Pozners

In early 1943, Haakon Chevalier (right), close friend of atomic physicist J. Robert Oppenheimer (left), privately raised the idea of sharing secret atom bomb research with Soviet spies. The so-called "Chevalier Incident" destroyed their friendship and derailed Oppenheimer's career

settled in until March 15, 1943—the day before the Oppenheimers left for an extended stay in Los Alamos (although their destination was unspoken). Pozner wrote:

> I also remember the reception at Opje's, in his house on Eagle Hill, the farewells he and Kitty made that day to their friends who did not know the reason and purpose of the trip while attaching to it the largest, and most obscure meaning.

The bond between the physicist and the Frenchman is evident in Pozner's recall of Oppenheimer's farewell gifts:

> He and his wife and son left for our baby, who was on the verge of being born, his first clothes and, for our daughter, toys: a giraffe, a rabbit, and a handsome gray mare with black mane, which she still possesses, like me, I kept the gift that Opje gave to me, a small volume bound in leather, with its name penned on the front page: Goethe's Faust. I was glad to receive this present, without attaching a particular meaning to it at the moment, without looking for an allusion to it, or even sensing a coincidence.

Not long before the Oppenheimers departed for Los Alamos, on an evening in January or February (neither Chevalier nor Oppenheimer pinpointed the date), the so-called Chevalier Incident took place at Oppenheimer's home. As Opje mixed his famous cocktails in the kitchen and the wives chatted in the living room, Haakon quietly shared their mutual friend George Eltenton's proposal that Oppenheimer's research could be easily and covertly shared with the Russians.

Eltenton, a scientist at Shell Development Corporation (then located near Berkeley in Emeryville), knew Oppenheimer and Chevalier through leftist social events as well as Opje's efforts to help unionize the local Shell scientists. Eltenton and his wife, both British, were also close friends with Grigori Kheifets, the Soviet vice consul in San Francisco, and Peter (Pyotr) Ivanov, the consulate's third secretary. Acquiring atom bomb secrets from UC Berkeley was one of Kheifets's main assignments.

Oppenheimer's political radicalization blossomed during the 1930s, stemming to some degree from his strong attraction to left-wing young women. Among his numerous lovers was pianist Estelle Caen, sister of renowned San Francisco newspaper columnist Herb Caen. Historians credit Jean Tatlock, a Berkeley girlfriend, with having the biggest influence on Oppenheimer's activism. The daughter of a University of California English professor, Jean was a Stanford-trained psychiatrist. She was also a member of the Communist Party and wrote for the *Western Worker* newspaper, a predecessor to *People's World,* the West Coast's leading Communist newspaper. Reputedly, Oppenheimer code named the first atomic bomb test, detonated July 16, 1945, "Trinity" as a reference to a John Donne poem and a secret homage to Jean, who'd committed suicide a year and half earlier.

After Jean, the next significant woman in Oppenheimer's life was Kitty Puening, whom he'd marry in 1940. The pair became lovers while she was still married to her third husband, a medical student named Richard Harrison. Her previous husband, Joe Dallet, a passionate young Communist, had died in Spain in October 1937, fighting with the Abraham Lincoln Brigade. Dallet's closest comrade in Spain, with whom Kitty stayed in New York after Dallet's death, was Croatian-born Steve Nelson (Stjepan Mesaros). In 1942, Nelson was named chairman of the San Francisco branch of the Communist Party of the United States, and was himself later implicated in Manhattan Project espionage. According to the FBI, in March 1943, Nelson obtained "highly secret information regarding [atomic bomb] experiments" from Joseph Weinberg, a scientist at Berkeley's Radiation Laboratory, and he "delivered this classified information to Soviet consular officer Ivan Ivanov for transmittal to the Soviet Union."

In the Bay Area, Oppenheimer, Chevalier, and Pozner were all active, often together, in left-wing political activities and fundraising efforts, attending or hosting parties for such causes as Spanish Civil War refugees and Russian War Relief. According to Pozner:

> At the end of the summer of 1941 on the verge of being autumn, we had the same anxieties, the same hope. Kitty's first husband had fought in the International Brigades in Spain; he had fallen. Opje was leading a group that had been trying to raise money for the Spanish Republicans and was still looking for refugees. For him and Kitty, as for me, the defeat of Spain had been the first heartbreak of our lives, which was followed by the fall of Paris.

Most accounts of Oppenheimer's time in Berkeley make no mention of his friendship with Vladimir Pozner. I believe this is because there were actually *two* Vladimir Pozners, both of whom were likely spying for Russia. This fact has befuddled Cold War historians as well as film biographers, who repeatedly conflate the two men.

A Pair of Pozners

Vladimir, the French writer, was born to Russian parents in Paris on January 5, 1905. His first cousin, Vladimir Aleksandrovich Pozner, was born almost four years later in St. Petersburg. After moving to Paris, Voldoya's cousin, V. A. Pozner, became an expert in film dubbing technology and served as chief engineer for MGM's European branch.

Both cousins ended up in the United States during World War II, working in the film industry. Voldoya became a screenwriter in Hollywood, while V. A. Pozner, based in New York, landed a position as general manager for MGM–Loews International and was head of the Russian film section for the US War Department. During the Red Scare, the younger Vladimir Pozner, long under FBI surveillance, was blacklisted and lost his job at MGM. In late 1948, he moved his family to East Germany. Later, relocated to Moscow, V. A. became a leading figure in the Russian film world.

In 1995, the US government allowed the first public release of the Venona transcripts, intercept-

Three Vladimirs (clockwise, from above left): The French-born writer Vladimir S. Pozner; his first cousin, Vladimir A. Pozner, a Russian-born expert in film dubbing; and Vladimir V. Posner, the son of V. A. Pozner, who, raised in the United States, became a familiar pro-Russia television spokesperson during the Glasnost era

ed Soviet spy transmissions from a highly classified US counterintelligence program that ran from 1943 until the end of 1980. The transcripts revealed that, while in the United States, Voldoya's cousin was spying for the Soviets with the codename Platon:

> We are planning to use Vladimir Aleksandrovich Pozner … He has contacts in the country which are of interest to us.

Some readers may remember V. A. Pozner's son, Vladimir Vladimirovich Posner (he Americanized the spelling), the accent-free Russian spokesperson for Mikhail Gorbachev during the Glasnost era who later cohosted a talk show in the United States with Phil Donahue.

Oppenheimer's friend, Volodya, was born in France while his family was in exile from Russia following the failed revolution of 1905. An amnesty enabled the family to move back to St. Petersburg, and there Pozner became active in literary circles. The family returned to Paris in 1921, and Voldoya graduated from the University of Paris three years later. It was in Paris, in 1933, that Pozner and his Russian-born wife, Ida, first met the influential and peripatetic Dutch documentarian Joris Ivens, a connection that would prove of long and great significance to the writer. According to Ivens's biographer, Hans Schoots, "Pozner and his wife were to become two of Ivens's most faithful friends."

In 1934, Voldoya was involved in organizing the first Congress of Soviet Writers in Moscow, where along with Aragon and Malraux he participated in the French delegation. Not long after, Pozner worked with the Hungarian writer Arthur Koestler, at the Paris-based anti-fascist propaganda INPRESS press agency run by another mysterious Hungarian, Alexander Radó. According to Koestler, "the news agency had an editorial staff of three: Alex, 'Volodya' and myself." Koestler believed that INPRESS might have been a Comintern[2] front operation, serving "as a cover address, or rendezvous place, for couriers of the network." Although unsure if Pozner was "in

---

2   Comintern, short for the Communist International, and also known also as the Third International (1919–43), was an international organization that advocated for worldwide Communism.

any way connected with Alex's underground activities," Koestler concluded that Radó "must have already been an important agent" during their time at INPRESS. In 1937 Radó moved to Geneva, and became, according to Koestler, "head of the Soviet espionage network operating from Switzerland."

It was a time of subterfuge and covert action. Ivens and Koestler were both "Münzenberg Men," intellectuals who provided creative support for the numerous propaganda projects backed by Willi Münzenberg. Known as the "Red Millionaire," Willi worked for the Comintern, as head of the International Workers Aid (IWA) organization, founding and funding pro-Soviet overt and covert activities around the world. One of the Münzenberg projects was the Mezhrabpom Film Studio in Moscow, where Joris Ivens went to work in late 1931. Two years later, in the spring of 1933, Ivens left Russia for Paris and there befriended Pozner. Koestler wrote of Münzenberg, "I became deeply attached to him—an attachment which lasted until he was assassinated in 1940."

In September 1936, Pozner made his first road trip across the United States to gather research for a journalistic critique of American capitalism during the Great Depression, acting as a sort of Alexis de Tocqueville with a Communist slant. At the time Ivens was living in New York, and Pozner stayed with him in Greenwich Village. The resulting book, *The Disunited States*, published in France in 1938, is compared by some to James Agee's *Let Us Now Praise Famous Men*.

It was during Pozner's second visit to the United States in 1938 that Chevalier first introduced the Frenchman to Oppenheimer. Pozner arrived in San Francisco, as he remembered, shortly after "great strikes had just shaken the harbor":

> University professors or union activists, they were dark, lost and asked me questions that suggested reassuring answers I could not answer. The one I knew best and who I traveled to Berkeley to see, where he was teaching, was named Haakon Chevalier. He told me that I had to meet his best friend, a remarkable man, to tell him everything, more precisely to tell him everything I knew.

In *Se Souvient* (1972), a collection of essays about the celebrated figures he'd befriended in his life, Pozner recalled:

> I see again, in the garden of Chevalier, the big party in favor of the Russian War Relief, attended by people from all parties, all the unions, all the faculties, and, of course, the Oppenheimers, and, needless to say, the Soviet consul from San Francisco whose daughter was a military doctor in Stalingrad.

When Hans Schoots interviewed the Pozners in early 1990, they confirmed to him that Ivens knew a Soviet vice-consul in California. They also admitted that they too knew the vice-consul well, but they couldn't remember his name. Schoots surmised that since Kheifets, like Ivens and the Pozners, was also friends with Bertolt Brecht and the composer Hanns Eisler, he was undoubtedly the Soviet official in question.

On March 17, 1943, the day after the Oppenheimers left for Los Alamos, *People's World* published a front-page profile of Pozner discussing his writing and his work at the Kaiser shipyards ("The shipwrights at the Richmond yard call him 'Nick,' because 'Vladimir' is hard to say"). The article noted that Pozner was currently at work on his next novel, *First Harvest*, scheduled for publication a month later.

Around this time, Chevalier, having left the University of California, was considering new employment and sent an application in early April to the Office of War Information in Washington, D.C. Chevalier's OWI clearance request was denied, but it would be years before he learned that it was Oppenheimer's testimony to federal security investigators that led to the rejection. On March 29, 1943, the *Oakland Tribune* announced that Pozner had been awarded a $2,000 Guggenheim fellowship to write his next novel. Little more than two months later, on June 10, 1943, newspapers reported that Voldoya had quit his job "at Permanente Yard 2 in Richmond to write of his experiences during this war." Next, the Pozners pulled up stakes and moved south to Los Angeles.

Pozner's new book, *First Harvest*, also translated by Chevalier, was reviewed by Ruth McKenney in *New Masses*, the leftist culture newspaper, on June 29, 1943. McKenney wrote that "Pozner is an artist of imposing stature. *First Harvest* is a beautiful book." This view was in stark contrast to Kay Boyle's review in the *New York Times* two months earlier. About his previous novel, *The Edge of the Sword*, Boyle wrote, "Last Spring a book appeared which in the opinion of one reviewer at least, took its place among the most interesting of the year." In comparison, she found the new work a "hasty job" and a "heedless little volume."

The Joris Ivens Connection

After arriving in Los Angeles, the Pozners moved into a house on Stanley Hills Drive, a few doors away from Joris Ivens, who lived around the corner on Stanley Hills Place in Laurel Canyon. Ivens was lecturing at UCLA and working on Major Frank Capra's US Army Signal Corps' propaganda film team. Pozner's first Hollywood screenwriting credit was for Warner Bros.' *The Conspirators* (1944), directed by Jean Negulesco. The job likely came through Joris Ivens's connections with the writer Elliot Paul.

In late 1941, Ivens was living in New York. With the demise of the German-Soviet nonaggression pact, Russia became America's ally against Hitler, and backed by Artkino, the US-based Russian film distributor, Ivens began work on a pro-Soviet propaganda documentary, *Our Russian Front*, assembled from war footage. Nicola Napoli, the Italian American Communist who ran Artkino, directed Ivens on themes and messaging. Writers on the the film, which helped raise funds for Russian War Relief, included Elliot Paul and Ben Maddow.

A 1947 FBI file on Communist infiltration in the film industry profiled Elliot Paul as "a member of the League of American Writers, a contributor to numerous Communist Party publications and active member of recognized Communist front groups." Ben Maddow, a poet turned writer for New York–based leftist film collectives and Frontier Films, wrote the commentary for *Our Russian Front*. In 1939, Maddow had rewritten Dudley Nichols's commentary for *The 400 Million*, Joris Ivens's documentary about Chinese Communists. In the case of *Our Russian Front*, released in 1942, Maddow's commentary was rewritten by Elliott Paul.

Ivens and Maddow first met in 1936, when Ivens, already a legend in leftist filmmaking circles, came to the United States as a guest of the New York Film Alliance. According to John Wakeman's *World Film Directors*, "Irving Lerner, Ben Maddow and other independent filmmakers in America gave [Ivens] a hero's welcome, afterwards recalling his visit as "a turning point … a shot in the arm."

Voldoya may have already met Elliot Paul in the 1920s in Paris when Paul first gained attention as editor of *transition*, an experimental literary journal. According to Paul, in addition to being the first to publish sections of James Joyce's *Finnegans Wake*, the magazine also "introduced all the Russians who have come up since the revolution over there, and most of the French writers." More recently, Paul had gained acclaim in leftist circles for his book *Life and Death of a Spanish Town*, published in 1937, which depicted village life in Ibiza at the beginning of the Spanish Civil War.

When the Pozners arrived in Los Angeles in 1943, Paul was writing the treatment and screenplay for *The Conspirators*. In short order, Voldoya was hired on to the film. He submitted his own first-draft screenplay on October 18, 1943, and continued to work on the script through February 1944. That October, Pozner was named as one of a handful of showcased "guests" at the historic Writers Congress in Los Angeles, along with such luminaries as Walt Disney, Theodore Dreiser, and Thomas Mann. In addition to Pozner, another presenter at the event was Sergeant Ben Maddow, First Motion Picture Unit, Army Air Forces, who spoke on documentary filmmaking.

April 1945 proved especially busy for Pozner. He sold the screen rights to his story *The Dark Mir-*

In 1938, the year after making *The Spanish Earth*, Joris Ivens (center), with his frequent collaborator John Fernhout (left) and photographer Robert Capa (right), traveled to China to film *The 400 Million* and report on the Japanese invasion of Manchuria. Ben Maddow (as "David Wolff") reportedly helped Ivens write the film's narration

ror to William Goetz (*Good Housekeeping* published it in two parts, in its September and October 1945 issues), and he was signed by Hal Wallis to write the screenplay for an unproduced project called *Dishonorable Discharge*. Also that month, Lester Cowan signed Pozner to help Joris Ivens and the leftist screenwriter Salka Viertel write a screenplay for a project called *The Woman of the Sea*. Ivens had earlier worked with Cowan as a consultant on *The Story of G.I. Joe* (1945), a feature based on the writing of war correspondent Ernie Pyle. Cowan had been impressed with the combat footage Ivens shot in Spain during the Spanish Civil War, used in *The Spanish Earth* (1937), a documentary coproduced by, among others, Lillian Hellman.

Intended as a return vehicle for Viertel's close friend Greta Garbo, *Woman of the Sea*, had it been made, would have been Ivens's first and only feature film. The unproduced picture, based on an idea Ivens credited to Pozner, was inspired by news accounts of a female Russian sea captain. The project fell apart when Garbo withdrew, accusing Viertel of being "under the influence of the Reds." According to Viertel, "the 'Reds' could only be Pozner and Ivens." After the Garbo project collapsed, Viertel recruited Pozner to join her and Bertolt Brecht as equal partners to write a screenplay called *Silent Witness*, about a wrongly accused female Nazi collaborator in France. This film also went unproduced; they couldn't find a studio willing to buy it or a female star willing to shave her head.

In the last year of the war, Ivens, like Chevalier, tried to find work with the US government, but his attempt to volunteer for the Office of Strategic Services failed. Ivens's biographer Hans Schoots wrote, "Did he hope to gather intelligence for the Soviet Union? Or did he simply want to contribute to the Allied war effort...?"

All the while, the FBI had Ivens under surveillance, ultimately compiling a 650-page file in which they identified him as a "dangerous Communist" who was "strongly suspected of being a Soviet espionage agent." A security report the FBI provided to the Netherlands Forces Intelligence Service described the documentarian as "one of the most dangerous Communists in the United States." Ivens left the country in 1946 to make a controversial documentary about the Netherlands and Indonesia.

With France liberated and the Red Scare growing, the Pozners relocated to Paris. Voldoya attempted to stay active in Hollywood, making occasional trips back to California. In February 1947 the *New York Times* reported that he was working on the treatment for Frank Borzage's *Moonrise*

To Russia, with Love

Beyond the astounding number of coincidences and accusations that connect Pozner, Lerner, and Maddow to documented attempts to steal atomic bomb secrets for the Russians, there is no smoking gun. There is, however, one known incident in which one of the players in this story was directly involved in smuggling A-bomb secrets to the Soviet Union.

Nicola Napoli was president of Artkino from 1940 until 1962. Though born in New York he was raised in Italy, where he graduated from the Royal Technical Institute in Palermo. He returned to New York and worked as a reporter for Italian newspapers. In the 1920s he reportedly edited *Il Lavoratore* (The Worker), a Communist newspaper published in New York. In 1929 he went to work for Amkino as assistant to the president. Amkino, founded in 1926, was the first distributor of Soviet films in the United States. In early 1940, Amkino shut down and Artkino Pictures opened for business with an agreement from the Soviet government giving it the "sole and exclusive distribution" rights in North and South America to Soviet-made films.

In 1945, Elizabeth Bentley, a New York–based American working as a spy/courier for the Soviets, defected and provided the FBI with the names of other members of her organization. Of the dozens of names she shared, 25 also appeared in the Venona transcripts, including that of Nichola Napoli.

In November 1944, 19-year-old Harvard student Ted Hall was invited to Los Alamos to work on the Manhattan Project. After being briefed on the atomic bomb, Hall returned to New York. There, along with Saville Sax, a friend and fellow member of the Young Communist League, he made some amateurish efforts to contact Soviet intelligence in order to share information about the new secret weapon.

Sax's mother knew of Napoli through her work for Russian War Relief; she suggested the boys contact him. When Hall and Sax met with him at the Artkino office, Napoli told the would-be spies to contact Sergey Kurnakov, a writer who covered military stories for the communist newspapers *Daily Worker*, *Soviet Russia Today,* and *Russky Golos*. Kurnakov was also a KGB agent. When the boys met with Kurnakov at his apartment in lower Manhattan, Hall gave him a folder "containing a report he had written on Los Alamos and a list of the scientists there working on the bomb." These were the first atom bomb secrets obtained by the Soviets. Hall continued his spying for the duration of the war and after. The secrets he shared included information about the "Fat Man" bomb and methods for purifying plutonium.

While the most famous Manhattan Project spy, Klaus Fuchs, provided the Soviets with information about uranium enrichment, Ted Hall (code name "Mlad" in the Venona transcripts) is reputed to be the only known Manhattan Project scientist to have given the Russian specific details on the design of an atomic bomb. The bomb used in the first Soviet atomic explosion—August 29, 1949—was a replica of the "Fat Man."

—*John Wranovics*

(1948). Later that year, the California legislative committee investigating un-Americanism named Pozner (and Dalton Trumbo, Ring Lardner Jr., and Abraham Polonsky, among others) as one of the leftist writers who had been assigned to write speeches for an FDR memorial held at the Hollywood Bowl in 1945. In 1948 Pozner became involved in another Lillian Hellman–related project when he was hired to write the screenplay for the film adaptation of her play *Another Part of the Forest*.

As the 1950s began, Pozner was essentially blacklisted. His Paris apartment became a regular meeting place for leftist expatriates and victims of McCarthyism, including Joseph Losey, John Berry, Michael Wilson, and Charles Chaplin.

The Red-Handed Heiress

At what are now remembered as the "Hollywood Ten" hearings, held on October 30, 1947, by the House Un-American Activities Committee (HUAC), the testimony of FBI investigator Louis J. Russell provided the first public accusation that Haakon Chevalier had served as a go-between for the Russians and Oppenheimer. Under oath, Russell also named Louise Bransten, a Berkeley-born heiress, as "the 'sharper' or 'loader' for the Commies." According to Russell, Bransten was the person who directed "the manner in which contacts" were made in the Oppenheimer case. He also testified that she had connections with people in Hollywood.

Bransten, a well-known Bay Area socialite and backer of left-wing causes, hosted numerous leftist fundraising events at her impressive home at 2626 Green Street in San Francisco, some of which were attended by the Oppenheimers and Chevaliers. The FBI believed that it was at one of these parties, in 1942, that "Ivanov contacted Eltenton and requested him to secure information regarding some highly secret work being carried on at the radiation laboratory." From two bugs planted in Bransten's house, the FBI also learned that Bransten was the mistress of Grigori Kheifets.

In 1929, Louise Rosenberg had married Richard Bransten, heir to one of the founders of the MJB Coffee company in San Francisco. She had her own wealth, inherited from her father, California's largest dried fruit shipper. After she and Bransten divorced in 1937, Richard married Ruth McKenney. As "Bruce Minton," Richard wrote for leftist newspapers and for a while was the owner of *New Masses*. In 1947, Louise married Lionel Berman, a founding member of Frontier Films—and a colleague of Ben Maddow and Irving Lerner. In 1942, Berman served as editor on Leo Hurwitz and Paul Strand's *Native Land*, for which Maddow was a cowriter. Berman also worked as a cultural section organizer for the Communist Party and on the cultural commission of the *Daily Worker*. He was known as an "important spirit … a fund-raiser, a participant and advisor on many of the films to come, a man alert and dedicated to the politics of the far left."

In 1948, when Louise Bransten Berman was subpoenaed to appear before HUAC, she refused to answer any questions, citing the Fifth Amendment. One of those questions was whether she knew Joris Ivens. The press, rarely failing to mention her red hair, tagged Louise "The Red-Handed Heiress" and the "Communist Angel." *Brotherhood of the Bomb*, a history of the building of the atom bomb, noted that it was probably at Bransten's house where the Soviet consul, Kheifets, first met Oppenheimer, possibly at a benefit for veterans of the Abraham Lincoln Brigade, the night before the attack on Pearl Harbor.

In 1944, the FBI got hold of Louise Bransten's address book, which included Oppenheimer's address and phone number and a listing for "Vladimir Pozner." The feds (and later historians) assumed the reference was to Voldoya's New York–based cousin. The following year, the FBI also obtained an address book belonging to Vladimir Pozner (which one is now unclear). The address book also listed Oppenheimer's address. On this basis, investigators believed they had successfully connected the dots between the New York–based V. A. Pozner, Bransten, and Oppenheimer, though I believe it more likely they confused the two Pozners.

A 1944 FBI file titled "Comintern Apparatus" (COMRAP) reported:

Poesner [*sic*] is known as a contact and correspondent of Haakon M. Chevalier. … An infor-

During the blacklist years, Lerner and Maddow worked on numerous projects as "surrogates" for producer Philip Yordan. In 1956, Lerner was supervisor on *The Wild Party*, a "lurid hostage melodrama" for Yordan's Security Pictures

mant has described Poesner as 'now active in this country as an undercover agent for the Russian G.P.U.

Another FBI report, while discussing Chevalier and Oppenheimer, identifies Voldoya as "a suspect in this case" and notes that in "August and September, 1944, while on a trip to Los Angeles, Chevalier and his wife and daughter, stayed at Vladimir Posner's home."

The COMRAP report also connected Lillian Hellman to Bransten, Steve Nelson, Chevalier, and Voldoya:

[Hellman] associates with prominent Communists and is considered pro-Communist and pro-Soviet. She has been observed in the company of Haakon Chevalier and is known to Louise Bransten and Steve Nelson. ... In 1943 she was one of the sponsors of Vladimir Poesner when he was awarded the Guggenheim Fellowship in the literary field and has maintained correspondence with Poesner.

Lerner and Maddow and the Cyclotron

This brings us to the second of the FBI's accounts of Berkeley atom bomb spying. Two fairly contemporary accounts of this incident exist, both from Irving Lerner. The first is from a *New York Times* piece published on September 30, 1945, a year after the incident:

Add to that still growing list of those who quite innocently came close to lifting the veil of secrecy on atomic research, the name of Irving Lerner, chief film editor and a producer for the OWI Overseas Motion Picture Bureau. It all began in August, 1944, when Mr. Lerner read "Men of Science in America," and was inspired to make a film on "the story of science in America." Lerner, together with Sgt. Ben Maddow, a scenarist with the First Motion Picture Unit of the Army Air Forces, whipped up a script for a two-reeler tentatively titled "The Question."

The story was to feature a young scientist who comes home from the wars to assist Dr. Ernest O. Lawrence, the famed atom-smasher and Nobel Prize winner. "We chose nuclear physics as one of the main themes, using a sequence on the cyclotron, because we planned to show the relationship of seemingly abstract science to everyday life in such fields as cancer research," Lerner said. However, it was shortly after Lerner and Sergeant Maddow visited Professor Lawrence's laboratory at the University of California that orders were issued banning the use of atomic physics and the atom-smashing cyclotron in the script. But the idea was still close to Lerner's heart, and he and Sergeant Maddow planned independently to develop it "into a dramatic feature film" in the future.

Three months later, in January 1946, "Death and Mathematics: A Film on the Meaning of Science," a treatment for the project referred to as "The Question" in the *Times* article, was published in the second issue of *Hollywood Quarterly*. The piece was credited to "Ben Maddow, in collaboration with Irving Lerner." In an afterword to the article, entitled "Director's Notes," Lerner wrote:

I spent one day at the Crocker Radiation Laboratory at the University of California, Berkeley. After a great deal of persuasion I was allowed to take a peek at the 60-inch cyclotron. It was common knowledge at that time, of course, that almost all the scientists connected with nuclear physics were engaged in secret military research. President Truman revealed the nature of that research on August 1, 1945! But to get back to the 60-incher. I was allowed my peek because this very unphotogenic machine was being overhauled.

At the time, Lerner was chief producer for the civilian-staffed Overseas Branch of the OWI's Motion Picture Bureau at 35 West 45th Street in New York's jewelry district, where he worked alongside a group of experienced filmmakers, many in the progressive documentary scene. These included Joris Ivens's girlfriend, Helen von Dongen, and Frontier Films veteran Sidney Meyers, both accomplished film editors. According to another veteran of the Motion Picture Bureau, film editor Ralph Rosenblum, Lerner, along with department head Robert Riskin, was one of "the group that hashed out ideas and assignments."

While Lerner was working in New York, Ben Maddow was in uniform in Los Angeles, having been drafted into the Signal Corps in the autumn of 1943. There, Maddow made an impact on postwar American film by giving many of his fellow filmmakers in the First Motion Picture Unit of the Army Air Forces their first exposure to the world of progressive documentaries.

Malvin Wald, co-screenwriter of Jules Dassin's *The Naked City* (1948) wrote that when he served in the First Motion Picture Unit, "one of the most talented of all was a young writer-director of documentaries named Ben Maddow." After discovering a profound ignorance of documentary films among the young Army writers, Maddow "organized a series of lunch-hour screenings of the early works of Robert Flaherty, John Grierson and Joris Ivens." Wald later wrote that when he told this story to Mark Hellinger, the producer of *Naked City*, Hellinger asked, "What's this got to do with Hollywood?" to which Wald replied, "Why doesn't Hollywood leave its sheltered studios and go out in the world … instead of using painted backdrops or street sets on back lots?" Hellinger must have taken Wald's comment to heart.

Irving Lerner began his documentary career working for the Anthropology Department at Columbia University in New York. He joined the Workers Film and Photo League (WFPL) in the early 1930s. In 1933 and 1934 he taught film at the Harry Alan Potamkin Film School, named after a leading leftist film critic who had died young. Between 1932 and 1938 he wrote dozens of film reviews for left-leaning and Communist newspapers and magazines, using his own name or the pseudonym "Peter Ellis," including *Workers Life*, *Daily Worker*, *New Masses*, *New Theatre*, and *TAC*. Lerner remained a key participant as the WFPL split up and morphed into NYKINO, and later, Frontier Films.

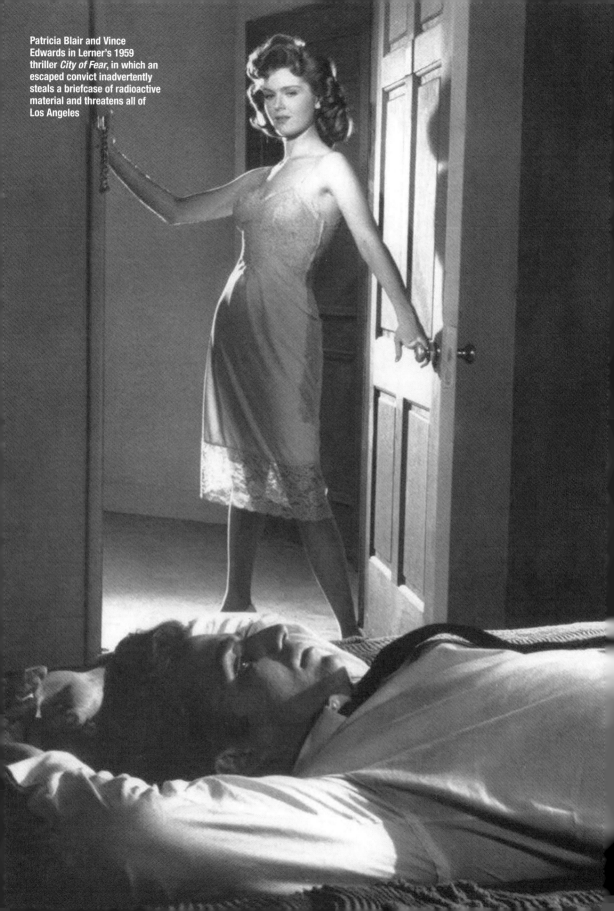

Patricia Blair and Vince Edwards in Lerner's 1959 thriller *City of Fear*, in which an escaped convict inadvertently steals a briefcase of radioactive material and threatens all of Los Angeles

In early 1945, with the war winding down, OWI film production slowed to a crawl. On August 30, 1945, President Truman shuttered the department; the State Department's Information Service (USIS) took over production of propaganda films. By the early 1950s, with the Red Scare in full effect, Lerner found it difficult to find work. Along with Ben Maddow, Bernard Gordon, and a few other blacklisted filmmakers, Lerner found employment through Philip Yordan, a notorious exploiter of blacklisted writers and directors. For Yordan, Lerner worked on low-budget features like *Man Crazy* (1953), *The Wild Party* (1956) *Men in War* (1957), and *God's Little Acre* (1958). In 1953 he also codirected *Edge of Fury*, which was finally released in 1958. Again working for Yordan, he helmed *Murder by Contract* (1958) and *City of Fear* (1959).

Murder by Contract, featuring a young Vince Edwards as a hired killer on assignment in Los Angeles, would have a major impact on Martin Scorsese, who cites it as "the film that has influenced me most." Years later, Scorsese hired Lerner as an editor on *New York, New York* (1977). After Lerner died during production, Scorsese dedicated the film to him.

The FBI report also connected Irving Lerner to Eric Bernay, owner of the radical record label Keynote Recordings, which recorded artists such as Pete Seeger, Hanns Eisler, and Paul Robeson (reputedly another of Louise Bransten's lovers). The label was taken over in 1948 by John Hammond, famed "discoverer" of Bob Dylan and Bruce Springsteen among *many* others. From 1936 to 1939, Bernay was advertising manager for *New Masses*. He and *New Masses* financed Hammond's famous landmark celebration of African American music.

In late 1948, Bernay made headlines when he was implicated in HUAC's investigation into a mysterious Russian "super-spy," Arthur Alexandrovich Adams, who had obtained "highly secret information regarding the atomic bomb plant at Oak Ridge, Tennessee." There were also accusations that Steve Nelson delivered "secret information from radiation laboratory at Berkeley, Calif." to "underground Comintern agent, Arthur Adams." Under oath, Bernay testified that "about the latter part of 1941–1942, I can't remember the date," he provided Adams with a salary, as an engineer, through Keynote Recordings. According to the right-wing newsletter *Counterattack*, Adams was paid $75 a week by Bernay. The US government interpreted these payments as proof of legitimate employment to cover for Adams's espionage activities. Adams, who successfully escaped to Russia without being prosecuted, was later described as "one of the most important Soviet agents … His assignment was the procuring of atomic and radar secrets."

In the FBI report "Soviet Activities in the United States," there's a claim that following the cyclotron incident, in the winter of 1944, Lerner "subsequently resigned from the Office of War Information to take employment at Keynote Recordings, Inc." Many citations on the internet seem to interpret this in a sinister manner, suggesting that Lerner immediately quit the OWI after being confronted by University security. In fact, Lerner was still working at the OWI until it shut down, overseeing production of propaganda films such as *Toscanini: Hymn of the Nations* (1944), *The Cummington Story* (1945), *Northwest U.S.A.* (1945), and *The Library of Congress* (1945). He also produced *The Pale Horseman* (1946), the last OWI production, finished and released by the USIS.

After the war, Ben Maddow went on to write the screenplay for the Glenn Ford picture *Framed* (1947) and such film classics as *Intruder in the Dust* (1949) and *The Asphalt Jungle* (1950). With Lerner and Philip Yordan, he worked on *Men in War* (1957), *Gun Glory* (1957), and *God's Little Acre* (1958), among others. For John Huston, he also scripted *The Unforgiven* (1960). Frustrated with the difficulty in finding work, Maddow reportedly came to an agreement with HUAC and named names. He also became an expert on photography and penned critical studies of photographers Edward Weston and W. Eugene Smith. Maddow's last collaboration with Irving Lerner was the astonishing docu-drama *The Savage Eye* (1960), written and directed by Maddow, Sidney Meyers, and Joseph Strick, about which the painter Edward Hopper is supposed to have said, "If anyone wants to see what America is, go and see a movie called *The Savage Eye*."

I have found no evidence, beyond the claim in the FBI report, that Lerner ever worked for Keynote Recordings. Nor have I been able to find any news reports, including contemporary issues of UC Berkeley's *Daily Cal* student newspaper, that mention the cyclotron incident. It's also clear that neither Lerner nor Maddow were arrested or prosecuted for anything related to the incident. ∎

Gabrielle (Gaby Rodgers) decides to make the acquaintance of The Great Whatsit in the closing moments of *Kiss Me Deadly*

THE WORLD OF TOMORROW

Nuclear Noir in the Atomic Age

Jason A. Ney

n the 1950s, the atomic and hydrogen bombs represented humanity's first existential threat of its own making, and in this era of "duck and cover," backyard bomb shelters, and millions of government-issued dog tags for school children (to more easily identify their charred bodies after a blast), Hollywood was quick to capitalize on America's fear of annihilation. After all, what makes a better villain than the bomb? Dozens of science fiction films dealt with the threat of nuclear weapons, from the giant mutated ants of *Them!* (1954) to the postapocalyptic wasteland of *The World, The Flesh and The Devil* (1959). While filmmakers only produced a handful of nuclear noirs, the films that emerged paint a more complicated picture of both the bomb and humanity's relationship to it. All atomic noirs ask variations on the same question: does the bomb push us into darkness or does it simply reveal the evil in our souls?

The nuclear family and friends under siege in *The Atomic City*: from left, Michael Moore, Nancy Gates, Lydia Clarke, and Gene Barry

The opening title card in *The Atomic City* (1952) reads "Alamagordo, New Mexico, July 16, 1945, 5:30 A.M." Footage of a mushroom cloud, the result of the first successful atomic bomb test, fills the frame as the narrator intones, "the Atomic Age begins." Scientists, he tells us, "have continued to work, to invent, to improvise, to improve the old weapons and develop new ones because the spirit of aggression is not yet dead in the world." If that sounds ominous, don't worry; he has good news. America's top minds aren't just building weapons of mass destruction because "isotopes and other atomic techniques are saving lives all over the world." All of this comes at a cost, as "absolute security is vital if the free world is to survive and if the Atomic Age is to at last free man from his long bondage to power"—a sinister sentiment that serves as a chilling thesis for what follows.

Nuclear physicist Dr. Frank Addison (Gene Barry), along with his wife Martha (Lydia Clarke) and son Tommy (Lee Aaker), live in Los Alamos—a seemingly idyllic, all-American community with picturesque suburban homes, good schools, and nice people. The film wastes no time stripping away the town's false veneer by highlighting how Tommy, no more than six years old, is already saying "*if* I grow up" rather than "*when*" and rattling his mother into questioning her husband's work on the hydrogen bomb, a weapon one thousand times more powerful than the bombs the United States dropped on Japan. The boy's troubling word choices soon become the least of her worries as Commie agents kidnap Tommy during a school trip and demand Frank's access to the H-bomb's secrets as payment.

Sydney Boehm's Oscar-nominated screenplay fearlessly dives into the ethical muck surrounding issues of state security versus individual freedom, capably illustrating the dehumanizing effects of the Atomic Age. The Commies callously kill their own and are willing to murder Tommy in pursuit of the bomb, but the Americans—ostensibly the good guys—don't come out clean, either. When FBI agents try

to persuade Frank to get his wife, the only person with a direct line to the kidnappers, to help, one agent appeals to Frank's nationalism at the expense of his son, claiming "the bomb means more than just one life." As Frank points out, his wife doesn't see it that way because to her "Tommy counts more than the millions. They're just numbers. Tommy's very real." Another agent counters, "Our job is to keep the bomb at home, to apprehend the kidnappers, and to bring your son back safely." Frank, impotent and defeated, asks, "That's the order of their importance, isn't it? One, two, three: Tommy's number three." In the next scene, that same agent's coldly utilitarian beliefs are on full display when addressing other FBI agents about their priorities: "You're probably asking yourselves, 'What about the boy? Isn't getting Tommy Addison back safely more important?' I'm giving you my answer to that officially: no."

Do the Commies eventually betray each other? Of course. Do the American agents eventually value Tommy enough to risk their lives to save him? Sure. Yet we still know they would have let him die to maintain state secrets, and while the bomb's corrosive power has not yet reached the total control over humanity's volition it displays in *Kiss Me Deadly* (1955), no amount of emotional uplift from Tommy's rescue can completely wash away the grime of the agents' core beliefs.

Split Second (1953), Dick Powell's directorial debut, takes an intimate, small-scale approach to the atomic threat. Sam (Stephen McNally) and Bart (Paul Kelly) escape from prison and take four hostages—newspaperman Larry (Keith Andes), down-on-her-luck showgirl Dottie (Jan Sterling), and couple Kay Garven (Alexis Smith) and Arthur (Robert Paige)—to a ghost town within the blast radius of a nuclear test scheduled for six o'clock the next morning. Sam doesn't care about the impending blast because he knows he can leave whenever he wants to chase down a $500,000 score—but first, he needs to get the bullet out of Bart's gut. Fortunately, Kay's husband is a doctor. Unfortunately, Arthur isn't her husband, so Sam calls the real Dr. Garven and tells him to get on the first plane out of California or Kay is toast. He also needs to decide what to do with his hostages. Does he kill them or let them go?

More so than *The Atomic City*, Powell's film posits a moral universe with fixed poles of right and wrong (no accident: a somber Bart requesting to hear "anything" from the Bible before Dr. Garven performs emergency surgery). Within the bomb's pressure-cooker environment, *Split Second* clearly delineates between love and lust, selfishness and altruism, compassion and violence, forcing every character to reckon with the choices they will make before doomsday comes at dawn. Will Kay fight for her marriage or let fear drive her toward Sam's false assurances of safety? Will Dottie stick with respectable Larry or fall prey to Sam's offer of a fresh start in Mexico? Will Larry stand up to Sam or sit passively by letting the chips fall where they may? By the film's explosive conclusion, the bomb, a vengeful deity, has laid bare every character's true nature—sparing the righteous but punishing the wicked—turning them not into pillars of salt but charred corpses littering a desolate landscape.

How quaint this morality tale seems when compared with the jagged cynicism of, as the infamous tagline puts it, "Mickey Spillane's Latest H-Bomb!"

ost films, noir or not, have at least one hero. *Kiss Me Deadly* has Mike Hammer (Ralph Meeker), and he is not, to put it mildly, a typical hero. After picking up Christina (Cloris Leachman), a frantic woman standing in the middle of a dark road late at night, and immediately disparaging her for almost wrecking his flashy convertible, it doesn't take her long to pin down the shortcomings of his character. "You have only one real lasting love," she smirks at him. "You. You're one of those self-indulgent males who thinks about nothing but his clothes, his car, himself. Bet you do push-ups every morning just to keep your belly hard." Screenwriter A. I. Bezzerides, no fan of Spillane and his source novel, decided to turn Spillane's controversial, conservative PI inside out, highlighting at every possible turn what he perceived as crippling character defects, not causes for callous celebration.

A hero would track down the men who tortured and murdered Christina in the film's unnerving second scene; he'd ensure they were brought to justice. (A hero also wouldn't take sadistic pleasure in slamming an uncooperative doctor's fingers in a drawer, but that's another scene.) Hammer, in true antihero fashion, is more interested in what the men wanted from her—what Velda (Maxine Cooper), his secretary/grifting partner, dubs "The Great Whatsit." His pursuit of a big payday that turns out to be the bomb gives the narrative its framework, but the film is primarily concerned with exposing the pointlessly brutal lengths to which men and women will go for the false promises of an unknown entity they do not respect or even understand. As Velda says to Mike, "Everyone everywhere is so involved in the fruitless search for what," including "the nameless ones who kill people for The Great Whatsit. Does it exist? Who cares."

In director Robert Aldrich's feverishly sweaty creation, people are either abusers or victims, leaving questions of any greater good to those who exist beyond the edges of the frame. Hammer takes advantage of Velda whenever he needs something, and in her insecure desire for a love he'll never give, she lets him. Lieutenant Pat Murphy (Wesley Addy), a far cry from Mike's genuine friend in Spillane's novels, gives Hammer just enough rope to hang himself and then lambasts him once he does. And what of Dr. Soberin (Albert Dekker), the man behind the curtain, the puppet master who has been making Mike dance? He gets a bullet to the gut, the victim of a double-cross from Gabrielle (Gaby Rodgers), the impersonator of Christina's former roommate who strings Mike along until the film's shocking final scene when she flips her victim persona on its ear and decides, against Soberin's Pandora-laden admonitions, to open the film's modern-day Ark of the Covenant, the box that holds humankind's most seductively deadly creation. Her decision results in one of the most famous endings in film noir history, signifying humanity's hopeless pull against our most horrifying instincts. From the film's viewpoint, the species that created the bomb cannot be trusted to live with it.

Mike Hammer (Ralph Meeker) tries to piece together a plot (with help from Lily Carver aka Gabrielle, played by Gaby Rodgers) that involves purloined atomic material in A. I. Bezzerides' reworking of Mickey Spillane's *Kiss Me Deadly*

E veryone knows about the atomic bomb and most are familiar with the hydrogen bomb. but what about a bomb so deadly no government has dared to detonate it? In February 1950, physicist Leo Szilard publicized the idea of the cobalt bomb, a dirty bomb that would coat the earth with weaponized cobalt-60. which has a radioactive half-life of over five years, rendering the affected areas uninhabitable for decades. Build and detonate a series of large enough cobalt bombs and you could theoretically render the entire planet uninhabitable.

City of Fear (1959), the second low-budget collaboration for director Irving Lerner and star Vince Edwards, takes the central conceit of *The Killer That Stalked New York* (1950) and *Panic in the Streets* (1950)—unwitting citizen carries deadly disease through densely populated city—and updates it for the Atomic Age. Edwards plays Vince Ryker, a fresh-on-the-lam con sprung from San Quentin with a canister he believes contains one pound of pure heroin—the drug the prison was using in experiments on prisoners. Once he meets up with June Marlowe (Patricia Blair), his old flame, he explains how selling it will set them up for life. However, his situation includes more shades of *Experiment Alcatraz* (1950) than he knows. During an emergency response meeting, after police Lieutenant Mark Richards (John Archer) informs scientific consultant Dr. John Wallace (Steven Ritch) that Ryker is actually carrying around granulated cobalt-60, Los Angeles Police Chief Jensen (Lyle Talbot) asks

Wallace how deadly it is. "In granular form," Wallace tells them, "it's the most deadly thing in existence. Contamination begins almost immediately. Within eighty-four hours, you're dead." He claims the steel casing in which the cobalt-60 is housed doesn't protect against radiation exposure, and if Ryker opens it? Goodbye, L.A.

The film quickly drills down to our utter helplessness against the unholy power of the bomb. During a follow-up meeting, the police discuss the possibility of notifying the entire city of Ryker's unintended threat to their existence and attempting an evacuation. Dr. Wallace responds asking the men how they would explain "calmly to three million people without touching off the worst panic in history" that if Ryker makes one simple mistake they will all face "hoarse coughing, heavy sweat, horrible retching. Then the blood begins to break down the cells. If you merely touch your skin, the watered blood just oozes out of your pores. Finally, you hemorrhage internally. Blood fills the lungs." In other words, a petty convict's ignorant mistake could easily result in the grisly suffering and untimely deaths of millions.

If *Kiss Me Deadly* posits a world in which the bomb's influence over our actions stems from our destructive desire for control, *City of Fear* puts forward an even more pitiful view—humans as rats in a maze, scurrying blindly down disorienting corridors, banging our heads in desperation against dead ends of our own design. As Vince and June deteriorate, suffering the gruesome symptoms described by Dr. Wallace, the cops close in on June, expose her to the truth, and convince her to flip on Vince. By the time they track him down, Ryker is writhing on the ground outside of a sandwich shop, sweaty, coughing, and convulsing, clutching the canister to his chest and screaming that "it's worth a million!"—an image of the nuke-hungry world in miniature. Jensen sneers at him just before Vince dies, "It's not even worth your life." A fitting message not just for Ryker, but for all those who cling to the false solution of the bomb's continuous proliferation.

An ironic postscript: the film contains numerous scientific inaccuracies about Cobalt-60's radioactive powers, methods of transmission, and effects on individuals in its vicinity. Instead of rendering the film ineffectual, these errors only underscore—albeit unintentionally—its dire warning about how far in over our heads we are.

ity of Fear was released in 1959 but copyrighted in 1958, the year the world witnessed 77 nuclear tests by the United States, 34 by the USSR, and five by the UK—more than double the previous highest number of annual nuclear detonations (55 in 1957). Beginning with that first mushroom cloud over Los Alamos, governments from around the world have detonated 2,056 nuclear explosions on our Earth's surface, underground, and in our atmosphere. The most recent six have originated in North Korea, widely seen as the world's most unstable nuclear power. Given recent political developments in both the United States and North Korea, this quartet of nuclear noirs, while dated in some respects, retain a renewed urgency about our failure to recognize the bomb's dreadful power, corrupting influence, and hideous reflection of our own worst instincts. If we do not wise up, these films collectively cry, we will be doomed to forever repeat our devastating nuclear history—until our weapons become too powerful and we no longer can. ■

Paul Schrader's creation of Travis Bickle, embodied by Robert De Niro in *Taxi Driver* (1976), would become one of the most iconic characters in noir, the epitome of "God's lonely man"

NIGHT WORKERS

PAUL SCHRADER EXPLORES THE LIVES OF GOD'S LONELY MEN

Danilo Castro

P aul Schrader hit rock bottom in 1972. The film critic and aspiring screenwriter was living in his car, fueled by a steady diet of drugs and alcohol. At night he cruised the streets of Los Angeles, soaking in the sights and sins through a dirty windshield. By day he found refuge in porno theaters. He carried a loaded .38 Special, but could never work up the courage to use it. In a last-ditch attempt at reform, Schrader turned his misery into art. He sat down with his typewriter and his .38 and vowed to either write a script or end it all.

Schrader's self-imposed ultimatum proved to be a defining moment. Not only did the script (eventually entitled *Taxi Driver*) make him a sought-after commodity in Hollywood,[1] but it established many of the themes he would revisit throughout his career: alienation, spiritual anguish, sexual depravity, and the self-destructive nature of man. Schrader is not the first storyteller to have recurring themes run through his work, nor is he the first to experience them in his own life. What he's managed to create with them, however, is unparalleled in the film noir canon.

Schrader's tetralogy of noir films, comprising *Taxi Driver* (1976), *American Gigolo* (1980), *Light Sleeper* (1992), and *The Walker* (2007), is essential viewing. It is the medium's answer to Monet's "Haystacks" series; it uses repetition of theme to bring out subtle differences in form. But instead of color and texture, Schrader traces the evolution of a character he calls the Night Worker—an archetypal loner, a man who lives outside of society and interacts with it only when providing a sometimes illicit service. Over the course of four decades, he tries to reconcile his isolation with an underlying desire for acceptance.

In many ways, the Night Worker is a surrogate for Schrader himself, who modeled each character's age and mindset after his own. "When he's twenty he's angry, and a taxi driver. When he's thirty he's narcissistic, and a gigolo," the filmmaker explained. "When he's forty he's anxious, and a drug dealer. [Then] he's fifty and he's superficial, and he's a walker." By taking such a long-term approach to a narratively compressed style like film noir, Schrader's tetralogy provides a fascinating look at the passage of time and how it can change self-perception. Where the fate of most antiheroes is decided in a tight 90 minutes, the Night Worker is given a lifetime onscreen to reflect and ultimately make peace with his existential hang-ups.

TAXI DRIVER

Travis Bickle (Robert De Niro) was the first to embody the Night Worker in *Taxi Driver*. He's also the most troubled. His inability to pick up on social cues, or comfortably interact with others, has left him marginalized, dwelling on the filth and ugliness he encounters on his taxi route. "All the animals come out

---

1 His next screenplay, *The Yakuza*, written with his brother Leonard, would sell at auction for $300,000, then one of the highest prices ever paid in Hollywood for a script.

Paul Schrader, Martin Scorsese, and Robert De Niro share a needed laugh during the shooting of *Taxi Driver*, one of cinema's most relentlessly grim films

at night," he bitterly fumes. "Someday a real rain will come and wash all this scum off the streets." These "animals" are his imagined targets whenever he practices his tough guy routine ("You talkin' to me?") or trains himself for combat. He's a man looking for a purpose, a time bomb waiting for an excuse to explode.

It's implied that Vietnam vet Travis suffers from post-traumatic stress disorder, but Schrader posits his actions as being more indicative of America's disillusioned youth, not its soldiers. The character longs for approval, and like so many angry young men he turns to acts of violence when he doesn't get it. He tries to assassinate a political candidate not because of his beliefs, but because one of the candidate's campaign workers rebuked his advances. The horrifically bloody climax, where Travis guns down a pimp and his goons, is similarly contradictory. Though he perceives the murders as a heroic act, his wrath stemmed from the humiliation of his being unable to "save" an underage prostitute who mocked him.

The film's coda brings the character's delusion full circle. Travis is seemingly reformed and has resumed driving a cab. But after dropping off a fare (the woman who had spurned him, now treating him like a celebrity), something behind him catches his eye. He snaps the rear-view mirror toward himself,[2] displaying the same twitchy agitation we'd seen before his cathartic explosion. Martin Scorsese's direction[3] has a dreamy quality that hints at the scene being imagined, but Schrader has denied it. The intention is simpler and more troubling: the bomb inside Travis has been reset, for he's not yet figured out how to defuse it. "The redemption or elevation or transcendence he seeks has no meaning for him," Schrader told *Film Comment*. "In time, the cycle will again come around."

2   A gesture cribbed, perhaps as homage, from Robert Ryan in *On Dangerous Ground* (1951).
3   Martin Scorsese directed *Taxi Driver*, while Schrader assumed directorial duties on the other three films.

EXPIRES MAY 31, 1976

De Niro's portrayal of Travis, a lost and lonely soul on a desperate search for meaning, touched a raw nerve in American culture

The luxurious light and textures of *American Gigolo* were, literally, hundreds of miles away from the mean streets of *Taxi Driver*—but Julian Kaye (Richard Gere) shared the existential ennui of lost and lonely Travis Bickle

Paul Schrader and Richard Gere on the set of *American Gigolo* (1980)

AMERICAN GIGOLO

Schrader uses this failed bid for transcendence as the jumping-off point for 1980's *American Gigolo*. As though determined not to make the same mistakes, Julian Kaye (Richard Gere) has abandoned any search for a higher calling. He's a male escort content with his louche lifestyle in Beverly Hills. He exists for the sole purpose of pleasuring women, and when they aren't around, he spends his time sculpting his body or learning different languages to broaden his client base. When he dresses, he lays out his clothes like a haberdasher, as if determining the best version of himself to sell. He's so good at it, in fact, there ceases to be a real Julian behind closed doors. Only when the he gets framed for murder does Julian's manicured facade begin to fall apart.

Schrader emphasizes the character's narcissism by making his spiritual crisis a physical one as well. As Julian's search for an alibi intensifies, his designer wardrobe becomes creased and dirty, his smooth face acquires stubble. He ransacks his apartment looking for planted evidence, trashing the costly possessions he once held dear. Julian's breakdown parallels Travis's earlier shooting spree; both depict a character trying to exert control through mindless destruction. Neither succeed. In a film brimming with sex, it's worth noting that Julian's howls of misery are the most passionate sounds we hear him make. Control was all he had, and without it, he is lost. Beaten, he accepts his frame-up with dead-eyed passivity.

In the end, Julian's fate is left for others to decide. He's too fragile to mend himself, and it's only through the mercy of Michelle (Lauren Hutton), a peripheral love interest, that he avoids prison. She sacrifices her reputation and her marriage to clear his name. Schrader borrows this "moment of grace" from Robert Bresson's seminal film *Pickpocket* (1959), and though unexpected, his version packs a similarly transcendent punch. Because of Michelle's selfless act, Julian may be able to shed his selfish hedonism and chart a path out of the darkness.

Willem Dafoe as drug dealer John LeTour in *Light Sleeper*, Schrader's Night Worker approaches middle age, still looking for redemption and reconciliation

LIGHT SLEEPER

The path toward redemption takes on a wistful tone in Schrader's third installment, 1992's *Light Sleeper*. Here we meet John LeTour (Willem Dafoe), a white-collar drug dealer who spends his nights making house calls to needy clients. As a reformed junkie, LeTour possesses a warmth and understanding that his Night Worker predecessors lacked. Underneath his placid exterior, however, he is looking for solace of his own. He can't sleep. He's nearing 40, and a lifetime of transgressions and criminal acts is starting to wear on his conscience. Call it the Night Worker's midlife crisis. He wants to make a positive change, but it's been so long he's forgotten how.

Schrader considers *Light Sleeper* his most personal film, and it's easy to see why, given the character's introspective manner. LeTour frequents street corners and Manhattan clubs that remind him of his troubled past. He fills up notebooks with memories and stray observations, all the while knowing he's near the end of his professional rope. "A DD told me when a drug dealer starts writing a diary it's time to quit," he reluctantly admits. LeTour is so desperate for a way out that he misreads a chance encounter with Marianne (Dana Delany), an old flame, as a fateful occurrence. He decides that winning her back will bring him salvation, despite her pleas to be left alone.

LeTour's attempt to reconcile the past with the present has predictably tragic results. Marianne is killed by one of his clients, and he responds by gunning him down in a vengeful display that recalls *Taxi Driver*. The act may seem like a moral regression on the surface, but in LeTour's malevolent world, it proves to be a blessing in disguise. Schrader uses the repetition of violence to show how the character has matured: where the shootings in *Taxi Driver* were fueled by adolescent rage, LeTour's is a cathartic release that restores his sense of agency. As he lies on a hotel bed, critically wounded, the character's anxiety dissipates and he discovers the capacity for change within himself.

LeTour is sent to prison for his crimes, and the brief exchange he has with his boss Ann (Susan Sarandon) harkens back to *Gigolo*'s ending. In this instance, though, the character is on equal footing with his prospective lover. "I've been looking forward," he affirms. The words of a man who's finally gotten a good night's sleep.

Schrader brings the tetralogy to a subdued close with 2007's *The Walker*.[4] Carter Page III (Woody Harrelson) has the cumulative wisdom of the men who came before, but he's decided to keep it hidden out of convenience. His life has been a reeling series of disappointments, and the best way to cope is to smile and crack a few jokes. His "work" supports this disingenuous outlook: Carter is a "walker," a man who escorts busy politicians' wives around Washington, D.C. He entertains his female clients with his amusing company rather than sex, and he has a knack for gossip, which he gleefully spreads at fundraisers and canasta tables. "I'm not naive, I'm superficial," he quips, as though it were a badge of honor.

Carter's blissful ignorance hits a brick wall when his favorite client (Kristin Scott Thomas) stumbles upon the body of a slain lobbyist. He decides to protect her by saying he found the body, but in doing so, he submits himself to the scrutiny of the outside world. The character's strained relationship with his father, a beloved senator, comes to the fore. His homosexuality, previously an open secret, becomes a point of vulnerability. The very gossip Carter thrived on has made him a pariah, and Schrader compounds the irony by having it stem from a decent act. In classic noir fashion, the character must choose between what's right and what's easy.

It's worth noting that *The Walker* doesn't end with a shootout or rueful rumination from behind prison glass. It ends on a quiet, hopeful note. By refusing to sell out his client to the police, Carter proves that he's more than a lowly servant of the night. He's a loyal friend and a decent man, capable of meaningful interactions he never thought possible. "I've spent my life without any real idea of why I behaved as I did," he says, subtly owning up to the sins of previous films. The character seizes his moment of clarity and leaves the big city behind, a loved one and the hope of a brighter future in tow. Schrader's lonely man has finally broken the cycle.

While each of the Night Worker films functions perfectly as stand-alone noir, their lasting power comes from how they echo one another, and how they encompass the various stages of life when taken as a whole. They provide a continuity that few of Schrader's stylistic peers can match. He may no longer write with a .38 Special in reach, but Schrader's talent for articulating the pain of tortured souls, and for baring his own soul in the process, has never waned. When we watch his Night Workers striving to reform, we're reminded that the greatest threat to achieving happiness most often is ourselves. ■

---

4   Schrader originally planned to make *The Walker* a direct sequel to *American Gigolo*, with Richard Gere reprising the titular role.

UNGENTLEMANLY CONDUCT

CONDUCT

NOIR AT EALING STUDIOS

Ray Banks

The end of Ealing Studios was marked by financial difficulties, a BBC buyout, and a plaque—its inscription composed by studio head Michael Balcon to commemorate the closing of an era: "Here during a quarter of a century were made many films projecting Britain and the British character." It was typical Balcon understatement; no other studio was more concerned with the often-contradictory elements of the British character, and nowhere was this more apparent than in Ealing's output during the Second World War.

As one of only three studios allowed to continue production during wartime, Ealing's remit was simple: develop features that boosted home morale and furthered the war effort. But while other studios churned out propagandist tales of officer heroism in the face of overwhelming odds, often attributing the imminent Allied victory to the stiff upper lip of the ruling class, Balcon's roster of documentary-trained filmmakers concentrated on the reality experienced by ordinary men and women. This was, after all, the first bona fide people's war, and the people deserved proper representation. And so, outside of a few initial efforts, the officers in Ealing's war films were exposed as collaborators (*The Foreman Went to France*, 1942), Nazis in disguise (*Went the Day Well?*, 1942), or else shoved out of the story to make room for working-class solidarity and collective decision making (*Nine Men*, 1943; *San Demetrio London*, 1943). These films represented the people's dream: that with victory would come an end to the inequality and grinding poverty that had characterized British life in the 1930s. By the mid-1950s, however, that dream had soured. Clement Attlee's postwar government might have given the country a welfare state, but the subsequent quartet of Conservative prime ministers would do their best to reestablish the prewar status quo.

"I know about ships. They're wood and metal and nothing else. They don't have souls. They don't have wills of their own. And they don't talk back." So begins *The Ship That Died of Shame* (1955), one of Ealing's final films. An adaptation of Nicholas Monsarrat's 1952 short story of the

Randall (George Baker) and Birdie (Bill Owen) escape the wreckage of the suicidal gunboat in *The Ship That Died of Shame*, one of the ex-Navy boats "cast" as MGB 1087 was later used as a smuggler's vessel before sinking in the Mediterranean

same name, *The Ship That Died of Shame* (released in the United States under the gung-ho alternative title *PT Raiders*) represents a seedy counterpart to the studio's previous Monsarrat adaptation, *The Cruel Sea* (1953). While that film is still seen as a prestige classic, albeit one saddled with an obligation to the truth and a sanitized Eric Ambler screenplay, *The Ship That Died of Shame* is a nimble and nasty slice of quasi-noir.

Lieutenant Commander Bill Randall (George Baker) was once the committed skipper of MGB 1087, a motor gunboat that prowled the coastal defenses of France and Holland in search of vulnerable enemy assets. But after an air raid kills his new bride and the end of the war means the decommissioning of MGB 1087, Randall finds himself at a loss. No longer wanting to return to his old career in a stuffy office and unable to make a living as a boat builder, he drifts into the orbit of his former first mate George Hoskins (Richard Attenborough), who offers him the opportunity to revive the old gunboat as a "fast freight" vessel smuggling contraband across the Channel. Randall reconciles the dubious legality of this new venture with the grim reality of postwar rationing—"our only aim in life was to make people happy"—but after run-ins with both customs and a rival smuggling operation, the adventure begins to lose its attraction. As Hoskins's greed escalates and the contraband switches from nylons and brandy to counterfeit currency and machine guns, the boat suffers technical failures. And when a job smuggling a child murderer out of Britain alerts the authorities on both sides of the Channel—including dogged customs officer Brewster (Bernard Lee)—the subsequent getaway attempt proves too much for the apparently conscience-stricken MGB 1087. After tossing the worst of her crew overboard, the boat finally scuttles herself on the rocks as a guilt-ridden Randall looks on.

While the war had naturally featured in director Basil Dearden's previous films, it was usually as a backdrop to docudrama (*The Bells Go Down*, 1943), social dramas about postwar prejudice (*The Captive Heart*, 1946; *Frieda*, 1947; "The Prisoner-of-War" segment in portmanteau film *Train of Events*, 1949), or as a counterargument to Irish nationalism (*The Gentle Gunman*, 1952). The liberal

ADVENTURE ON THE HIGH SEAS!

THE J. ARTHUR RANK ORGANIZATION
presents
NICHOLAS MONSARRAT'S

THE SHIP THAT DIED OF Shame

(by the author of The Cruel Sea)

starring

RICHARD ATTENBOROUGH · GEORGE BAKER
BILL OWEN · VIRGINIA McKENNA · with ROLAND CULVER · BERNARD LEE

Produced and directed by MICHAEL RELPH and BASIL DEARDEN · A Michael Balcon-Ealing Studios Production · A Continental Distributing, Inc. Release

LITHO. IN U.S.A.   49849

What a gas! Weaver (Norman Bird), Porthill (Bryan Forbes), Stevens (Kieron Moore), Lexy (Richard Attenborough), Rupert (Terence Alexander), Mycroft (Roger Livesey), and Race (Nigel Patrick) run gas mask drills under the watchful eye of Hyde (Jack Hawkins)

Dearden might have supported the war effort, but he was also reluctant to present the conflict in a jingoistic light. *The Ship That Died of Shame*'s opening hit-and-run attack on an enemy gasworks fits loosely into the Boys' Own adventure formula just as it is undermined by its ungentlemanly nature and Hoskins's gleeful attempt to rack up kills, confirmed or otherwise. Similarly, MGB 1087's later engagement with a German bomber might seem successful, but it also forces the plane to drop its payload on a nearby recreation ground, leading to the death of Randall's wife. Even the film's most apparently nostalgic moment—a female singer (Yana) leads a group of misty-eyed and clearly inebriated ex-servicemen in a rendition of Vera Lynn's wartime anthem "We'll Meet Again"—is given ironic counterpoint by Hoskins and Randall discussing their criminal enterprise.

Victory in war has, therefore, been replaced with marginalization and financial desperation, particularly for the officers now struggling to adapt to a civilian world that has little use for them. Working-class Hoskins might have managed to parlay his amoral opportunism into a new career as an upmarket spiv, but Randall is little more than a vagrant with a cut-glass accent. And while he never admits it, Randall has much in common with the villain of the piece, Major Fordyce, who set up his own bootlegging business because he "got a bit tired of working for the plebs after fighting for them." This sense of class entitlement pervades the film, even as Randall plays off his spiral into criminality as a more existential search for meaning.

MGB 1087 knows better, of course. In his 1956 *New York Times* review, Bosley Crowther theorized that the boat contained the soul of Randall's wife (who had hitherto represented Randall's moral compass), and while there is certainly room for a more supernatural reading, the boat's resistance to her work and eventual self-destruction is reflective more of internal epiphany than external conscience. The film is told squarely from Randall's point of view, and so it is more likely that MGB 1087's engine troubles are a representation of Randall's escalating self-hatred. By the time she dashes herself on the rocks, MGB 1087 is a suicidal statement of Randall's own loss of pride and moral superiority: "She gave up and died. In anger and in shame."

It was a sentiment shared by Britain's erstwhile officer class. Post-war austerity coupled with a rash of former colonies winning independence and Prime Minister Anthony Eden's disastrous handling of

The spiv spy and the Cyprus sociopath: Lexy and Porthill discover being gentlemen doesn't preclude them from grunt work

the Suez Crisis had made a mockery of Britain's self-image as a strong and stable imperial nation. By 1957, Harold Macmillan had taken over from the disgraced Eden and attacked the "doctrinaire nightmare" of the Labour policies that had brought the country standardized health care and its new welfare state while taking credit for the postwar industrial boom, telling his party that the people of Britain "never had it so good." The people would disagree, and the culture would reflect it. War films took on a decidedly skeptical tone: *The Bridge on the River Kwai* (1957) scratched the surface of the officer class to reveal the stubborn, self-defeating streak beneath, while films like *Yesterday's Enemy* (1959) and *The Long and the Short and the Tall* (1961) openly presented British forces torturing enemy prisoners.

In 1960, Basil Dearden would offer his own, albeit lighter, take on this newfound cynicism in one of his greatest films: *The League of Gentlemen*.

Lieutenant Colonel Norman Hyde (Jack Hawkins) has been "suitably rewarded after twenty-five years of service by being declared redundant." As revenge (or simple restitution), he has spent a year planning an audacious heist partly inspired by an American crime paperback titled *The Golden Fleece*. But he can't do it alone, and so baits a collection of former officers with the promise of "no further financial worries." His hand-picked crew all share the same disgrace: each was cashiered from the forces. Captain Porthill (Bryan Forbes, who also wrote the screenplay) shot political prisoners in Cyprus; Captain Mycroft (Roger Livesey) was found guilty of "gross indecency in a public place"; Lieutenant Lexy (Richard Attenborough) spied for the Russians; Major Rutland-Smith (Terence Alexander) had to be bailed out of gambling debts by his promiscuous wife; Captain Weaver (Norman Bird) caused the deaths of four members of his bomb disposal squad while drunk on duty; Captain Stevens (Kieron Moore) is a former Mosley blackshirt and subject of a homosexual scandal; and Major Race (Nigel Patrick) ran a black-market ring in postwar Hamburg. The men are sequestered to Hyde's decaying country house and prepare for the two-part job. The first part is a weapons raid on an Army training center (to be blamed on the IRA), with a comic diversion provided by Mycroft disguised as a high-ranking officer performing a spot check. The second part is the heist itself, an armed robbery of used notes from a London bank, performed with military precision under cover of smoke bombs and jammed communications. Hyde's

plan is perfectly executed, and were it not for a little boy's hobby and an inauspicious visit from a boorish neighbor, the robbery would have been an unmitigated success.

The League of Gentlemen was the first feature from the short-lived production company Allied Film Makers, founded in 1959 by Dearden, his producer partner Michael Relph, Jack Hawkins, Richard Attenborough, and Bryan Forbes. Forbes had conceived the film as a comic dig at the stiff-upper-lip school of officer heroics (the first choice for Hyde was Cary Grant), and the film finds further irony in casting war movie stalwarts as the heist crew, some of whom (Hawkins, Patrick, Alexander) attained officer ranks themselves. Hawkins in particular had become a star portraying gruff-but-fair authority figures in the likes of Angels One Five (1952) and The Cruel Sea (1953), and the film brilliantly subverts this image by making him an embittered and entitled relic. Indeed, notwithstanding their obvious talents as men of action, the whole league represents a collected crisis of masculinity. Hyde and Race frequently adopt the mannerisms of a long-married couple; outside of Stevens's homosexuality, there are hints of further sexual fluidity in both Race (who calls everyone "darling" and speaks wistfully of the boys at the YMCA) and Mycroft, whose "gross indecency" is a common euphemism for cottaging. These are men for whom romantic heterosexual relationships are loveless (Hyde, Rutland-Smith, Weaver) if not downright predatory (Porthill, Lexy), and who yearn for the comfortable camaraderie of the officer's mess.

This codependency forms both the league's primary asset and its fatal flaw. Traditional heist movie pitfalls do not apply: no woman can tempt the men from their path or guilt them with moral superiority, and Hyde's principle of "equal shares for all" means no single member of the crew is ripe for betrayal. Yet their arrogance for the plebs (including the small boy who takes their number plate) and their marrow-deep deference to a superior officer—the bluff and ridiculous Brigadier Bunny—are what lead to their undoing. Had the gentlemen's sense of decorum not insist they join the blithering old coot in a drink, they might have jetted off to sunnier climes as wealthy men. As it happens, their inertia gives the police ample time to surround the house. Hyde's only consolation is that nobody betrayed him; when he emerges from the besieged house, he finds the rest of the gentlemen "all present and correct" in the back of the waiting police van.

The League of Gentlemen was an early success for Allied, and managed to trounce the more traditional war movie *Sink the Bismarck!* at the box office. While Dearden's future films would struggle to replicate its success, he would continue to present the hypocrisy of the British conservative classes in social-issue films like *Victim* (1961) and *Life for Ruth* (1962), as well as aim one final dig at the officer class in the con-man comedy *Only When I Larf* (1968). Ealing Studios might have been long gone, but Balcon's commitment to "projecting Britain and the British character" lived on. ■

PROFILES

SECTION TWO

GRAHAM

THE GRIM "ENTERTAINMENTS"

Sharon Knolle

In the noir landscape, nestled between hard-boiled writers synonymous with the genre–Dashiell Hammett, Raymond Chandler, James M. Cain– are the works of literary giant Graham Greene, who parlayed his own experiences with the British Secret Service into novels that included *Our Man in Havana* and *The Quiet American*. The classic film noir films based on his work–*This Gun for Hire* (1942), *Ministry of Fear* (1944), *Brighton Rock* (1947) and *The Third Man* (1949)–all bear his particular brand of profound cynicism and moral conflict.

Made by four different directors, these films reached the screen with varying degrees of fidelity to their sources. Greene himself wrote the screenplay for *The Third Man* and cowrote *Brighton Rock*'s script with dramatist

GREENE

Terence Rattigan (*Separate Tables*). Not surprisingly, Greene was happiest with those adaptations.

The world-weary way Greene ended most of his novels was typically considered too downbeat for moviegoers; the films based on his books have endings ranging from slightly less bleak to positively upbeat. The final shot of *The Third Man*—where after Harry Lime's funeral, Anna (Alida Valli) walks inexorably toward an increasingly optimistic Holly Martins (Joseph Cotten) … and then right past him, without breaking stride—remains one of the most stingingly bitter endings in film history.

Oddly, it was Greene who advocated for a finale in which Anna and Holly end up together. For once, Greene was the odd man out in desiring a happy ending.

THIS GUN FOR HIRE (1942)

As Greene writes in his 1980 autobiography, *Ways of Escape*, this 1936 novel was born out of a sense that patriotism—and his favorite John Buchan novel, *The Thirty-Nine Steps*—had lost their appeal. "It was no longer a Buchan world," wrote Greene. "The hunted man of *This Gun for Hire*, which I now began to write, was Raven, not [Richard] Hannay: A man out to revenge himself for all the dirty tricks of life, not to save his country." Transplanting the film to 1942 America changed things considerably: now patriotism was the point and Raven (Alan Ladd, in his breakout role) dies with a smile, having furthered America's cause in the war as his last redemptive act. The novel's harelipped assassin is transformed on-screen into the strikingly handsome Ladd, who now, instead of facial disfigurement, has a deformed wrist, the result of an abusive childhood.

"Raven the killer, seems to me now a first sketch for Pinkie in *Brighton Rock*," Greene reflected in *Ways of Escape*. "He is a Pinkie who has aged but not grown up. ... They have something of a fallen angel about them, a morality which once belonged to another place."

The screenplay for *This Gun for Hire* was cowritten by Albert Maltz (later one of the Hollywood Ten) and W. R. Burnett, who wrote such classic crime novels as *High Sierra* and *The Asphalt Jungle*.

In a 1983 interview, Maltz, who earned his first screenwriting credit on this film, dismissed it as "a creaky melodrama" and "very contrived." He recalled telling director Frank Tuttle, "Well, you can't do a thing like that, it's ridiculous," and Tuttle responding, "We'll find an answer." Added Maltz: "Well, we did find answers, but they were very contrived." Many of these contrivances are in the novel itself, however, with everyone involved—the hired gun, the damsel in distress, the Nazi schemer who betrays Raven, and the policeman on Raven's trail—all constantly crossing paths. The novel was published the year after Alfred Hitchcock's film of *The Thirty-Nine Steps* came out, a film Greene felt "ruined" the novel. In his side job as a film reviewer, he accused Hitchcock of an "inadequate sense of reality" and "'amusing' melodramatic situations"—some of the same faults one could argue hinder *This Gun for Hire*.

MINISTRY OF FEAR (1944)

Greene categorized his books as either "entertainments" or "novels." Among his "entertainments" he considered his 1943 book *Ministry of Fear*, in which a man recently released from a mental institution for the mercy killing of

Greene set *A Gun for Sale* in the British city of Nottingham, where a munitions magate hires an assassin to kill a British minister; the film version, starring Veronica Lake and Alan Ladd, moves the story to California, undermining the book's geopolitical relevance

Menace... BEHIND EVERY SHADOW!

Suspense... IN EVERY MOVE!

MINISTRY OF FEAR

Starring RAY MILLAND · with MARJORIE REYNOLDS

and
CARL ESMOND · HILLARY BROOKE · PERCY WARAM
Directed by FRITZ LANG · Screen Play by Seton I. Miller · A PARAMOUNT PICTURE

his wife becomes embroiled in a Nazi plot, his favorite, although he wished "the espionage element had been less fantastically handled."

Per Glenn Kenny's Critierion DVD film notes, at a retrospective in 1984 "Greene counted *Ministry of Fear* as one of several 'very bad' adaptations. He told an anecdote where the film's director, Fritz Lang, approached him at a bar years later and personally apologized for having made it."

As Lang told Peter Bogdanovich in 1968, he hated the film, saying he was "terribly shocked" about what had been done with the script and that he had tried and failed to get out of his contract. "I saw it recently on television where it was cut to pieces, and I fell asleep," the director related. Lang's first biographer, Lotte Eisner, dismissed screenwriter Seton I. Miller, who won an Oscar for cowriting *Here Comes Mr. Jordan* (1941), as "a former saxophonist and bandsman." But noir fans might consider him partially redeemed by 1950's *The Man Who Cheated Himself*, which he cowrote with novelist Philip MacDonald. (He also shared an Oscar nomination for the 1930 screenplay of *The Criminal Code* and was a major contributor to the Warner's bullpen in the 1930s.)

Lang scholar Joe McElhaney notes (in an interview on the Criterion DVD) that Miller was also the producer of the film, one who was "reportedly not intimidated by Lang at all." By some accounts, Miller was brought in by Paramount specifically to hold a tight rein on Lang in terms of time and budget.

The biggest omission in the screen adaptation is the novel's amnesiac hero Arthur Rowe (changed to "Stephen Neale" in the film) discovering he's in a mental hospital run by Nazis; this would have been rich material for the director of *The Testament of Dr. Mabuse*. These were also Greene's favorite scenes, but they never made it into the script. Still, Lang elevates the film with his visual style. An eerie séance where the medium reveals that Milland's guilt-ridden character killed his wife is on par with anything Lang ever shot, recalling the operatic sense of the sinister shown in his Dr. Mabuse films.

Although the film version of *Ministry of Fear* takes liberties with Greene's novel that remove much of its noirness, Lang's visual elan provides for a fast-paced thriller in which the artifice of the art direction lends a stagebound surreality to the affair

Near the finale, when Milland has tracked the Nazi spy ring to a tailor shop where villainous Dan Duryea works, Langs adds a macabre flourish. Duryea pretends not to recognize Milland, then makes a phone call and delivers a calm speech about his not being able to "repeat the trousers"—exactly as written in the book. Except that Lang has Duryea dial the phone with a ridiculously oversize pair of scissors—which he'll employ momentarily to commit suicide off-camera. Duryea's final line, "Personally, sir, I have no hope ... no hope at all," is one of the most faithful moments to Greene's book, and one that speaks for the entire story.

Other major omissions from the novel include the main character's oddly proud identification as a murderer. After he's nearly killed for the cake he's won at a county fair, he hires a detective, Mr. Rennit, to track the people responsible. It's a ridiculous story, but he's angered that Rennit fails to take him seriously. He demands, "In all your long career as a detective, have you never come across such a thing as murder—or a murderer?" Rennit responds, "Life isn't a detective story. Murderers are rare people to meet. They belong to a class of their own." Rowe then boldly states, *"Perhaps I ought to tell you that I am a murderer myself."* He seems to take pride in the notoriety, saying, "That's what makes me so furious. That they should pick on me, *me*. They are such amateurs."

The novel's ending is also radically different: after Nazi spy Willi Hilfe kills himself, Rowe, who's fallen in love with Willi's sister, Anna, is left wondering whether she is as innocent as she seems. In the film, Anna (renamed Carla and played by Marjorie Reynolds) shoots her own brother to save the man she loves. There's no question which side she's on. Cut to Milland and Reynolds driving happily by the seaside, discussing their upcoming wedding. She declares she wants a "big cake." "Cake?" yells a horrified Milland in the film's comedic final line.

Contrast this to the novel, where Rowe knows that by not questioning Anna further after her brother's death, he is "pledging both of them to a lifetime of lies... they had to tread carefully, never speak without thinking twice; they must watch each other like enemies because they loved each other so much. They would never know what it was not to be afraid of being found out."

BRIGHTON ROCK (1948)

Pinkie Brown, the vicious 17-year-old who takes over his small-time Brighton gang, is one of Greene's most memorable antagonists. He was played—to Greene's satisfaction—by Richard Attenborough in the 1948 film version, directed by John Boulting. A grimly religious Catholic in his own way, Pinkie strides through life with a purity of purpose that lends him an almost God-given right to his crimes.

The novel is not just told from Pinkie's perspective; but also from the viewpoint of newspaperman Fred Hale, whose murder sets the entire story in motion; Ida, the blowsy good-time girl who's determined to get to the bottom of Hale's death; and Rose, the naive waitress whom Pinkie must marry to secure her silence. Although his pursuit of Rose is purely mercenary, Pinkie sees in her the same purity that he believes sets him apart from the rest of the lowlifes. When he spots her rosary, he tells Rose, "These atheists don't know nothing. Of course it's real. Hell, damnation, flames, torments."

In the novel, Pinkie always carries a bottle of vitriol (acid) in his pocket, often caressing it as if anticipating the moment when he can use it next. On his first date with Rose, in which he tries to determine how easy she will be to intimidate, he mentions another woman whose looks were "spoiled" after she got "splashed" and reaches into his pocket briefly. But the vitriol, which actually speaks to him in the novel, isn't ever shown.

The film finds another way to convey the implied threat: When we first see Pinkie Brown, we see only his hands, idly forming a cat's cradle. He continues to toy ominously with the string when they first confront Fred, as if he'd like nothing better than to wrap the string around Fred's neck.

In the novel, Pinkie's cohorts merely report back that Fred has been killed. The film stages his death in far more dramatic fashion: Trying to hide from Pinkie and his crew, Fred boards a seaside amusement park ride: As the ride starts, Pinkie suddenly sits down next to him. We don't see Fred's demise in the tunnel of terror—it's determined to be from "natural causes"—we just see Pinkie emerging from the ride alone.

This is just the start for Pinkie, who is soon seeing traitors at every turn: *He trailed the clouds of his own glory after him: hell lay about him in his infancy. He was ready for more deaths.*

As he prepares to marry Rose, who knows he's far from innocent, Pinkie is almost giddy, not from love, but his own audacity. *He had a sense now that the murders of Spicer and Hale were trivial acts, a boy's game, and he had just put away childish things. Murder had only led up to this—this corruption. He was filled with awe at his own powers.* After they're married, Pinkie makes a record at Rose's request. Alone in the soundproof booth as she looks on, he says, "You want me to say I love you, but here's the truth. I hate you, you little slut. You make me sick."

Pinkie nearly succeeds in convincing Rose to commit to a suicide pact—in which only she'll die—on the lonely Brighton pier. With the police on their trial, she panics and throws the gun into the ocean. As the police close in, a trapped Pinkie falls to his death over the railing. To please the censors, the film ends with a ray of hope for Rose: as she listens to the record for the first time, it sticks on the phrase "I love you..." and keeps repeating.

The ever-cynical author later said, "Anybody who had any sense would know that next time Rose would probably push the needle over the scratch and get the full message."

Although 25-year-old Richard Attenborough wasn't exactly the callow youth of Greene's novel, his performance as devout Catholic crook Pinkie Brown was a revelation

Orson Welles and director Carol Reed on the set of *The Third Man*, a story conjured up by Greene when asked if he had a thriller up his sleeve

THE THIRD MAN (1949)

As a reviewer, Greene had trashed Alexander Korda's work just as thoroughly as he'd trashed Hitchcock's. Despite that, the two got along like a house on fire once they met. After the success of their collaboration with Carol Reed on *The Fallen Idol* (1948), Korda asked Greene if he had a thriller up his sleeve.

Greene had something he'd penned on the back of an envelope—the opening lines of what would become *The Third Man*.

It was Korda's idea to set the film in the Four-Power Allied occupation of Vienna. "So to Vienna I went," Greene wrote, to soak up the necessary atmosphere. He didn't intend *The Third Man* to be a book, merely "the raw material for a picture," one he had to flesh out by actually getting to know the postwar city.

It would have been a completely different film if David O. Selznick had had his say. According to Greene, on his and Reed's first meeting with Selznick the legendary producer said, "I don't like the title. Listen, boys, who the hell is going to see a film called *The Third Man*? ... What we want is something like *A Night in Vienna*, a title which will bring them in."

Reed stopped Selznick there by saying, "Graham and I will think about it." Greene would hear that sentence repeated frequently because, as he explained, "the Korda contract had omitted to state that the director was under any obligation to accept Selznick's advice. Reed, during the days that followed, like an admirable stonewaller, blocked every ball." Among the changes Greene agreed to, however, was renaming Joseph Cotten's naive writer. Cotten objected to the name "Rollo," which is what Holly Martins is called in the novel. "To this American ear [it] apparently involved homosexuality," Greene noted.

For a novelist who embraced the bleakest side of humanity, it's surprising that Greene favored a happier ending than did Korda and Reed: "I held the view that an entertainment of this kind was too light an affair to carry the weight of an unhappy ending." The original ending, in which Martins joins Anna in silence and they walk off together, Korda regarded as "unpleasantly cynical," coming right after Harry's second (and this time real) funeral.

Greene was sure no one would sit through the long take of Anna walking toward and past Martins, but he admitted, "I had not given enough credit to the mastery of Reed's direction." After viewing the completed film, he added that the choice "proved triumphantly right." In a 1972 interview, Reed noted that Selznick also objected to the bleak ending, saying "Jesus, couldn't we make a shot where the girl gets together with the fella?" As Reed told the interviewer, "The whole point with the Valli character is that she'd experienced a fatal love—and then along comes this silly American!"

However, according to Charles Drazin's 2007 Criterion article "Behind the Third Man," Reed's notes indicated that Selznick argued against the "happy ending" of Greene's story, in which Martins and Anna unite after Martins kills Harry: "Selznick felt this very strongly, that Anna's love for Harry should be fatal, especially since it seems impossible for her to be with Rollo immediately after the shooting of her lover."

In his memoir, Greene charitably acknowledged that Reed's film is better than his novel: "The reader will notice many differences between the story and the film, and he should not imagine these changes were forced on an unwilling author: the film in fact is better than the story because it is in this case the finished state of the story." ∎

HANDLE
WITH
CARE

The Ordeals of Gene Tierney

Steve Kronenberg

I t was 1958, a spring day in New York, and Gene Tierney was in crisis. Perched on the ledge outside her mother's 14th-floor Manhattan apartment, the star of *Laura* (1944) and *Leave Her to Heaven* (1945) was about to leap to her death. Her intended suicide was the culmination of a seemingly incurable depressive disorder that had plagued her for years.

Tierney gazed across the city's skyline to Sutton Place, the exclusive building in which another star-crossed actress, Marilyn Monroe, resided. After several life-or-death moments, Tierney gamely swept away the cobwebs that clouded her reason; she climbed back inside and sought the medical care she desperately needed. "I wasn't at all certain I wanted to take my own life," she wrote years later in her autobiography, *Self-Portrait* (Wyden Books, 1979). "There's a point where the brain is so deadened, the spirit so weary, you don't want any more of what life is dishing out. … If I was going to die," she recalled, "I wanted to be in one piece, a whole person, and look pretty in my coffin."

Looking pretty was never a problem for Tierney; *feeling* pretty was another matter entirely. Blessed with elegant bearing and beatific beauty, Tierney could transcend cinematic genres. But her tortured psyche seemed especially suited to the twilight fringes of film noir.

A PRIVILEGED LIFE

From her birth on November 19, 1920, in Brooklyn, Gene Eliza Tierney lived a pampered life in Westport, Connecticut. Her father, Howard Tierney, Sr., owned a thriving insurance brokerage, with several film studios among his clients. He sent his daughter to elite private schools and presided over her debut into New England's *haute monde*. But it was Hollywood, not high society, that fascinated the 18-year-old debutante. While accompanying her mother, brother, and sister on a guided tour of Warner Bros., the alluring teenager caught the eye of director Anatole Litvak, who sparked a fire when he told her, "Young woman, you ought to be in pictures." A thrilled Tierney tested with the studio and was offered a contract—which her father quickly rejected. "Father considered Hollywood to be the moral equivalent of purgatory," she said.

Undeterred, the would-be thespian pursued a career on Broadway. At age 18, Tierney made her acting debut in 1939 in the play *Mrs. O'Brien Entertains*, written, produced, and directed by stage legend George Abbott. The show was short-lived, but Tierney received excellent reviews and eventually inked a deal with Columbia Pictures. When the studio was unable to find work for her, she returned to the New York stage in 1940 and became the toast of the Great White Way with a captivating performance in the hit comedy *The Male Animal*. Her flawless, perpetually pouting face became a fixture in fashion magazines from *Vogue* to *Harper's Bazaar*. After 20th Century–Fox chief Darryl F. Zanuck caught a performance of *The Male Animal*, he was determined to sign Tierney to a contract. Later that night, his eye was drawn to a beautiful woman at the Stork Club. It was Tierney, but out of character and unrecognizable; Zanuck didn't realize she was the woman who'd dazzled him on stage hours before. "I always had different looks," Tierney said. "It was a quality that proved useful in my career." Zanuck, properly introduced, told Tierney her unusual overbite was what clinched the deal. "In a time of glossy, look-alike glamour," she mused, "my imperfect teeth became an asset."

Fox became Tierney's Hollywood home. She began her film career with 1940's *The Return of Frank James* under the direction of legendary Teuton tyrant Fritz Lang, who called her "a little bitch" when he mistook her overbite for a bit of mugging. The picture tanked, and *Harvard Lampoon* named Tierney "The Worst Female Discovery of 1940." Tierney agreed, and thankless roles in *Tobacco Road* and *Belle Starr* (both 1941) did little to improve her fragile self-image. She hated her high-pitched voice and took up smoking in hope of it making her sound sultry and sexy.

Tinseltown had already begun to take a toll on Tierney. She suffered chronic stomach pains and an unbearable skin disease later diagnosed as angioneurotic edema, a condition equal parts psychological and physiological. At age 20, she impulsively defied her parents' objections and eloped with philandering fashion designer Oleg Cassini, who promptly persuaded Tierney to permanently estrange her family. Howard Tierney, Sr., retaliated by suing his daughter for breach of contract, claiming he was her agent and demanding $50,000 in damages. She prevailed in court, only to discover her father had frittered away all of her personal savings. Tierney's Hollywood dream was unraveling.

AN EMPTY GESTURE

"I don't know that I ever went into a movie more excited," Tierney revealed, "with what turned out to be less cause than I did for *The Shanghai Gesture*." Her deflated optimism was understandable.

The 1941 picture, directed by taskmaster Josef von Sternberg, was greeted with groans by U.S. critics and audiences (Tierney was shocked at the film's successful reception in Europe). Tierney's stopover in *Shanghai* barely brushed the outskirts of noir, though it provided the young actress with a role that tested her physical and emotional range. The movie was sourced from John Colton's scandalous 1926 Broadway play about the habitués of an opium-hazed house of ill repute run by the mysterious Mother Goddamn. Hollywood censors forced some severe changes: the brothel became a casino, Mother Goddamn became Mother Gin Sling (played by a Medusa-coiffed Ona Munson),

The Shanghai Gesture did not score with audiences in 1941, but this nearly-noir drama gave Tierney a chance to show her range and make a vivid impression

The "wonderfully brittle" Clifton Webb as Waldo Lydecker opposite Tierney in the title role of *Laura*

and the addiction *du jour* morphed from narcotics to gambling. A stunning, sloe-eyed Tierney exudes haughty hauteur as the aptly named Poppy Smith, a thrill-seeking rich kid whose frosty allure catches the eye of Victor Mature's exotic (and toxic) Dr. Omar. Bedecked in bejeweled costumes by Cassini, Tierney's Poppy is an airy, elegant confection, purring von Sternberg's inscrutable dialogue in a tone both arrogant and aloof: "Does he sleep with his fez?" she asks of Omar. She questions Mother Gin Sling about her name: "Why Gin Sling? Why not whiskey and soda?" Tierney convincingly conveys Poppy's gradual descent into dissolution, lapping up liquor and coolly losing thousands at Mother Gin Sling's gaming tables. Ravaged by booze and bad luck, the gorgeous gamine soon swaps fancy for frowsy. Tierney effortlessly segues from stunning sophisticate to vicious viper, her face furrowed by drink and decadence. *The Shanghai Gesture* plays like a louche fever dream, a cryptic combination of racist Asian stereotypes and febrile overacting. Tierney's performance lends the film a measure of depth and darkness.

Despite her growing fame, Tierney shied away from stardom and its trappings. She and Cassini "drove inexpensive cars and put on a show for no one." Yet, behind the humble facade was an easily bruised ego. The critical drubbing she received in the early 1940s sapped her confidence and amplified her inherent insecurities. "Most of the time I suffered from a fear I couldn't explain or control," she recalled. "I was born shy and still am." She saw acting as a shield from self-doubt: "You have the protection of a script and the other actors. My problem had less to do with feeling unreal than feeling alone."

FATEFUL CONTACT

These incipient symptoms of depression worsened when Tierney, pregnant with her first child, paid an ill-fated visit to the Hollywood Canteen to entertain U.S. soldiers. A few days later she was diagnosed with rubella, which caused the premature birth of her daughter, Daria, on October 15, 1943. The

Tierney lent depth and dimension to what was seen as a shallow role in *Laura*, and fame came knocking

Laura Hunt (Gene Tierney) stands up to the third degree delivered by Mark McPherson (Dana Andrews)

child weighed two pounds and was born deaf and cognitively impaired, requiring permanent institutionalization. A year after Daria's birth, Tierney attended a party and was approached by a woman with a confession: it was she who had exposed Tierney to the rubella virus when she broke quarantine in order to meet the actress at the Hollywood Canteen. "Everyone told me I shouldn't go," the woman admitted, "but I just had to. You were my favorite." Tierney was too shocked to angrily confront the thoughtless woman, but her daughter's tragic disability irreparably damaged her fragile psyche. "The main cause of my difficulties," she wrote, "stemmed from the tragedy of my daughter's unsound birth and my inability to bare my feelings." Though Tierney received moral and monetary support from close friend Howard Hughes, Daria's affliction strained her marriage and drained her finances.

Needing a solid part in a hit film, Tierney landed the title role in *Laura* (1944) by default. Jennifer Jones thought the character was insubstantial. Hedy Lamarr disliked the screenplay ("they sent me the script, not the score," she later quipped). Bound by her contract with Fox, Tierney was obliged to play Laura Hunt despite her own misgivings: "Who wants to play a painting?" she fumed.

Director Otto Preminger thought the character of Laura was "a nothing, a non-entity." The film's trailer teases: "Who is Laura? What is Laura?" Tierney supplies her an aura of mystery; she's ethereal, a ghost, the dreamy embodiment of the painting that introduces her in the story (actually a photo of Tierney by Fox photographer Frank Polony, touched up with oil paints to simulate a work on canvas). The plot concerns itself less with Laura than with the men in her orbit. Each objectifies her, artificially, as an ideal of female "perfection." To Mark McPherson (Dana Andrews), she's a beautiful bauble. Shelby Carpenter (Vincent Price) admires her elegance, vivacity, and material success. Waldo Lydecker (Clifton Webb) sees her as Galatea to his Pygmalion, someone with "innate breeding" to be reinvented in his own image. All three are shaken, stirred, and stunned when Laura proves to be her own woman.

Tierney with then-husband Oleg Cassini, admiring some costume designs he most likely created for her

None of them knows the real Laura Hunt, and Tierney cannily embodies the character's puzzling persona. Her responses to the men who worship her are detached, bloodless. It's easy to initially dismiss Tierney's performance as robotic and one-dimensional. Yet Laura is more than a vacuous beauty. Tierney endows her with the qualities Waldo finds irresistible: warmth, magnetism, poise, and charm (cinematographer Joseph LaShelle gives her a nearly angelic glow). She suggests Laura's inner strength and unmistakable self-assurance, either challenging McPherson when he suspects her of murder or scolding Waldo for investigating Shelby's seedy past: "I'm closer to despising you than I ever thought I would be." Tierney's eyes—and that petulant overbite—convey subtle contempt to anyone who courts Laura's displeasure. Those same eyes can register shock (as when Laura returns to her apartment and learns someone was murdered there) and pathos (wondering why Waldo so cruelly reveals that Shelby's two-timing her).

Tierney admired costar Clifton Webb's "wonderfully brittle edge," and even praised the despotic Otto Preminger: "Otto held us together. Pushed and lifted what might have been a good movie into one that became special." Tierney herself became the muse for David Raksin's celebrated theme music. "When I was working on the score, I kept looking at her all the time," Raksin remembered. "I'd run sequences and there's this fabulous creature. You come across something marvelous, and it inspires you."

Tierney was modestly dismissive of her work in *Laura*: "I never felt my own performance was much more than adequate." Her friend and costar Vincent Price disagreed: "No one but Gene Tierney could have played Laura. There was no other actress around with her particular combination of beauty, breeding, and mystery." It's Tierney's delicate, understated style that lends *Laura* its silvery, razor-sharp sheen.

Tierney, opposite Cornel Wilde, in the role she regarded as her favorite: *Leave Her to Heaven*'s Ellen Berent

TECHNICOLOR TERROR

Darryl F. Zanuck once described *Leave Her to Heaven* (1945) as the story of a woman who "deliberately kills her own unborn child, drowns the crippled brother of her husband, and endeavors to send her own adopted sister to the electric chair. And yet despite all of this, there are certain things about her that you rather like." Zanuck succinctly summarized the nuance Tierney brought to her finest—and most noirish—cinematic portrayal. The role of Ellen Berent nearly slipped through her fingers. Tallulah Bankhead, Ida Lupino, Linda Darnell, Paulette Goddard, Joan Fontaine, and Lauren Bacall were all considered before Tierney begged Zanuck to let her play Laura Hunt's evil twin. "The role was a plum," she recalled, "the kind of character Bette Davis might have played, that of a bitchy woman. I quickly told Zanuck that he would never regret it if he gave me the part."

Few noir antagonists are as eerie or insidious as Ellen. She's a woman stricken; her obsession with possession makes her insanely jealous of her husband and her privacy. There's no room in *Heaven* for this fallen angel! Ellen's beauty masks a treacherous passive-aggressive disorder that Tierney never overplays. Ellen's composed compulsiveness is revealed in a subtly widening or constricting of her eyes, a tightening of her overbite, an extra tilt to her head or lilt in her voice as she smoothly segues from love to loathing. She gazes at future husband Dick Harland (Cornel Wilde) with predatory lust; fixes a smug, icy glare on spurned fiancé Russell Quinton (Vincent Price); shoots imaginary darts at anyone invading the guarded space she shares with her mate.

Tierney's restrained style is chilling, and it dominates the film's most unnerving scenes: Ellen calmly observing the drowning of Harland's disabled brother Danny (Darryl Hickman); her aborting her

Watch that last step: Tierney lobbied hard for *Leave Her to Heaven*'s lead role, playing a woman who will go to any lengths to control the man she loves

own pregnancy with a calculated collapse down a flight of stairs; the unsettling serenity with which she plots her suicide to frame her half-sister Ruth (Jeanne Crain) for murder. Tierney manages to mix the pathology with pathos. When Ellen realizes she's losing Harland, she begs forgiveness for Danny's death: "I didn't plan it, I swear I didn't!" she lies. Tierney allows just enough sincerity to peek through her deceptive facade: "I love you so," she declares—and we know she means it. Tierney doesn't overdo Ellen's poignancy; her sadness is believable and genuine, presaging other such psychologically intricate performances as Jessica Walter in *Play Misty for Me* (1971) and Glenn Close in *Fatal Attraction* (1987).

Some find it difficult to square *Heaven*'s noir cred with its gorgeous landscapes and lush Technicolor palette, but lensman Leon Shamroy's radiant lighting and panoramic photography provide smart contrast to Tierney's dark, seductive performance. Beneath Shamroy's shimmer and glimmer lies the ugly truth of Ellen's psychosis. Her world is too beautiful, too tranquil, too good to be true. The camera loves her, but it also accentuates her delusional duality. Martin Scorsese marveled at how Shamroy's work is "matched to the strange perfection in Tierney's face, her presence." The Tierney/Shamroy synergy proves that not all noir is black and white.

Ellen Berent remained Tierney's favorite role, an exemplary moment in which an actress channeled her own emotional turmoil into a character. "As much as any part I played," Tierney wrote, "Ellen had meaning for me as a woman. She was jealous in a sad and destructive way. She believed herself to be normal and worked at convincing her friends she was. Most emotionally disturbed people go through such a stage, the equivalent of the alcoholic needing the bottle."

José Ferrer's mesmeric manipulator casts a hypnotic spell over a vulnerable Gene Tierney in the bizarre noir *Whirlpool*

Leave Her to Heaven garnered Tierney her only Academy Award nomination, though the gold was grabbed by Joan Crawford for *Mildred Pierce*. Tierney was disheartened, but not dissatisfied: "My own disappointment was lessened by the convention, new to me, that I had developed a difficult character and not just a pretty face on the screen."

DOWNWARD SPIRAL

Several months after Tierney's triumph in *Leave Her to Heaven,* her marriage to Cassini crumbled and the couple separated. She sought solace in the arms of rising politician John F. Kennedy, who met her on the set of 1946's *Dragonwyck*. The two became inseparable until Kennedy told her he had no intention of marrying her. A heartbroken Tierney reconciled with Cassini while reuniting with Dana Andrews for 1948's *The Iron Curtain*, helmed by William A. Wellman (whom Tierney cited as her favorite director). Andrews plays real-life Soviet defector Igor Gouzenko; Tierney is his stolid, steadfast wife Anna. The noir-stained film was the first of the "Red Menace" pictures that emerged from Congress's Communist witch hunts. In *The Iron Curtain*, Tierney's beauty is buried beneath a severe coiffure and drab wardrobe, her face bearing no makeup. Yet she enlivens the somber mood with an engaging blend of strength, sincerity, and gravitas—a welcome contrast to Andrews's stiff-necked *apparatchik*.

Five months after *Curtain*'s June 1948 release, Tierney gave birth to her second daughter, Christina, and the healthy baby temporarily buoyed her spirits.

A vulnerable, suggestible Gene Tierney appears in the bizarre noir *Whirlpool* (1949), a reunion with Otto Preminger. Tierney's Ann Sutton, well-heeled wife of a prominent psychiatrist (Richard Conte), is a secreted kleptomaniac who falls under the mesmeric spell of quack David Korvo (José

Ferrer). Korvo wins her trust by saving her from a jewel-theft rap—so he can hypnotize her and frame her for the murder of the ex-lover who is blackmailing him. Tierney registers the painful awareness of a woman who seeks perfection but knows her mental state is warped; she's a perfect foil for Ferrer's smooth-talking swindler. She explores a wide emotional arc, morphing from fragile and frightened to fiery and furious. Ann's innate fear is that she's not who she appears to be. The character seemed to offer the actress a catharsis, an exorcism of her own inner demons.

While Jules Dassin was polishing Jo Eisinger's script for *Night and the City* (1950), he got a call from Darryl Zanuck asking a favor. Zanuck was aware of Tierney's mounting depression and asked Dassin to write in a part for her. "She's going through hell and she's a good kid," Zanuck told him. "Save her." Tierney's casting may have been an afterthought, but her performance is a vital complement to Richard Widmark's frenetic portrayal of Harry Fabian. As Mary Bristol, Fabian's loyal-but-exploited girlfriend, Tierney projects warmth, empathy, and steely determination, continually admonishing the manic grifter to change his ways: "You can't go on forever. Always running, always in a sweat." Surrounded by characters steeped in corruption, Mary is the film's conscience, its beacon of compassion. Her heartrending devotion to him makes Fabian all the more pathetic. "I didn't know how to help you," she tearfully tells him. "No one could have loved anybody the way I loved you." Tierney's own sadness is integral to the film's bleak tone; her sweet and sour byplay with Widmark gives Dassin's noir the pall of Shakespearean tragedy.

Where the Sidewalk Ends (1950) re-teamed Tierney with Dana Andrews and Otto Preminger. The picture is owned by Andrews as ruthless homicide detective Mark Dixon, who accidentally kills murder suspect Ken Paine (Craig Stevens) then tries to cover up the crime. As Paine's abused wife, Tierney basically replicates her work in *Night and the City*. She's there mostly to console Dixon, providing a shoulder for him to lean on and balm for his wounded conscience. The actors share an emotional rapport that was oddly missing from *Laura*, but Tierney has little to do. One morning, real life mirrored the film: Tierney had to feed and comfort the hungover Andrews, who'd spent all night in an alcohol daze.

INTO THE DARKNESS

By 1952, Tierney's melancholia was overwhelming. She divorced the womanizing Cassini and a year later became engaged to Aly Khan, who'd just ended his own marriage to Rita Hayworth. But Khan's father refused to allow the royal scion to marry another "movie star." Tierney's breakup with Khan was devastating. While shooting 1953's *Personal Affair*, she reached a dangerous point. "I could not remember the words. My mind was a wilderness," she recalled. A minor role in the indifferently filmed mystery *Black Widow* (1954) was a sad coda to Tierney's sojourn in noir.

Beyond her growing depression, Tierney began suffering from paranoid and suicidal ideation. She refused mental care, fearing its stigma would ruin her in Hollywood. A turning point (of sorts) came in 1955 while filming *The Left Hand of God* with Humphrey Bogart. Tierney credited Bogart with the encouragement she needed to finally seek psychiatric help. Other sources claim that Bogart's sister, Frances, herself a victim of mental illness, bonded with Tierney and referred her to a psychiatrist.

At New York's Harkness Pavilion, Tierney received 27 doses of electroshock therapy. It shattered her memory and left her confused and disoriented. When Tierney recovered from the temporary amnesia, she reluctantly admitted herself to the Institute of Living, a Connecticut sanitarium where she was treated more as a prisoner than a patient. She was trapped in a tiny room, ignored by staff, and denied visitation from friends and family. "It was the most hellish experience of my life," she later said. She made one frantic attempt to escape the facility, was forcefully apprehended, and subjected to 32 more electroconvulsive treatments. After eight months of abuse, an anesthetized, amnesiac Tierney was released into her mother's custody.

Tierney's memory returned—but so did her depression and paranoia. Convinced her condition was incurable, she found herself on that narrow ledge outside her mother's apartment. After climbing back to safety, she was soon admitted to the Menninger Clinic in Topeka, Kansas, where she endured a

Gene Tierney returns to Fox Studios for a hopeful Hollywood comeback

sometimes-torturous regimen of therapy. When finally released, a relieved Tierney accompanied her mother to Aspen, Colorado. There, she met and fell in love with oil tycoon Howard Lee, who had recently dissolved his marriage to Hedy Lamarr.

With renewed confidence, Tierney visited the Fox lot in Hollywood and was warmly welcomed by friends, actors, and technicians. Unfortunately, a return to acting provoked anxiety attacks, forcing her to drop out of the 1959 film *Holiday for Lovers*. "My departure from Hollywood was seen as a walk-out. No one understood that I was cracking up." Tierney re-admitted herself to Menninger for another year, and her second enlistment turned the tide.

While an outpatient, she accepted a position as a salesperson at a local Topeka dress shop. "Working at the dress shop was a tonic for me," she said. Her full release from care in 1960 brought her back to the film industry and to a happy marriage with Howard Lee.[1] Now 41 years old and uninsurable, Tierney found few employers in Hollywood until old friend Otto Preminger fought to have her cast in 1962's *Advise and*

---

1   The couple remained together until Lee's death in 1981.

Consent. She appeared in three more films and one TV movie before calling it quits. "The Hollywood I knew was gone," she reflected.

Tierney retired to Houston with her husband and became an outspoken advocate for humane and effective treatment of the mentally ill. She died of emphysema on November 6, 1991.

"If what I have learned can be summed up in one sentence it would be this: life is not a movie." Those words concluded Tierney's autobiography. Sometimes, however, Tierney's own troubled life seemed inseparable from the roles she played in film noir. She didn't possess the bravado of a Barbara Stanwyck or the sexuality of a Gloria Grahame. Instead, Gene Tierney brought to the screen her own distinctive style, boldly baring her soul and enhancing noir with its subtlety and sophistication—and a just a dash of sinfulness. ■

Jonathan Latimer
A Writer in the Wheelhouse
by Ben Terrall

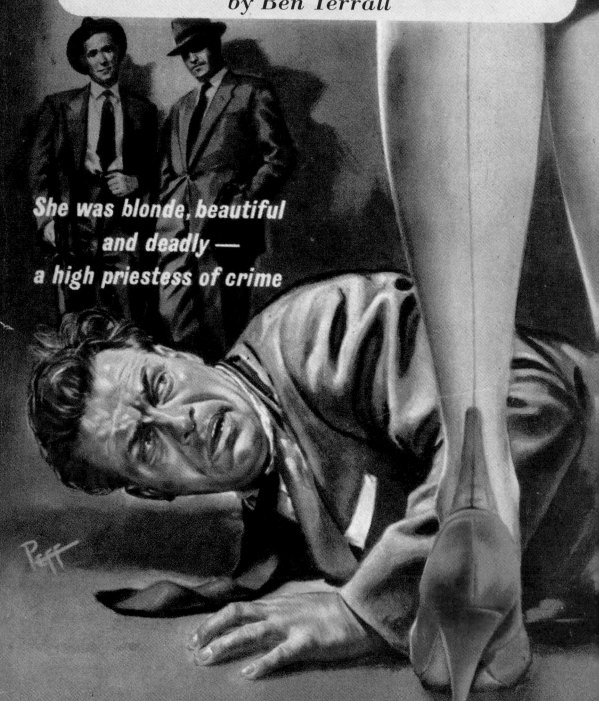

She was blonde, beautiful and deadly — a high priestess of crime

T hough Jonathan Latimer isn't well known today, his impressive career spanned crime reporting and hard-boiled fiction in the 1930s, well-oiled studio screenplays in the '40s and '50s, and workmanlike scripts for television shows such as *Perry Mason* in the late '50s and early '60s. His Hollywood work included several classic noir titles, including *The Glass Key* (1942), *They Won't Believe Me* (1947), *The Big Clock* (1948), and *Alias Nick Beal* (1949). Latimer was born in Chicago in 1906. He graduated Phi Beta Kappa with a degree in English from Knox College in 1929 and spent the following summer bicycling around France and Germany. Upon returning to the States, he caught on as a reporter for the Hearst-owned *Chicago Herald Examiner*. In a 1983 interview, the writer recalled covering "Criminal matters: gangland slayings, kidnappings, more or less routine homicides, race riots, bank embezzlements and such. I knew Al Capone, George 'Bugs' Moran and assorted other gangsters, as well as whorehouse madams, pimps, dope peddlers and con men." The crime beat clearly suited Latimer who recalled, "One Sunday when I was the only rewrite man in the *Herald Examiner* office, I established some sort of record by writing about ten thousand words in six hours about the machine gun slaying of Chicago's second most prominent union labor boss on his way home from church and the escape of John Dillinger, at the time the country's most notorious outlaw, from the Crown Point, Indiana jail."

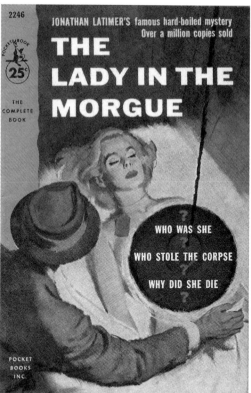

After voraciously reading Dumas, Dickens, and Victor Hugo as a child, Latimer was convinced to follow their lead. Newspaper work afforded him excellent training for his later writing career. He moved from the *Herald Examiner* to the Windy City's largest newspaper, the *Tribune*, before relocating to Washington, D.C. to take a job as staff editor in the Department of the Interior's publicity department. It was there he ghostwrote *Back To Work - The Story of PWA* (1935) for Interior Secretary Harold Ickes.

THAT SAME YEAR Latimer sold his first novel to Doubleday—*Murder in the Madhouse*, the first of five books in the William Crane detective series. The sale enabled a move to Key West, Florida, where he'd write fiction full time. "I used to write mornings until I had a thousand words or so," Latimer later recalled, "Then I'd return to rewriting or blocking out the next day's work. About six hours a day in all. … I did a lot of rewriting, not so much plot changes as sharpening scenes and dialogue and condensing description."

James M. Cain was an early inspiration, as was Hemingway, who Latimer knew briefly while living in Key West in 1936 and 1937. Another important influence was Dashiell Hammett, evidenced when Latimer's protagonist Bill Crane requests an issue of *Black Mask* (for which Hammett was the star contributor); in the fifth Crane book, *Red Gardenias* (1939), there's a reference to the William Powell-Myrna Loy *Thin Man* movies, in which Nick and Nora Charles drank at the same gargantuan levels as the alcoholic Crane. There are also parallels between Crane's unnamed detective agency and the Continental outfit for which Hammett's Op worked.

The Crane stories are careening concoctions consisting of equal parts Hammett-influenced stylings and whatever variety of boozy libations are at hand. The writing is often uneven, but at times achieves a frenzied, off-kilter lunacy. As critic Geoffrey O'Brien wrote in his essential survey *Hardboiled America*, "At their best the books have the tempo of a 1932 Warner [Bros.] movie; you can almost hear

Lee Tracy or Roscoe Karns spitting out the dialogue." O'Brien also observed, "In Latimer's parodistic books … whiskey drinking is the central activity, occasionally interrupted by the plot."

Variety said of *Murder in the Madhouse*, "It is rough and loaded with action and gore. Setting is a bit unusual and more gruesome than most whodunits, but tops for those readers who can take it. Not for films." The unnamed reviewer was prescient, as the book was never turned into a movie, though three of the later Crane mysteries became Universal Bs on which Latimer did no writing: *The Westland Case* (1937) was adapted from *Headed for a Hearse* (1935); *The Lady in the Morgue* (1938) from the 1936 Crane book of the same name; and *The Last Warning* (1938) from *The Dead Don't Care* (1938). All three serviceable programmers starred Preston Foster as Crane.

Murder in the Madhouse begins with Crane, throughout the series assisted by (hard-) drinking buddy and fellow detective Doc Williams, being committed to an asylum for claiming to be C. Auguste Dupin (Edgar Allan Poe's famous detective). The reader only finds out many chapters in that Crane is, in actuality, a detective. His assignment, issued by his boss, "The Colonel," is to locate a missing strongbox containing $400,000 worth of bonds. As with all the books in the series, between gulps of booze Crane lets loose with a stream of wisecracks which don't always hit their mark. He also indulges in wanton violence when given half a chance; after felling the sanitarium's bodyguard for no particular reason, "Crane put his right heel in the exact center of the upturned face and threw his entire weight onto his right leg. Then he spun clockwise. There was a cracking sound, and under his heel it felt juicy."

The second Crane book, *Headed for a Hearse*, again drew praise from *Variety*, which exulted, "It's one of the best whodunits in some time: terse, tough, and intelligently plotted and keyed."

The best-remembered Crane is the third entry, *The Lady in the Morgue*, which *Variety* called "a pip" and which ultimately sold more than 2,000,000 copies. A corpse is stolen from the Cook County morgue while Crane is on the scene, resulting in the police treating him as a suspect. Included is one of the more deranged scenes in Latimer's oeuvre. While casing an apartment, Crane is interrupted by the police. He climbs out a window and into the next apartment, where a couple is asleep in bed. The man is drunk, and Crane carries him into the bathroom after tying up the woman. When the cops come to the door, Crane throws them off by pretending to be the drunk husband.

This kind of gallows humor is, unfortunately, marred by racist slurs not confined to the characters—the third person narrative at one point employs "the N-word." Casual racism played cute is a factor elsewhere in the Crane books, which led critic James Naremore to point out Latimer's "manifestly racist treatment of black people." Crime fiction historian Woody Haut has argued that Naremore's take unfairly singles out one writer for a tendency prevalent throughout the thirties. Latimer's stereotypes, however, are played for laughs in a mean-spirited fashion that goes beyond a reflection of the times. It's impossible to ignore this glaring problem, even while acknowledging Latimer's importance to crime fiction and film noir.

Latimer's best-remembered novel is probably *Solomon's Vineyard*, which was published "unexpurgated" in England in 1941, but did not appear in an uncensored U.S. edition until 1988. Naremore declares it Latimer's best, "a synthesis of *The Maltese Falcon*, *Red Harvest*, and *The Dain Curse* … It deserves to be put alongside Paul Cain's *Fast One* (1933) as one of the toughest, most sadomasochistic Hammett imitations of all time."

Solomon's Vineyard is prefaced by a note from its fictional protagonist, Karl Craven, which reads in part: "*Listen. This is a wild one. Maybe the wildest yet. It's got everything but an abortion and a tornado.*" The first sentence kicks things off in characteristically unrestrained fashion: "From the way her buttocks looked under the black silk dress, I knew she'd be good in bed." The case study in hetero male-gazing goes on, "She had gold-blonde hair, and curves, and breasts the size of Cuban pineapples."

In his reference guide to classic mysteries, *1001 Midnights*, Art Scott wrote of *Solomon's Vineyard*, "It has *everything!* A private eye; a shoot-out at a roadhouse; necrophilia; a shoot-out in a steam bath; mobsters; a crooked police chief; a bizarre religious cult; a knife fight in a whore-

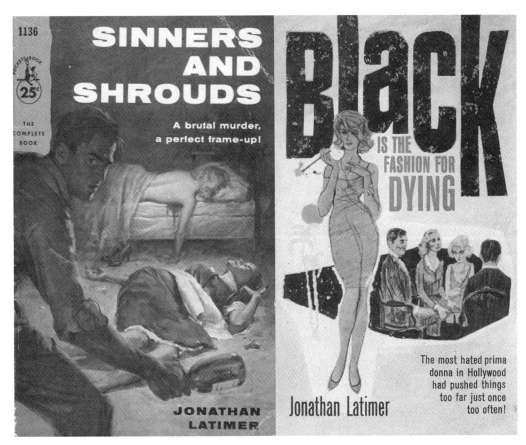

house; kidnapping; a mystery woman with a taste for kinky sex; human sacrifice; crypt robbing." Scott felt that the novel "deserves to be ranked with the best of Hammett, Whitfield, Cain and Chandler *et al.*"

Latimer's most famous novels are the Crane books and *Solomon's Vineyard*, but my favorites are the later offerings *Sinners and Shrouds* (1955) and *Black is the Fashion for Dying* (1959). The two are more cleanly written than his earlier work, and Latimer's humor has matured and is less non-stop knockabout.

Sinners and Shrouds shares similarities with Sam Fuller's *The Dark Page* (1944) and Kenneth Fearing's *The Big Clock* (1946). After a blurry night out, newspaperman Sam Clay wakes up in a strange bed with a dead woman at his side. After a hasty retreat, he is assigned by his paper to find the killer. Clay is put through the proverbial ringer and, after a number of plot twists, he takes stock of his situation while looking at "the face dimly reflected on the plate glass, a face a poltergeist would have hesitated to claim, twisted lips sucking air, eyes glazed like a dead halibut's, skin blotched from blows, cuts, and sundry conditions: the face of an insane toadstool." Elsewhere, Latimer describes a cup of coffee that's "black as tar, as pungent as garlic, as clear as dry sherry, as hot as Bisbee, Arizona." *New York Times* critic Anthony Boucher called *Sinners and Shrouds* "a too-long delayed comeback that ranks as a major event in crime fiction," and the *Chicago Tribune* called it "a shrewdly concocted blend of exciting suspense." The novel didn't hit commercially, however.

Black is the Fashion for Dying is a mystery set in Hollywood at the end of "Golden Age" filmmaking. Each chapter is from the perspective of a different character, all involved in making an overwrought safari adventure called *Tiger in the Night*. Protagonist Richard Blake is a veteran screenwriter bemused by his trade. He sees studio policy toward writers changing: "No more contract writ-

Warren William, as Michael Lanyard (aka The Lone Wolf), irritates Ida Lupino by flirting with Rita Hayworth in *The Lone Wolf Spy Hunt*

ers. He was the last one, the last shaggy buffalo of a nearly extinct herd, and they were only waiting until option time to shoot him, stuff him and hang him over the studio gates."

As *Black is the Fashion for Dying* begins, Blake is cranking out pages to keep up with the production schedule for the jungle picture. The plot is thickened by tensions between an up-and-coming ingénue and an older star desperately hanging on; machinations of a wily producer to gain control of his father-in-law's studio, and a murder investigation which occurs after a real bullet is found among blanks on the *Tiger in the Night* set.

Late '50s filmmaking is described with acerbic wit and zero sentimentality. The studio system is on the way out, and so are old-school ways of making movies. Troubled director Josh Gordon bemoans the fast-moving, multiple-camera assembly line approach borrowed from TV: "Television monitors. Six cameras. Four sets. Simultaneous action," Gordon muttered as he outlined the production assistant's scheme. "What you need is the ringmaster from Ringling Brothers' Circus." Among the book's more stable traditions is the Academy Awards ceremony, in which Latimer uses real-life movie people (Kim Novak presents an award to one of the book's characters) to comic effect.

Latimer hated the title *Black is the Fashion for Dying*; his preference, *The Mink-Lined Coffin*, was used only for the British edition. Under whatever title, the book deserves reissue.

WHEN HE WROTE *Solomon's Vineyard*, Latimer's Hollywood career was already underway. In 1937, he'd married Ellen Peabody in Key West[1], and, in 1938, they moved to the Southern California

---

1 Latimer and Ellen had three children, but later divorced; Latimer married Jo Ann Hanzlik in 1954.

town of La Jolla. There, he met and drank with Raymond Chandler, whom Latimer described as "a sharp, crusty man with a heart of ice." Producer Joseph Sistrom, then at Columbia, approached the writer to do an original treatment for a spy movie, which became *The Lone Wolf Spy Hunt*, Latimer's first script job in Hollywood. The picture, released in January 1939, is a fast-moving adventure featuring Warren William as a retired jewel thief working himself out of a frame-up while recovering weapons plans stolen from the War Department (an earlier more honest title than the "U.S. Department of Defense").

The Lone Wolf Spy Hunt features a stellar cast, including Ida Lupino, Rita Hayworth, and Ralph Morgan. Also included is a "surrealist party," which William attends by swiping an invitation from a drunk and breaking off tree branches and stuffing them into the neck of his suit; he explains that he is costumed as "the forest primeval."

Latimer quickly churned out three more screen stories: an original Nick Carter detective yarn, *Phantom Raiders* (1940), with another writer, William Lipman, tackling the screenplay; *Topper Returns* (1941), the second sequel to the comic ghost picture *Topper*, and *Night in New Orleans* (1942). Then, Latimer got a plum assignment at Paramount—adapting *The Glass Key*, Dashiell Hammett's favorite of his own novels. Latimer's screenplay was top-notch. The 1942 film, directed by Stuart Heisler, was the second film version of the story and *Variety* enthused, "New version of the yarn has been refurbished to overcome major faults in the 1935 film version. Scripter Jonathan Latimer has materially strengthened the story with vigorous writing."

Alan Ladd does a credible job portraying Ed Beaumont (Ned in the novel), "fixer" for ward boss Paul Madvig (Brian Donlevy); both men fall for high society bombshell Janet Henry (Veronica Lake). Lake and Ladd were fresh from their successful pairing in *This Gun for Hire* (1942); studio ads described Lake as "Little Miss Dynamite" and tagged *The Glass Key* as a "Battle of the Sexes."

Latimer hewed closely to the novel's narrative structure, and preserved period slang like "Ain't you a pip?" and references to "roscoes." He also added some of the best dialogue of his career. When William Bendix, playing a thug known simply as Jeff, is asked, "What's the matter, don't you like your steak medium?" he says, "Nah, when I bite a steak I like it to bite back at me." Bendix asks his sidekick, "Where'd you learn how to cook?" and the guy replies, "My first wife was a second cook in a third-rate joint on Fourth Street."

Ladd and Lake develop a palpable romantic on-screen chemistry while trading some great lines:
Ladd (seeing Lake at his apartment door): "What is this, a social service call?"
Lake: "You don't like me, do you?"
Ladd: "I think I do."
Lake: "I'm pleased, even with such qualified approval."

Brian Donlevy, in a role reminiscent of the one he played in *The Great McGinty* (1940), responds to the entreaty "I can't make my boys vote the reform ticket" with "Why not? Most of 'em come from a reform school." Latimer seemed to have a field day writing in the long shadow cast by his hardboiled mentor.[2]

Latimer's movie work was interrupted when he joined the U.S. Navy in 1943. During the war, he was executive officer on a destroyer doing escort duty in the Atlantic. Postwar, his first assignment was for freelancing producer Joan Harrison at RKO, working on a screenplay based on a story by Frank Fenton and Rowland Brown called *Nocturne* (1946).

George Raft stars as police detective Joe Warne out to find the killer of a womanizing composer whose death is ruled a suicide. Warne steps on so many toes (and leans so hard on suspects) he gets kicked off the force. Of course, he perseveres in his quest and eventually nabs the killer. The cast included Lynn Bari, Virginia Huston, and, in his film debut, future director Joe Pevney. *Variety* predicted

---

2 Paramount agreed; it next assigned Latimer to adapt Hammett's *Red Harvest* as another vehicle for Ladd and Lake. Although he completed the script, the screenplay was never filmed. Legal battles over ownership of the film rights have prevented the novel from ever being directly adapted, although films ranging from *Yojimbo* to *Last Man Standing* to *Miller's Crossing* have lifted the basic small-town gang war plot line.

George Raft, as detective Joe Warne, displays characteristic cool in *Nocturne*

Jane Greer and Susan Hayward have womanizer supreme Robert Young surrounded in *They Won't Believe Me*

the movie was "headed for a good payoff," which proved accurate; *Nocturne* turned a tidy $500,000 profit, acceptable by RKO standards.

Joan Harrison, who'd been a valued script collaborator with Alfred Hitchcock, appreciated Latimer's handiwork. She hired him to write the screenplay for her next production, *They Won't Believe Me* (1947), based on a story by Gordon McDonell (*Shadow of a Doubt*). It featured Robert Young as supreme cad Larry Ballentine, whose voiceover narration relates a tale (in flashback) that in true noir fashion goes from bad to worse then keeps on going. Ballentine's downfall begins when he cheats on his rich wife Greta (Rita Johnson) with Janice (Jane Greer), whom he drops when Greta sets him up with a cushy job in a brokerage on the opposite coast thinking the move will save their marriage. Enter secretary Verna Carlson (Susan Hayward), whom Larry notes "looked like a very special kind of dynamite, neatly wrapped in nylon and silk." More philandering ensues. About an hour in, Ballentine's voiceover sets us up for a major plot twist with the immortal line, "Then, one day in the hotel, fate opened up a brand-new deck of cards." Suffice it to say: fate is less than kind to our narrator.

The Big Clock (1948), Latimer's next assignment, was the author's favorite among his movie scripts. Adapted at Paramount from Kenneth Fearing's classic novel, *The Big Clock* did well at the box office and garnered positive reviews. Bosley Crowther of the *New York Times* wrote, "This is a dandy clue-chaser of the modern chromium-plated type, but also an entertainment which requires close attention from the start. … Ray Milland does a beautiful job of being a well-tailored smoothie and a desperate hunted man at the same time." Gossip columnist Louella Parsons promised, "You'll be taut as a Heifetz fiddlestring."

In a studio promotional biography from the late 1940s, Latimer said of Fearing's novel, "That

George Macready, Ray Milland, Dan Tobin, Richard Webb, and Charles Laughton all excel in *The Big Clock*, which Latimer adapted from the Kenneth Fearing novel of the same name

was a wonderful book. Practically swept you out of your seat. But when I started to transpose it for the screen, I found there wasn't any third act. In the book, after building up the huge manhunt for Suspect X, who was the hero, the villain commits suicide because a rival publisher has grabbed control of his Empire. That ending wouldn't hold up on the screen. I had to smoke the guy out into the open and have him commit suicide because Suspect X had outwitted him."[3] Latimer streamlined some of the book's plot strands and made Fearing's metaphorical clock into an actual giant timepiece that the hero, George Stroud (Milland), hides in as the trap devised by villainous Earl Janoth (Charles Laughton) closes in on him.

The Big Clock was also significant for being the first of *ten* collaborations between Latimer and director John Farrow. Their next was another flashback-laden noir, *Night Has a Thousand Eyes* (1948). Latimer wrote the script with playwright and screenwriter Barré Lyndon (a pseudonym for Englishman Alfred Edgar), who had also written the screenplays for *The Lodger* and *Hangover Square*. *Night Has a Thousand Eyes*, based on a Cornell Woolrich novel, shifted the focus of the story from two young lovers (the book's central characters) to the clairvoyant John Triton (Edward G. Robinson), who suffers the onus of being able to see the future. The film garnered lackluster critical response and meager box-office returns. In his autobiography, Robinson dismissed the film as "unadulterated hokum I did for the money." Nonetheless, his performance carries the movie. Gail Russell is convincing and John Lund does a credible job as her fiancée. Lund also sets up William Demarest's police detective with his best

---

3 This isn't actually true; Janoth accidentally falls down an elevator shaft, since the Production Code forbade suicide as a means of escaping justice. A similar change befell *They Won't Believe Me*, where Ballentine's climactic suicide attempt in the courtroom is thwarted by a bailiff's fatal gunshot.

Edward G. Robinson in *Night Has a Thousand Eyes*, screenplay by Latimer and directed by John Farrow

Nick Beal (Ray Milland) eyes a justifiably wary Donna Allen (Audrey Totter) in the Latimer-scripted knockout *Alias Nick Beal*

line—when Lund exclaims "Then it's *murder*," Demarest snaps, "It ain't table tennis!"

The only Latimer-Farrow collaboration to rank alongside *The Big Clock* is *Alias Nick Beal* (1949), based on a story by *Black Mask* veteran Mindret Lord entitled "Dr. Joe Faust." The title went through several iterations, including *Strange Temptation* and *Beyond Evil*, before Latimer settled on *Dark Circle*, which Paramount later changed to *Alias Nick Beal*, a crime film spin on "Beelzebub," as the title character is Satan in mid-twentieth-century form. Brilliantly portrayed by Ray Milland, Beal appears onscreen immediately after crusading district attorney Joseph Foster (Joseph Mitchell) swears that he would give his soul to take down the corrupt machine running his (unnamed) city. Beal operates on the assumption that "In everyone, there's a seed of destruction, a fatal weakness." His eternal task is to expose it.

In one of several drafts of the *Beal* script, Latimer introduced the title character in flashier form than he appears in the finished film: "Nick is closing the pier door behind him. He moves toward the bar, apparently oblivious of the men's stares. He is oddly dressed. His houndstooth [sic] suit might be that of a gambler, or a race tout, but there is a foreign quality about it, too."

Early drafts also included a scene, subsequently cut, in which a knife-wielding Beal "presses a button so that the ugly blade flies out, holds the weapon low, ready for a belly threat." Ultimately, Milland and Farrow made Beal smoother than that, and the actor did more with his eyes than lesser thespians manage with their entire bodies. Latimer never leaves Beal without a pithy comeback; when he hears a soapbox proselytizer describing God defeating the Devil, Nick comments, "I wonder if he knows it's two falls out of three?"

1953 photo: Latimer relaxing in his home reading a script
Photo courtesy of Latimer's grandson Jonathan

Diana Dors radiates trouble as Phyllis Hochen in *The Unholy Wife*

Variety's review noted that the "Subject has been approached interestingly in the script by Jonathan Latimer" and "It doesn't preach with pointed dialog or situations, letting the moral speak for itself, and that is an aid." The industry bible summed up: "Theme has strong church exploitation angles, which will prove the best-selling measure outside of Ray Milland's name on the marquee." Unfortunately, the film disappointed at the box office. Thanks to its revival at NOIR CITY film festival screenings in recent years, the movie has wowed a new generation of filmgoers, but it has not yet received a quality DVD or Blu-ray reissue.

Latimer followed with another Farrow-Milland effort, *Copper Canyon* (1950), a serviceable Western which features Hedy Lamarr sporting an odd Southern accent and Percy Helton playing against type as a grizzled Civil War veteran. Latimer now left big-screen crime behind, penning *The Redhead and the Cowboy* (1951), the Farrow-helmed WWII adventure *Submarine Command* (1951), the Alan Ladd-at-sea period picture *Botany Bay* (1952), and *Back from Eternity* (1956), about a plane crash in South America. One of his more entertaining screenplays of the decade was *Plunder of the Sun* (1953), which involved the smuggling of antiquities and featured Glenn Ford squaring off with nefarious characters in Zapotecan ruins near Oaxaca. Times had changed; *Variety* complained that Latimer spoiled things by "backing into the story via flashback." The closest Latimer came to noir in his 1950s pre-television career was the turgid melodrama *The Unholy Wife* (1957), yet another Farrow-directed production. The story opens with Phyllis Hochen (Diana Dors) describing her wicked past in—you guessed it—a flashback. A pity there wasn't a bigger role for Marie Windsor, playing Phyllis' good-time pal who vanishes too quickly. We do get plenty of Rod Steiger as hapless grape-obsessed vintner Paul Hochen, who marries Phyllis and then is betrayed by her; Tom Tryon plays Phyllis' rodeo-riding lover. "*Femme* star turns in an excellent account of herself and Steiger is on a par," claimed *Variety*, but the *New York Times* was less kind, concluding "*The Unholy Wife* is a dull, unholy mess, and an absolute waste of anyone's time."

LATIMER'S FIRST TELEVISION credit came in 1958, a story for the series *Pursuit*. He wrote for TV for the rest of his career, with scripts for *Hong Kong*, *Checkmate*, Ray Milland's one-season crime series *Markham*, and a 1972 episode of *Columbo*. His longest-running TV gig, however, was turning out 32 scripts, from 1958 until 1965, for the hugely popular *Perry Mason*.

Erle Stanley Gardner, *Perry Mason*'s wildly prolific creator, had trouble writing TV adaptations of his own books. Ultimately, the show's producers (which included former screen star Gail Patrick) hired Latimer and a stable of other writers to handle scripting chores, which Gardner insisted on approving throughout the show's run.

The show was a change of pace for Latimer, given that, as producer Ben Brady noted, Mason "is not a smart aleck." The stoic Mason (Raymond Burr), ably assisted by secretary Della Street (Barbara Hale) and investigator Paul Drake (William Hopper), ended each episode squaring off in court with and defeating District Attorney Hamilton Burger (William Talman). Latimer managed to provide a few wrinkles to the formula, including a story set in a mining town that includes no courtroom scenes, and an episode that had Mason's client found guilty of murder in the show's opening scene (although Mason hunts down the actual killer and eventually clears his client).

Latimer's "The Case of the Startled Stallion" features this exchange:

> Drake: "Don't tell me you're defending the horse!"
> Mason: "That's exactly what I'm doing."

At the end, the horse's grateful owner hasn't the money to pay Mason, to which Mason says, "That's all right." In another episode, "The Case of the Blushing Pearls," Mason launches his investigation on a retainer of five yen. These low-end paydays are unintentionally hilarious given that Mason never hesitates to send Drake off on chartered planes to track down potential witnesses, and Drake routinely employs a crew of investigators (whom Mason calls "your people") to pursue any obscure lead. But Drake always earns his salary, as in another Latimer-scripted episode, where he quickly responds "Yes" when Mason asks, "Paul, do you have a portable ultraviolet light in your office?"

Despite prejudices that are glaring today, Jonathan Latimer provided more than thirty years of entertainment for readers of hardboiled fiction, movie audiences, and TV watchers. His output was prodigious, and his talent for fast-moving action and his ear for pithy dialogue has earned him a lasting place in American pop culture. ∎

INTERVIEWS

SECTION THREE

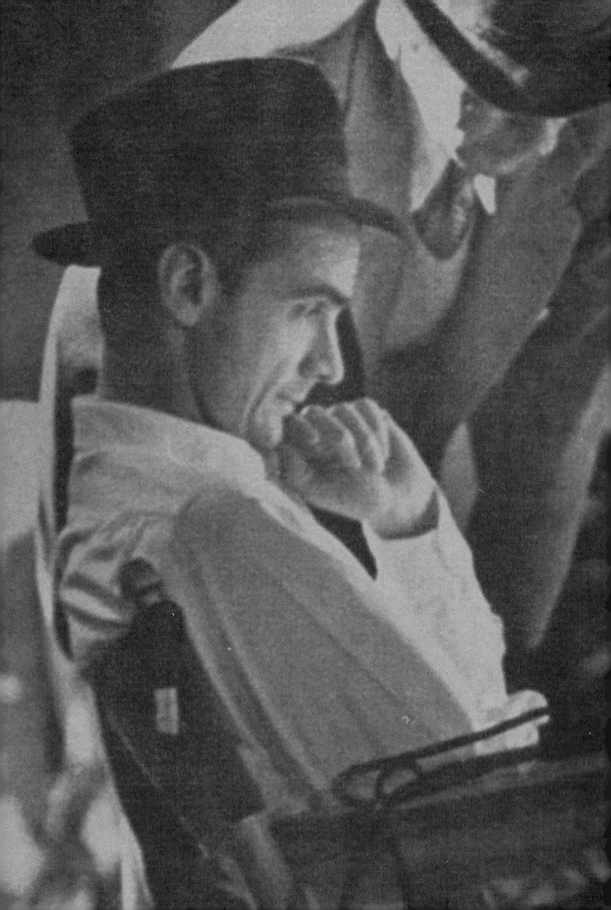

SED UCT ION

Karina Longworth on Howard Hughes's Hollywood

by Vince Keenan

"The Many Loves of Howard Hughes" was an essential early series of Karina Longworth's acclaimed podcast *You Must Remember This* about "the secret and/or forgotten history of Hollywood's first century." These episodes spotlighting several women involved with the renowned filmmaker and aviator form the foundation of Longworth's new book *Seduction: Sex, Lies, and Stardom in Howard Hughes's Hollywood*. Telling the story of the figure who personified the male gaze from the perspective of the women drawn into his orbit proved an ambitious undertaking; after two years of research, Longworth said, "I learned much more than I ever could have predicted." She unearthed enough material to spawn a six-episode season of *You Must Remember This* diving deeper into subjects only touched on in *Seduction*, including the careers of director Rupert Hughes (Howard's uncle) and actress Linda Darnell. *NOIR CITY* spoke with the former film editor at *L.A. Weekly* and critic at *The Village Voice* about Hughes' life and work, beginning with his impact on film noir.

NOIR CITY: Jane Russell emerges as *Seduction*'s secret heroine. Many of the actresses Howard Hughes had under contract resembled her physically, and you recount many incidents where she shows initiative and agency, even outwitting him. How was she able to forge her own persona while in his stable?

KARINA LONGWORTH: Obviously, her ability to work while under contract to him was limited to what he allowed her to do, but she does show more agency than a lot of the actresses in that situation. Part of it is that she became more famous, and she does owe that to Hughes. She would probably not have had the career that she had if he had not mounted this many-year-long campaign for *The Outlaw* (1943) with her at the center of it. She was incredibly famous before anyone had ever seen her in a movie. She was able to take the privilege and the platform of fame and build her own persona, as someone who didn't take any bull from anybody and was an independent, ballsy woman. She was unique in that case.

NC: You're so strong on Russell's presence in *Macao* (1952), one of the films she made with Robert Mitchum. In *Seduction*, you include Hughes' quote about the actor, which I suppose is a compliment: "(You're) like a pay toilet—you don't give a shit for nothing." What accounts for Hughes' infatuation with him?

KL: The way it was described by people who knew both of them was in a lot of ways Robert Mitchum was everything Howard Hughes could not be, and that idea of not giving a shit is a large part of it. Howard Hughes was able to foster a public persona as somebody who didn't want publicity, and was a rebel who didn't care about the convention of society. But behind the scenes, he was working very hard and paid a lot of publicists because he cared very much about what people thought about him. There's that, and there's the fact that Robert Mitchum had this incredible physique where he looked like a boxer without ever actually working out. (laughs) He had effortless virility. He wasn't just Howard Hughes' idol. For a lot of men and women, he was an iconic figure of his time.

NC: Hughes called *His Kind of Woman* (1951) "the best picture I've ever made" and in some sense you agree, describing it as "a B-movie through and through, but it was the most thematically substantive—and possibly personal—movie Howard Hughes had anything to do with." Can you explain why?

KL: *His Kind of Woman* is a hybrid of a couple of different genres. Film noir is one. It's sort of a Hollywood satire and sort of a romance. It's about these people who are walking around behind false fronts and basically negotiating the lies they're telling all the time. (laughs) The version of Howard Hughes I came to know through reading many documents having to do with him was someone who told so many lies he—I don't want to use clinical terms, but he kind of lost his mind. It's dangerous to say somebody was insane when they weren't diagnosed as such, but he lost some semblance of sanity trying to keep all of his lies straight. I don't know what was the chicken and what was the egg; I don't know if he started pathologically lying because he was already having mental problems or if he lost touch with reality because he told so many lies. That's a defining feature of his life from the 1940s on, and it's something that feels like it's pulsating out of the screen in that movie. (laughs)

NC: You shed a lot of light on aspects of Ida Lupino's career that are not well known, specifically her relationship with the FBI during the blacklist era and how that affected what you describe as "the Trojan horse act" she had to engage in professionally. What did you learn about her and how did you learn it?

KL: Ida Lupino obviously was the star of many great film noirs and other films. She was also the only female member of the DGA in the 1950s and the only woman directing mainstream Hollywood movies during that time. But what I discovered through reading her FBI file, which was made available through a Freedom of Information Act request, was that she collaborated with the FBI during

The tempest over Howard Hughes' censor-baiting build-up of his discovery Jane Russell's debut in *The Outlaw* allowed Russell's career to flourish, as did her several films with Hughes favorite Robert Mitchum, including 1951's *His Kind of Woman*

the blacklist era. Not only was it a situation where the FBI asked for help, but she volunteered it. She did this at least initially because she was concerned about her own citizenship. She did name names, and all the names she named were people who ended up being blacklisted. I'm absolutely positive she was not the only person to name any of these names. It's very probable all of these people would have been blacklisted if she had not done this. But she did do it. The fact she did it is surprising because she always presented herself as a liberal. Today we see her as a feminist icon because of her directing career. But one thing very clear to me from doing research about her was she never presented herself as a feminist. She was very careful while she was doing this thing that was absolutely pioneering for women to always say, "Oh, it's not a big deal, I'm just a good wife and mother." She played down her professional success as a director and played up the maternal and domestic aspects of what she was doing.

NC: And you believe she did that because she felt it was a necessity.

KL: Yes, but it's not like she's the only one. There are several stories in the book of women only being able to wield significant power in Hollywood by aligning themselves with a man. In her career, she was able to get a start as a producer, writer, and director because she married someone who became her producing partner. In terms of the division of labor, Ida was doing much more of the creative work, but she was able to domesticate this work by being part of a husband-and-wife team. That's the way a lot of women were able to negotiate those minefields.

NC: Did learning this alter your opinion of her?

KL: It's extremely complicated, but it's absolutely a problematic legacy to grapple with. What I tried to do was rationalize it and think logically about why she would have done it.

NC: Hughes' business relationship with Lupino is compelling. He sees a kind of simpatico between her career and his early success with *Scarface* (1932). He respects her ability to tackle socially relevant material while still making money.

KL: He doesn't care about the social issues. For him, it was 'Do whatever you want to do as long as you turn a profit.' Definitely for him it's the capitalism, not the social justice aspect. They're simpatico in that he's interested in making money off of controversy. Any stated ideals Howard Hughes had he was stating them for the money.

NC: Howard Hughes became the thinly-veiled antagonist of a film noir in *Caught* (1949), a movie that only exists because of his business practices. What insights does *Caught* offer into Hughes?

KL: It was directed by Max Ophüls, an immigrant filmmaker initially hired by Hughes' then-producing partner Preston Sturges to direct a movie called *Vendetta*, which was supposed to be a showcase for one of Hughes' girlfriends, a young brunette named Faith Domergue. After shooting for a few weeks, Ophüls ran way behind schedule and over budget, and Hughes decided to fire him. Ophüls was then hired to adapt a novel called *Wild Calendar*, and he used that to make a thinly-veiled portrait of his experience with Howard Hughes. He directed screenwriter Arthur Laurents to do a vague adaptation of this novel that was really about the way Howard Hughes treats women. Ophüls pulled from his own experiences and stories he probably learned second- and thirdhand from other women in Hollywood. Arthur Laurents himself spoke to a woman named Lynn Baggett who'd had an interesting experience being flown to Las Vegas to be one of two dozen women who were, unbeknownst to them, competing to be Howard Hughes' date for the evening. The movie ended up starring Robert Ryan as a character named Smith Ohlrig who is pretty clearly based on Hughes. Hughes knew the movie was being made; he had dailies sent to his house every day. He did request some changes to the character, but they were superficial changes, like 'I don't him want wearing tennis shoes because then everybody will know it's me.' (laughs) Robert Ryan physically really resembles Hughes. They have

Ida Lupino behind the camera of 1950's *Outrage*. The actress and filmmaker benefitted from a professional partnership with Howard Hughes, but Longworth's research unearthed Lupino's troubling relationship with the FBI during the blacklist era

the same sort of lanky stature and a similar jaw, and it really does feel like you're watching an actor playing Howard Hughes.

NC: Is there a Hughes movie you feel is underrated?
KL: I would say *Macao*.

NC: The timing of the book is uncanny. Were you working on it during the revelations about Harvey Weinstein and the rise of the #MeToo movement; and, if so, did they affect the way you wrote it?
KL: The book was almost finished by the time the Harvey Weinstein stuff came out. I turned in the first draft in September 2015. Nothing changed because of the #MeToo movement. There's one line in the introduction I wrote the morning after Trump was elected because I was angry about the idea that a man who had openly abused his power with women was being rewarded for it, so I wrote kind of a statement of purpose in the introduction. ("As we move into an era in which there is frank public discussion of the exploitation, subjugation, manipulation, and abuse of women by men in positions of power, it's time to rethink stories that lionize playboys, that celebrate the idea that women of the twentieth century were lands to be conquered, or collateral damage to a great man's rise and fall.") A year and a half after writing [the book], in November 2016, I woke up and had that sentence in my head.

NC: The contemporary stories we're hearing now are rife with unsavory details, but Hughes' system of exploiting women in his employ was even more elaborate and controlling. What exactly would happen to a woman who signed a contract with him thinking she was about to become a star?

KL: In most cases, they were really young—maybe eighteen, nineteen years old. They were often accompanied by their mother to Hollywood. Hughes would put them in the Beverly Hills Hotel, the Sunset Marquis Hotel, the Chateau Marmont, or maybe he would get them an apartment. He would have every moment of their lives accounted for. They would be given acting, dance, and voice lessons all day long. At night, they would be required to go out to dinner with Hughes' chauffeur as their date, although these were very chaste dates. Drivers were not even allowed to touch them to help them out of the car. Usually, eventually, the mother would be convinced to leave so the girl's family couldn't exert any control over her because Hughes wanted that control. In most cases, the women would never work; they would stay on this cycle of being "trained to work" for months or even years until they usually figured out how to get out of their contracts and left. In some cases, they would be put into a couple of movies. The book goes into the story of Faith Domergue in detail. She believed Howard Hughes was going to marry her. He gave her father and her grandfather jobs, and basically strung her along for five or six years. He did eventually put her in a movie, but it's the movie Max Ophüls got fired from directing (*Vendetta*). Two or three other directors, including probably Hughes himself, took turns trying to make this movie. It was finally released about ten years after she first met Hughes, and it was a disaster. As far as I can tell, it's not commercially available. I was able to buy a bootleg DVD from Europe. Hughes put a lot of his movies in a vault and then they'd never be in public circulation again. *Hell's Angels*, *Scarface*, the more classic films, they're only in circulation because they were released by his estate after he died.

NC: So how was *Vendetta*?

KL: Not good. (laughs) It's really not good, but

Hughes was fictionalized during his lifetime by jilted filmmaker Max Ophüls in 1949's *Caught*. Robert Ryan, here with Barbara Bel Geddes, "physically really resembles Hughes," according to Longworth

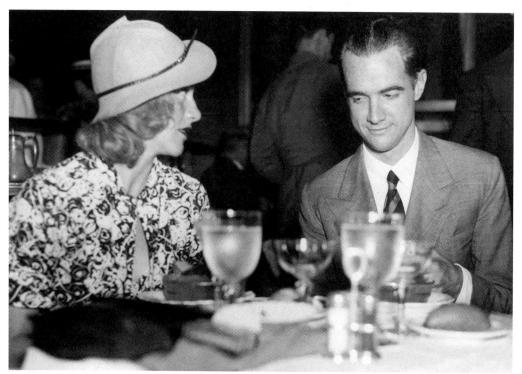

Howard Hughes cut a swath through Hollywood, his paramours including some of the silver screen's most famous faces like Katharine Hepburn, Bette Davis, and, shown above with Hughes, Ginger Rogers

fascinating in its way because it's transparently an incest fantasy. So, yet more shades of things Howard Hughes was interested in.

NC: Hughes goes from dating women of substance like Katharine Hepburn and Ava Gardner to being "so secretly afraid of failure that he couldn't approach a woman unless he was certain she was a sure thing." What accounts for that transformation? Was it his age and insecurity or something more?
KL: It's probably a combination of things. He had an ideal of himself that was larger than life, which he did a very good job of putting out there in the media, but his actual personal life was increasingly hermetic over time. This really increased after 1946, when he had a major plane crash in which he should have died. He had horrible injuries, but he'd already been in a lot of crashes by that point and this wasn't just another head injury. I personally believe some of the things that look like mental illness in him maybe were that, but you can't have that many head injuries over the course of your life and come out unscathed. I talk about half a dozen car and plane crashes in the book.

NC: Hughes has been the subject of multiple films, viewed variously as heroic and tragic. What is his legacy?
KL: One of the reasons why I wrote that sentence in the introduction is I didn't want anybody to think I was saying, "Wacky Howard Hughes, that crazy playboy!" I think that's some of the way he's remembered or perceived. "What a weirdo, but he had sex with a lot of dames!" Ultimately, he was a human being and there's tragedy in his life that I think is fine to think of as tragic, but I don't think he's a hero. People may recall him as an aviation pioneer, but don't remember specifics. Certainly, he wanted to be remembered that way, but there isn't a great record he held onto or a single major achievement people could easily point to. He developed airplanes during a period when some of the innovations he designed or paid for led to the rise of the jet age, but you can't say Howard Hughes specifically invented this.

The July 1946 crash of the Hughes XF-11 reconnaissance plane prototype in Beverly Hills almost killed Howard Hughes; the accident would have long-term physical and psychological effects on the movie mogul and aviator

NC: The book and your podcast use contemporary references to help make these movies relevant to audiences coming to them for the first time: speculating on how many Instagram followers Billie Dove would have, calling out Hughes for "negging" women. What do you want these newer and younger generations of film viewers to take away from Golden Age Hollywood?

KL: I just want them to watch these movies. I want [these films] to not disappear. If I have an undying and unquenchable enthusiasm for anything, it's being able to continually discover new films and be excited by this trove of material. I keep thinking I'm going to run out of stuff, and then I don't. (laughs) There's so much to be excited about. And if talking about things in modern terms will make someone watch *His Kind of Woman*, that's great. That would make me happy and feel like I had done my job. I'm happy people listen to the podcast, but I hope they seek out the movies. ■

BUDAPEST NOIR

by Brian Light

Budapest, 1936: a locomotive belching dense plumes of steam pulls slowly into Keleti train station, transporting the body of Hungarian Prime Minister Gyula Gömbös, who—after being inspired by a trip to Germany—had intended to install himself as a fascist dictator in his own country. Among the throng of mourners are dozens of soldiers who reverently offload the coffin. There to report on the event is Zsigmond Gordon (Krisztián Kolovratnik), a crime beat reporter who has seen his share of death. "There are many different means, but the end is always the same," he laments in voiceover. He is a sullen, unrepentant cynic who smokes cigarettes—often—like he's mad at them. Leaving the depot, he has a chance meeting in a café with an alluring woman who sticks him with her tab. When he next encounters her, she's dead—murdered in a dicey part of town, a Jewish prayer her sole possession. When he soon uncovers the victim's photo in an unexpected place, he reasons that learning her identity could move her death from a brief back-page paragraph to front-page news.

Krisztián Kolovratnik portrays the newspaper reporter who doggedly unravels the murder of a young woman with a mysterious past

With the city virtually shut down and the police pressed into service guarding the funeral procession, Gordon conducts his investigation with impunity. Displaying a shamus' eye for detail and a set of stealthy fingers, he sifts through clues to the victim's identity. When her body goes missing from the morgue, he snags an autopsy report, then a pilfered love letter from a rabbi's son, both deepening the mystery. Once he uncovers a servant's license from a humble dressmaker, Gordon begins to narrow his focus.

Budapest resonates as a supporting character in the film, and Elemér Ragályi's cinematography captures the old-world elegance of Buda and the oppressive squalor of Pest as though they're frozen in time. Director Éva Gárdos is also a veteran editor, and her skills in the cutting room serve her well behind the lens. Her camera placement, supple tracking, and compositional sense indicate she's a keen pictorial stylist, and the pacing and seamless transition shots advance the narrative with brisk resolve. The art direction is superb, and there are a number of exquisite set pieces throughout: a photographer's studio populated with mannequins bearing silent witness to his sordid trade, a sports club featuring a boxing ring amidst a lavishly appointed cocktail lounge; an upscale brothel, aptly named *Les Fleurs du Mal*, catering to high-level politicians. In addition to Kolovratnik, the casting is uniformly fine. Gordon's independently minded love interest, Krisztina, is played by Réka Tenki—Hungary's most talented, in-demand young actress. She brings depth and emotional nuance to what was essentially a one-dimensional character in the novel. As Fanny, the object of Gordon's obsession, Franciska Töröcsik incandesces in only a few brief moments. Zsolt Anger is solid as Gellért, the circumspect police commissioner, and Janos Kulka as Mr. Szöllösy delicately offsets his character's vanity with a veneer of fastidiousness. Adél Kováts as Mrs. Szöllösy provides a galvanizing display of conflicted emotions.

Although set in 1936, the film is strikingly contemporaneous. Hungary was about to enter the darkest period in its recent history and placed within the broader historical context—a shifting alignment of powers within Hungary and the rising tide of Nazism just across the border—*Budapest Noir* is imbued with a substrate of moral opacity, redolent with political peril. Mr. Szöllösy, a successful business entrepreneur desperately trying to curry favor in a rapidly changing political landscape—while keeping his family history a secret—unintentionally sets unforeseen wheels in motion and becomes the architect of his own demise. Complexities such as these elevate this from brooding film noir elegy to the dimensions of Shakespearian tragedy. The book hews closely to the well-worn tropes of a conventional crime thriller which requires retribution for the killer. The film, however, shifts the focus by exploring a tangle of complicity and indemnity that rises all the way to the government's upper echelons.

Ultimately, Gordon—once fired from a newspaper for printing a lie—decides to exact his own form of moral justice with a simple stroke of his pen. He may have solved the case, but his cynicism proves to be little more than a survival mechanism and his pitch-perfect final pronouncement (a sly nod to *Chinatown*) indicates the steely reserve needed to face the storm troopers gathering next door.

Éva Gárdos INTERVIEW

Interviewed by Brian Light for NOIR CITY

NOIR CITY: I've read the book and viewed the film, and I think this is one of the rare cases where the film is better than the book, considerably better!

Éva Gárdos: I'm glad you said that because that was the only criticism—strong criticism I got in Hungary. Some people preferred the book and they didn't like the changes I made from the book which I thought it really needed … badly.

NC: How did the book first come to your attention?

EG: People knew I was Hungarian and someone said to me arbitrarily, "Do you know there's a book called *Budapest Noir*?" I read the book and submitted it for development to The Hungarian Film Fund. The author, Vilmos Kondor, writes under a pseudonym so the first task was to find him.

NC: What was it about the book that inspired you?

EG: I wanted to make a film where Budapest was a real character—not Budapest substituting for Paris or Berlin, but Budapest as Budapest. I also liked the subtext that people don't want to see what's happening. I think that's very relevant to today, in Hungary and the United States and elsewhere in the world. Plus, as a female director, I wanted to get away from doing a "personal" movie and do a good genre film.

Hungarian location shooting: Director Éva Gárdos and DP Elemér Ragályi setting up a scene inside an authentic period tram

Four minutes of screen time: Fanny (Franciska Töröcsik) sets her sights on Gordon and leaves an indelible impression

NC: What were the challenges in adapting a popular book?

EG: Obviously, a book is different from a film; a film has to have some drama. I worked with screenwriter András Szekér—via Skype mainly since he was in Budapest and I was mostly in L.A. We spent two years fleshing out the characters and the events that build the drama. We became very close, and I was saddened when he died suddenly last October (2016). I wanted the film to appeal to younger audiences as well, so we changed the relationship between Krisztina and Gordon from where she was much more in service to Gordon, doing what he asked her, etc. We created a situation where they clearly have a history—when she shows up unexpectedly at his door—without having to show it all. You know they love each other, but they ultimately can't be together. She's sort of his Achilles' heel. It's good for him to have moments of weakness.

NC: In the book, Krisztina is simply the girlfriend, and it's just a routine relationship.

EG: Exactly! That's right. You've read the book.

NC: In the book, Krisztina designs Penguin book covers. In the film, she's a more independent-minded character—a photojournalist devoted to documenting the realities of Nazi detention camps.

EG: In the book, she sort of *knows* more about what's happening in Germany than Gordon is aware of, and I thought making her a photographer would be really interesting. We based her character on Gerda Taro (Robert Capa's colleague and longtime companion). Another change we made was with Fanny and her father, Szöllösy. We felt we had to introduce him much earlier than in the book, and we wanted Gordon and him to have a connection, so Gordon had more at stake. In the book, it seemed Szöllösy was more concerned about his business interests than his daughter's welfare, and we wanted to avoid the cliché of portraying him as a money-grubbing Jewish businessman. We also felt Gordon had to *meet* the girl whose death becomes his obsession . . . so did the audience. She had to make an impression, and our actress, Franciska Töröcsik, certainly does that.

NC: Tell me about her—the actress who played Fanny.

EG: Franciska has starred in several movies, and is far more recognizable than the two leads. When she came in to do a short test video, she conveyed so much emotion she sent shivers down my spine. I said, "I know it's a small part, and you're really well known, but if you're interested in doing it . . ." and she said, "Well, the movie's really all about me so why not?"

NC: She didn't mind only having four minutes of screen time?

EG: No—she even came and did publicity with us!

NC: I understand Krisztián Kolovratnik, the actor who plays Gordon, is mainly a stage actor?

EG: Krisztián had been contracted to a top Budapest theater, but then he stopped acting seven years ago because of family issues. He has a production company and is also a photographer. DP Elemér Ragályi, who shot *An American Rhapsody*[1], and I met him quite accidentally in a café, and Elemér said he was a great young actor. We had looked at a lot of actors in Budapest, but nobody seemed quite right. People had told us there was no such type . . .

NC: Like an American equivalent . . .

EG: Well, yeah—he's kind of an American equivalent. He's a guy who can box, he's a musician, and he's very cool. So, we sent him the script. He came in to do some screen tests and he was perfect. We also tested different girls for the role of Krisztina, but hadn't decided on anyone. I had seen Réka Tenki in a play and my casting director and good friend Helga Mandel, with whom I worked closely for several months, also knew Réka. When she came in to audition, she did a scene with Krisztián on the tram and in response to his line: "Let's pretend we're married," she unexpectedly smacked him across the face. That was the "spark" we didn't get from the other actresses.

NC: How does your experience as an editor shape how you direct a film?

EG: I think it's fairly easy for me to visualize how things are going to look. I'm very familiar with post-production and we spent a lot of time in the editing room. The composer, Attila Pacsay, and I worked on the music, which won an award in Los Angeles for Best Foreign Film Score. I had a great production designer, Pater Sparrow, and a very experienced cinematographer in Elemér Ragályi.

NC: Since Ragályi's career dates back to the late 1960s, how did your professional paths cross?

EG: We first met in the late '80s on a Brian Gibson documentary about Simon Wiesenthal.

NC: *Murderers Among Us: The Simon Wiesenthal Story* (1989).

EG: Yes, he was the DP and I was the editor, and we both won ACE (CinemaEditor) awards for that. He was also the DP on *An American Rhapsody* (2001).

NC: *Budapest Noir* was shot in Budapest; *An American Rhapsody* was shot in Hungary and America, and you've edited movies in both countries, as well. How would you compare the two experiences?

EG: That's an interesting question! There were many years between the two films and things had changed a lot in Hungary due partly to the Film Fund now being run by Andy Vajna. Ridley Scott has made three films there. I had a terrific producer, Ildikó Kemény, who really knows how to get things done. When I worked here, we just worked in the San Fernando valley with a low budget and a small crew. In Hungary, the artistry was great, and we were able to get really good people because we had a good script . . . it's not always about the money. I haven't really worked here in the U.S. enough to be able to compare, but the people were good. *Budapest Noir* was made with an all-Hungarian crew; we only spoke Hungarian, and it was great to work there.

NC: This film and *Rhapsody* are set approximately twenty years apart—mid-1930s and mid-1950s, respectively. The period costumes and set designs are superb. What kind of research did you do to get the look so right?

EG: I like to look at a lot of photographs, and in both films I had great costume designers, Beatrix Aruna Pasztor on *American Rhapsody* and Andrea Flesch on *Budapest Noir*. They were both in-

---

1 Gárdos' first feature, released in 2001.

Gárdos and her leading man Krisztián Kolovratnik, whom she coaxed out of temporary retirement for the film, share a laugh on location

volved in the whole look of the actors—hair, makeup, etc. I try to avoid doing things that are very typical of the period. We don't have to be *that* strict.

NC: How did you scout locations? You capture parts of the city that looked almost frozen in time. Was it difficult to get permits?
EG: Budapest has lots of great locations, but due to our small budget we couldn't always shut down streets and hold up traffic. The bridge scene near the end was important to me so we did get to have it for a day.

NC: . . . where Inspector Gellért pulls up and hops out of the police car.
EG: Yes—I liked the location, so I really pushed for that, and a lot of scenes were shot in alleys and doorways. We also built a lot of sets for a movie this size. One of the best sets was the photography studio with all the mannequins—that was completely (production designer) Pater Sparrow's idea. He also built the sports club. András Szekér and I came up with the idea of having a club where there was boxing. There were a lot of nightclubs in that era, but we integrated the two. I don't know if that really existed, but it gave Gordon and Szöllösy a reason to be acquainted. They both like bourbon and boxing.

NC: And it's certainly the type of venue that would attract high-level politicians, as well.
EG: Exactly. And another great set was the Bauhaus-inspired house. That was the hardest fight I had because I had looked at lots of beautiful villas all over Budapest, but I felt they were so typical and had been in so many movies. I did research on what the architecture was like in the thirties, and discovered that there were a lot of Bauhaus homes in Budapest during this period. Then, the Christmas before we started shooting, my son and I went to the Bauhaus museum in Berlin and I was struck by what a huge figure László Moholy-Nagy was in the Bauhaus movement. I felt, if we wanted to show Budapest, we had to show that part of the great city, too. We looked at a bunch of houses, but they had all been renovated, so we decided to build it. It was a huge job for the art department.

NC: The austerity of the interior suits Szöllösy's personality.
EG: I had also been worried about that big scene because there's so much dialogue, but it turned out to be great. There's a lot to see and the actors and the camera could really move, so that turned out very well.

NC: After this scene, the book has a final act concerning the murderer, but you chose to focus on the father/daughter relationship.
EG: I thought it was tragic that he wants to protect his daughter because he knows what's coming politically, and he reveals he's Jewish and he converted probably after the first World War. In my family, I only found out I was Jewish six years ago, and so many people in Hungary had that experience. The screenwriter András Szekér had the same experience.

NC: The actress who plays the wife/mother, Adél Kováts, has only two scenes in the movie and she's galvanizing.
EG: Adél was great. András Szekér and I struggled with her part in that scene . . . to get it real. I wanted her to react as a mother. That was one scene that we rehearsed for most of the day before we shot anything because we knew we had to get it right.

NC: What about those period trams and subway cars? Are they still active in Budapest?
EG: Well, the Metro is still there. I wanted to use the Metro and the Tram because it's difficult to fit a camera in those old cars, plus there were not a lot of cars on the streets back then. There is a museum of old trams, trains, and metro cars and they brought them to the location in the middle of the night. It was the same with the train at Keleti Station in the beginning when the coffin arrives, and at the end when Krisztina leaves, which we had to do very quickly so they could get the train out and reopen

As in most detective fiction, Gordon's inquisitiveness leads to a conflict with upper-class suspects and the police who protect them

the station. It was extremely cold, and difficult, but Krisztián and Réka knew exactly how to play it.

NC: Did the issue of Jewish identity during that politically unstable period enrich the story and was that an important aspect for you?

EG: It was very important and we wanted to integrate it into the film without making it totally didactic. And we fought very hard for the last sentence in the film where Gordon just kind of pushes it away and the man replies, "I have a newsstand and I have only one arm, and that's okay, but lately I am Jewish and that's too much of a good thing."

NC: Even though he may have lost his arm fighting for his country, he's now being marginalized.

EG: Exactly, and suddenly he's Jewish . . . I liked that aspect of the film—the political statement which I thought was important.

NC: And Gordon's final pronouncement?

EG: After all he has been through—over the course of just a few days—all he wants to do is go back to the café, have another bourbon and coffee and a pack of cigarettes . . . it's a survival mechanism. I suppose that's the cynicism of noir. András Szekér and I really liked that—we fought quite a few people to keep that ending.

NC: Is film noir a genre that you have an affinity for? Any particular film that may have informed your approach to filming *Budapest Noir*?

EG: Well, I know about film noir by going to noir festivals in San Francisco and L.A., and watching TCM. One of my favorites is *In a Lonely Place*, but right from the beginning we didn't want to make a replica. I wanted it to be more of a neo-noir like *Chinatown* or *L.A. Confidential*, where the city itself is also a character.

NC: Do you read a lot of this type of crime fiction?

EG: I've read Raymond Chandler and Dashiell Hammett ... particularly Hammett.

NC: Speaking of Hammett, there is a scene in the book where Gordon pumps Red Margo for information that is lifted almost verbatim from a similar scene in *Red Harvest*.

EG: Well, I have been nothing but polite about Kondor, but when I started to get all these comments about how much better the book was, it took all my restraint to not say . . .

NC: . . . to not call him out?

EG: Perhaps I should have, I don't know.

NC: What was the author's reaction to the film?

EG: His objection was the Krisztina and Gordon relationship. He felt that he wanted that part of Gordon's life not to have conflict. I think their relationship with all the complications is true to life. Because of this, we see Gordon in a more raw, emotional way. Kondor didn't like that we "invented" a fancy club that had boxing because it wasn't real. But it could have been, and I like to show things that haven't been seen before.

He failed to comment on important changes that made the film work—Gordon's meeting the girl who became his obsession, and revealing the "killer" earlier. There are elements that we dramatized about the killer—"showing" rather than "telling."

NC: The book was a bestseller, so there's an audience in Hungary for crime fiction. How has the movie been received there?

EG: It opened in October 2017 and it's still going strong which is great considering all the American films that open every week. We did quite a few Q & As in different towns and people really responded to them. There had not previously been this type of movie and people were really interested in seeing it.

NC: Do you have any other projects lined up?

EG: I have a script I developed, *Cindy in Iraq*, which is about U.S. contractors working in Iraq. It's a great story, but for a long time everybody was afraid of it. I also have a lovely memoir, *More was Lost*, by Eleanor Perenyi about a young American's love affair with a Hungarian baron before and during World War II. I'm also very interested in directing some of the great shows on Netflix, Amazon, Hulu, etc. The word in Hollywood is that it's the year of the woman!

ADDITIONAL INFORMATION

An American Rhapsody released by Paramount Classic in 2001. Éva Gárdos wrote and directed this autobiographical tale about her family's escape from Stalin-occupied Hungary in the early 1950s to start a new life in America. The film won the Hollywood Discovery Award for Best Feature and earned two honors at the Nantucket Film Festival—Audience Award for Best Feature and Bubbling Under Award for a promising first-time director. In addition, the Young Artist Awards cited the film for Best Ensemble in a Feature Film.

Krisztián Kolovratnik is an actor and director. Prior to *Budapest Noir*, he took a seven-year break from acting to form his own production company. He is also a photographer, a musician, and he has a vegan restaurant in Budapest.

Réka Tenki's film roles include István Szabó's *The Door* (2012) and the 2017 Oscar entry for Best Foreign Film, Ildikó Enyedi's *On Body and Soul*. She was voted one of the "10 Europeans to Watch" in 2017 by *Variety*, and in 2018 she was among those chosen for *The Shooting Star* award at the Berlin International Film Festival. ∎

APPRECIATIONS
SECTION FOUR

MY CONNECTION TO THE WORLD OF NOIR?

Fade in. I was about to experience an event that would have a profound influence on my childhood and my future: a movie theater, my first—a unique circumstance if you consider that, in those days, commercial television did not exist. Radio was *the* medium, especially for a poor, urban family existing on government food stamps.

We lived in a brick-and-tarpaper matchbox house my father built. During winters, a kitchen coal stove heated the three rooms in which we lived. Times were so tough, we couldn't even afford a nickel tablet for me to sketch on. Instead, I used the heat of my fingertips to draw pictures in the ice that formed on the inside of windows.

It makes complete sense that Orson Welles' visual virtuosity, on full display in *The Lady from Shanghai*'s fun-house scenes, would inspire Steranko's graphic corollaries to such cinematic sequences

The theater had seen better days, too. Nonetheless, I was awed by the huge cavern we entered, with aisles flanked by terraces of plush chairs. As we were seated, the room faded to darkness and curtains at the front parted to reveal a massive screen as high as a two-story building. At five years old, and with a very unsophisticated background, I was spellbound! Suddenly, the screen came alive with music and pictures of gray faces that were thirty-feet high! Intimidating and exhilarating! My heart pounded in response to the most bizarre incident of my young life—and one of the most formative. Words appeared (I'd been reading for three-and-a-half years) and they heralded THE MASK OF DIMITRIOS. My connection to the World of Noir. Fade out.

It's terminally unreasonable to reduce a lifetime of noir favorites to a finger count, so I may have to repeat the ordeal sometime when Muller has a weak moment—or too much wine! But, for what they're worth, a few noir thoughts...

Quick backstory: I painted about thirty Shadow book covers for HBJ/Pyramid, most under famed AD Harris Lewine (known to those under him as Harass the Swine). He was killer tough, opinionated, demanding—but talented, one of the reasons we hit it off. One day, he called me into his office where he was surrounded by cigar-store trappings (a Lewine obsession).

"Your paintings have *no basis in reality*," he said with his usual tact. "They create their *own reality*," I riposted. After a beat, he said, "Explain that!" It was unsound to confront Lewine on his turf, so I

Steranko and Welles briefly spoke about *The Lady from Shanghai*, with Welles revealing Columbia chief Harry Cohn made him include a Rita Hayworth musical interlude

A passel of bright boys: Charles McGraw, director Robert Siodmak, producer Mark Hellinger, and William Conrad on the set of *The Killers*, the only Hemingway adaptation to earn a thumbs up from Papa

took him into mine: "Why would I waste your valuable time? There's only one critical question: Do they sell?" He paused again. "Maybe they'd sell *better* if you painted from model photos." I nodded. "Maybe they'd look like everything else on the newsstand. Maybe they'd lose their *magic!* Can you afford to risk it?" He pondered a moment. "Get out of here—and impress the hell out of me next month!"

IT'S THE SAME REASONING WHY THE LADY FROM SHANGHAI works—it creates *its own reality*, in a class unlike any other noir film. It's the 1947 Orson Welles Magic Show, layered with hallucinatory illusions, a terminally convoluted puzzle that only Welles' logic can unravel. Yet, upon accepting that logic, it all works with uncanny precision and pristine beauty.

Wish I could say I discussed SHANGHAI with Welles, but the subject never arose during our conversations about CITIZEN KANE, the challenge of narrative technique, The Shadow, or the elusive world of magic (we were both members of the Witch Doctors Club)—except for his comment that Columbia czar Harry Cohn made him include a glamorous Rita Hayworth vocal sequence, and that the funhouse climax (including the mirror-shattering scene) was scheduled for 20 minutes and *cut to three* by the studio. Aside: Was Black Michael's soliloquy about the sharks an inspiration for Robert Shaw's recollection in JAWS?

IT'S NO SECRET THAT ALL ERNEST HEMINGWAY wrote of THE KILLERS is the opening diner scene with the "bright boy!" dialogue. Anthony Veiller—with uncredited John Huston [and Richard Brooks—ed.]—extrapolated on the short-short story, creating the quintessential non-linear, flashback-puzzle thriller, a device that became synonymous with noir cinema (perhaps with a nod

Burt Lancaster makes a memorable debut and meets a memorable end opposite Ava Gardner in *The Killers*

Steranko admits that he learned more about tempo, scene structure, camera placement, and character movement through the frames of director Michael Curtiz' *Mildred Pierce* than any other film

to CITIZEN KANE). DP Woody Bredell matched the plot complexity with evocatively tense images (the brilliant Prentiss Factory heist sequence tracking shot may have piqued Welles' envy), as did the dark orchestrations of Miklos Rozsa (listen for the inspiration of the DRAGNET theme in the Green Cat sequence). Burt Lancaster nailed his big-screen debut as the Swede in the 1946 Robert Siodmak-helmed masterpiece—in which almost everybody dies double-crossed. But isn't that the reward for those who ride the nightmare? Of all his film adaptations, Hemingway is said to have given KILLERS his only thumbs-up cinematic sanction.

IF ONE FILMMAKER COULD BE CITED as the architect of the Warner Bros. style, it would be Michael Curtiz, whose bravura direction fashioned so many of the studio's hits, from CASABLANCA to YANKEE DOODLE DANDY. It was a natural to graft him to James M. Cain, a writer often credited, along with Dashiell Hammett and Raymond Chandler, as the triumvirate who evolved the hard-boiled idiom (my apologies to Carroll John Daly). The premise is arguable; Cain's work spurned the stripped-down compression of the former and the clever metaphors of the latter. He employed no literary slight of hand, just solid, narrative skill—which would seem to qualify him as the superior wordsmith. MILDRED PIERCE may have been his masterpiece.

Assembling a first-class cast and crew, Curtiz shaped the bestseller into cinematic gold—including a 1946 Oscar® for Best Actress Joan Crawford. The picture still packs as much entertainment punch as it did 70 years ago. Confession: I learned more about tempo, scene structure, camera placement, and character movement through the frames from this film and director than any other.

FOR YEARS, 1941's THE MALTESE FALCON topped my noir list (John Huston told me that Bogart ad-libbed the line, "It's the stuff that dreams are made of!"), but over many viewings, it began

Robert Mitchum in *Out of the Past*, which brought new levels of sophistication to the tropes and traditions of noir

to tarnish to the point where I subsequently stopped watching it. FALCON set the bar for noir flicks for years—and spawned many imitations. But OUT OF THE PAST took those tropes and traditions to an increasingly sophisticated level, from flashback complexity to nuanced sexuality to ultra-expressive cinematography. And who else but Robert Mitchum could deliver the throwaway line (and the title of the Daniel Mainwaring source novel), "Build my gallows high, baby!"—and make us believe it?

ALTHOUGH I'VE NEVER SEEN 1948's THE TREASURE OF THE SIERRA MADRE on any noir list, it's high on mine because the cardinal elements of greed, paranoia, alienation, betrayal, and revenge are driving factors in one of the most compelling American films ever made. Writer-director Huston topped FALCON in the hard-boiled idiom by adapting B. Traven's conflicted neo-Western to the screen. I once baited Huston, telling him I'd scoured flea markets all over the country *hoping to find those pesos Bogart bummed from him* in the first act. He laughed, "Wouldn't mind having one of those myself!" He also revealed Bogart directed the "putting-the-bite-on-a-fellow-American" scene. Now you know.

DURING THE AGE OF DOUBLE FEATURES and beyond, Hollywood generated a tidal wave of crime/suspense pictures set in the Big Apple, many of which exploited Manhattan to superb dramatic advantage. Ironically, it took Brit director Alexander Mackendrick—paired with cinematographer James Wong Howe—to visualize the Broadway labyrinth of 1957's SWEET SMELL OF SUCCESS with the kind of stark chiaroscuro Yank filmmakers seldom canned. Like many Scorsese denizens, everyone in SUCCESS is twisted (even the protagonists are insipid and incompetent), mirroring the multiple personas of Burt Lancaster, who, in turn, qualifies Tony Curtis as, "A man of not one, but forty faces!" Razor-sharp dialogue (but not a single curse word) is delivered with understated corruption and malice. "Match me, Sidney!"

I CANNOT SUBMIT MY FAVORITE NOIR FLIX without listing at least one Sam Fuller (he pronounced it Full-ah) picture. As a fan and friend—dinners at Hollywood's Musso & Frank Grill or served by his beautiful actress-wife Christa Lang at their Hollywood Hills home—I knew his work better than the LA freeway. Whenever I sat close to Sam, he'd often accentuate a point by kicking the sole of my shoe, sometimes my calf. From anyone else, it would have been an insult; from Sam, a compliment! His garage—aka The Shack—was his personal museum piled with film souvenirs

John Huston directs Humphrey Bogart and his father Walter Huston in *The Treasure of the Sierra Madre*, which boasts enough greed and betrayal to land on Steranko's noir list

Pickpocket Richard Widmark and his mark Jean Peters in the movie J. Edgar Hoover hated, *Pickup on South Street*

and WWII gear, including a bookcase heavy with Fuller scripts—most of which were unproduced! He read the look on my face. "I settle in behind the typewriter *every morning* and generally work all afternoon," he said, behind a cigar almost as big as he was. We were standing next to *a hundred, unmade Fuller films*. Again, he anticipated my question. "Why do I continue turning out scripts? Can't help it—I'm a writer!"

Fuller loved pulp fiction, and it showed in 1953's PICKUP ON SOUTH STREET, which is riddled with noir-driven characters (rewritten from Dwight Taylor's screenplay BLAZE OF GLORY, but the title change is strictly Fuller), such as small-time cannon Richard Widmark coldcocking B-girl Jean Peters, stealing her cash, and reviving her by splashing a bottle of beer in her face. The hard-boiled thriller's most memorable scene: worn-out stoolie Thelma Ritter admitting she's "an old clock running down," just before Commie agent Richard Kiley puts a bullet in her brain to the poignant strains of *Mam'selle*. Cinematographer Joe MacDonald contributed heavily to the picture's taut atmosphere, and Leigh Harline's flyweight jazz score adds cool counterpoint to the gritty action. Fuller seemed to take some pride in the fact that J. Edgar Hoover hated the film.

HARD-BOILED ELEGANCE WITH COMPELLING dialogue, sharp performances, tight direction—LAURA defines its own noir category. One prime reason is the title theme, perhaps the most haunting, film-related melody ever scored: "That was Laura, but she's only a dream!" It was composed by my pal David Raksin. We're both from the Philly area, but we hung out in Hollywood, often at his Glendale home. After he graduated from the University of PA, he moved to the West Coast, studied with Arnold Schoenberg, and began background work at Hollywood studios, eventually apprenticing at 20th Century–Fox under the brilliant Dimitri Tiomkin.

Then, in 1944, director Otto Preminger asked Tiomkin to compose music for a new thriller. Tiomkin declined, suggesting Raksin for the job. The director bristled about the notion of some kid scoring his film, but he called Raksin in and assigned him the work—provided he'd bring in the theme *by the next morning!* It was a dirty Preminger trick, a blueprint for failure, but Raksin was elated. It was the break he'd dreamed of! He rushed home—couldn't wait to tell his wife he'd finally snared the brass ring.

When he arrived, the house was dark. Raksin entered, discovered it was empty. But, in looking around, he found an envelope on the piano stand addressed to him from his wife. He opened it and discovered she had left him. He read the note over and over—then, he began *to play it*. And what he played became the haunting, unforgettable LAURA theme.

True story. He told it sitting on the piano bench in his home, and I asked him to play the theme— just for me. And he did, as I stood there leaning against the piano, listening to music that changed my life years ago when I first saw the film. The moment was one of the most powerful and riveting in memory. Hundreds, probably thousands, of hours spent watching movies coalesced in this singular, unexpected experience. Raksin was playing for me...

While Waldo Lydecker (Clifton Webb) and Mark McPherson (Dana Andrews) are haunted by the image of Gene Tierney in *Laura*, audiences are bewitched by the theme composed by Steranko's pal David Raksin

The man who would eventually score FORCE OF EVIL, THE BAD AND THE BEAUTIFUL, TWO WEEKS IN ANOTHER TOWN, and so many others was delivering a command performance! A lifetime of cinematic harmony resonated as he articulated the keyboard. Raksin looked up, saw tears shining in my eyes. "Jim, what's the matter?" I shook my head, nodded to the keyboard. And he layed it in. His grand piano, 88 keys, become a symphonic orchestra. Afterward, we laughed. But I can never forget the emotional impact LAURA had on my young psyche. David is gone now, deeply missed—but he'll endue as long as his creative genius resonates in our minds, in our hearts.

MORE THAN ANY OF HIS CONTEMPORARIES, Steranko brought the *noir* sensibility to a range of contemporary visual mediums: In his characterizations (heroes and villains alike driven by alienation and psychotic obsession), narrative themes (cynicism, paranoia, eroticism, tragic irony, fatalism), and the visual style (chiaroscuro, montage, symbolism, metaphor, expressionistic rendering) he used to develop them. As critics implied, he transferred his troubled youth to the page, treating it as a forum of self-expression.

Driven by creative ambition, he engaged a multitude of mediums, including films, graphic novels, interactive games, comic-books, animated series, and electronic formats. His mastery of visual storytelling made a longtime friend of filmmaker Federico Fellini, and led to major cinematic collaborations with Francis Coppola, Steven Spielberg, and George Lucas, for whom, as production illustrator on RAIDERS OF THE LOST ARK, he created the look of Indiana Jones.

As a historian, his THE STERANKO HISTORY OF COMICS volumes have sold more than 100,000 copies each. His death-defying performances as an escape artist inspired the character Mister Miracle and, according to Pulitzer Prize-winning novelist Michael Chabon, Steranko was the man upon which the protagonist of his book THE AMAZING ADVENTURES OF KAVALIER & CLAY was based.

Steranko credits range from the psycho-architectonic OUTLAND film adaptation to the Harlan Ellison 3-D TICKTOCKMAN portfolio to the hard-boiled cinematic graphic novel CHANDLER. As writer-illustrator of Marvel's NICK FURY: AGENT OF SHIELD, CAPTAIN AMERICA, and X-MEN, he rocked the comic-book world with a revolutionary narrative approach using more than 150 original graphic innovations, a *tour de force* that changed the direction of the medium. *Wizard Magazine* credited Steranko as the 5th Most Influential Artist in the history of the form.

His paintings, ranging from Luke Skywalker to The Shadow, have appeared as book covers, movie posters, record albums, and magazine illustrations. As an editor-publisher, he helmed the entertainment magazine PREVUE for its impressive 25-year run. Musician, photographer, male model, ad agency art director, carnival fire-eater, typographer, magician, designer ... the list goes on.

He was inducted into the Eisner Hall of Fame, and given the prestigious Julie Award for his Lifetime Contribution to the Fantastic Arts. Steranko has won numerous awards in both Europe and America, lectured on popular culture, and exhibited his work at more than 350 international exhibitions, including The Louvre in Paris. ∎

Jim Steranko's print of his character Chandler that was included in his noir graphic novel *Red Tide*

COBELCINÉ présente

PIERRE VANECK
MIJANOU BARDOT
ROGER HANIN
et
PAUL FRANKEUR

Un film de
CHARLES GÉRARD
MICHEL DEVILLE

UNE BALLE
DANS LE CANON
DE WEG VAN DE MISDAAD

UNDER SURVEILLANCE

A Closer Look at Forgotten Film Noir | **Gary Deane**

Une balle dans le canon
aka A Bullet in the Gun Barrel (1958)

Film noir as a "thing" made its debut in the late 1930s, the term being coined by a right-wing French press inflamed by the dispiriting narratives and questionable morality darkening the nation's movie screens for a decade. The long-gathering storm—reaching from Jean Renoir's corrosive *La Chienne* (*The Bitch*, 1931*)* to Pierre Chenal's cold-blooded *Le dernier tournant* (*The Last Turning*, 1939)—had hit critical mass. One reviewer, having had enough of doomed men obsessed with little more than money and sex, or women too vulgar to qualify as *femmes fatales*, assailed the films as "sordid and bestial noir, with characters who are black down to the third basement of their soul."

The unsparing bleakness of wartime and postwar releases like Henri-Georges Clouzot's *Le Corbeau* (*The Raven*, 1943), Henri Decoin's *La Fille du diable* (*Devil's Daughter*, 1946), Clouzot's *Quai des Orfèvres* (1947), and Yvés Allégret's *Manèges* (1950) would draw still more critical fire; likewise, a cycle of gangster films even less graced by pathos—among them Jacques Becker's *Touchez pas au grisbi* (1954), Jules Dassin's *Du rififi chez les hommes (1955)*, and Jean-Pierre Melville's *Bob le flambeur* (1956). Both right *and* left took aim at what was seen as an American-styled glorification of conspicuous consumption and cheap criminals in two-toned Cadillacs.[1] Caught up in all this Gallic sucking and blowing was Michel Deville, an aspiring director and contemporary of the insurgent "New Wave" of French cinephiles like François Truffaut, who'd taken to denouncing classical moviemaking as *le cinéma de papa*. Among those shamed for their lack of artistic conviction and "authorship" were veteran directors Julien Duvivier, Henri Decoin, Henri Verneuil, Jean Delannoy, André Cayatte, and Gilles Grangier. Deville had already worked under Decoin on several studio productions, including *Razzia sur la chnouf* (1955), a shimmering film noir starring Jean Gabin and Lino Ventura, which is now part of the French film canon.

However, like Jean-Pierre Melville and Louis Malle, Deville wanted to plot his own course while attempting to remain on good terms with *La Nouvelle Vague*. With his apprenticeship behind him, he jumped at the chance to direct an intriguing crime story called *Une balle dans le canon* written by Albert Simonin. For years, Simonin's novels and adaptations, including Becker's *Touchez pas au grisbi*, helped to sate French hunger for big-shouldered *polars* (crime thrillers) and *policiers* (police procedurals).

---

1   Following WWII, several French writers on the left began assigning the term *noir* to American productions such as *This Gun for Hire* (1942), *Laura* (1944), and *Phantom Lady* (1944), movies unseen in France during the war. These films, with their dream-like states, gloomy romanticism, and transcendent male protagonists, were seen as reflective of French cinema's surrealist and poetic-realist traditions; hence, the term's 're-branding,' later enshrined in Borde and Chaumeton's *A Panorama of American Film Noir 1941-1953*.

No turning back: Mijanou Bardot, younger sister of Brigitte Bardot, plays Brigitte Geoffrain, Tony's guileless girlfriend in 1958's *Une balle dans le canon*

Simonin's convoluted yet enveloping storyline, in which motives and actions are either suspect or unknown, is one of best things about *Une balle dans le canon*. The film's protagonists, Dick (Roger Hanin) and his pal Tony (Pierre Vaneck), veterans of the war in Indochina, have returned to Paris with twenty-five million francs in hand to be delivered to a local crime boss. They soon succeed in blowing their commission on everything in general and nothing in particular; the rest they invest in a cabaret, Club Tip-Tap, on the understanding they can cash out when needed. But Pépère (Paul Frankeur), the mobster who'd sold the club, tells them they're going to have to pull a job for him if they want see the money again. Pépère also says that he'll split the proceeds of the robbery, but the pair suspect he has other plans—which he does. Dick, the more brazen of the two, thinks they'll get away with it all; Tony doesn't and just wants to get away. By this time, there's no turning back, including for Tony's guileless girlfriend, Brigitte (Mijanou Bardot). Roger Hanin, a fierce charmer both on- and off-screen, is in full fettle in *Une balle dans le canon*. Hanin was a movie and TV star in France for more than five decades, often playing take-charge types you don't want to mess with. He's best known for his role in *Navarro*, a realistic, comfortless police drama which ran from 1989 to 2006. His appearances in classic noir included those in Robert Hossein's dire *Les Salauds vont en enfer* (1955), the stylish *Le Désordre et la nuit* (1958) directed by Gilles Grangier, and Jean-Luc Godard's provocative pastiche *Breathless* (1960).

Hanin's partner-in-crime, Pierre Vaneck, was first introduced to filmgoers as "the new Gérard Philipe." As time went on, the blonde pretty boy would develop a more mature handsomeness and go on to star in both film and TV, as well as the theater. In *Une balle dans le canon*, one of his first films, Vaneck never musters more than a bland vigor—though Tony has troubles beyond the money as his relationship with Brigitte becomes increasingly precarious.

For her part, Mijanou Bardot isn't much more than a winsome presence. The younger sibling of Brigitte, she more resembles Bridget Fonda than *la Bardot*, showing only occasional flashes of her sister's bombshell allure. As one might guess, Mijanou was never given a real chance to mature as a performer. She's best known for her part as a frisky French exchange student in Albert Zugsmith's weirdly awful *Sex Kittens Go to College* (1960), sharing the bill with Mamie Van Doren and Tuesday Weld. Only in Éric Rohmer's lushly seductive *La Collectionneuse* (1967), do we get an idea of the actress she might have been.

As compensation, *Une balle dans le canon* provides a terrific supporting cast: the waggish Jean Rochefort as the club's bartender; American jazz pianist Hazel Scott, the venue's featured *artiste* (see sidebar); Michel Lonsdale, a dogged cop; and Paul Frankeur, the gang's chilling puppet-master Pé-père. Frankeur was a welcome fixture in French noir, usually operating on one side of the law or the other. The beefy actor shared the screen with his friend Jean Gabin more than a dozen times, and later with Lino Ventura in Jean-Pierre Melville's elaborate thriller *Le deuxième souffle* (1966).

Une balle dans le canon was the right project at the right time for Deville. With its tangled and compelling narrative, it was a perfect launch point from which to make a few waves of his own. The fact that *les enfants terribles* of the New Wave had the blood of his mentors on their hands couldn't be avoided. Deville was not about to end up as collateral damage by making a film for which he'd be skewered as *un traditionaliste*. Stylistically, *Une balle* has a lot going on, including the flamboyant use of hand-held cameras, extreme close-ups, jump cuts, extended tracking shots, and idiosyncratic editing. The film has a raw, graphic energy overall and often, within its frames, moments of drama independent of the story. While there's some occasional clumsiness, Deville never trips and hurts himself; he does a good job mopping up the narrative clichés expected in cheaply made genre thrillers. *Une balle* is the kind of film whose minor-key B movie refrains are uncommon in French productions (not to mention for international audiences who assume movies from France will be "works" of something, rather than something that just works). But then that's the great conjuror's trick—and not just of B movies. Most classic cinema was created not by self-styled *artistes* but by gifted artisans and craftsmen—who once might have conceived and built cathedrals.

Hazel Scott, a Trinadadian-born beauty and jazz pianist extraordinaire, fled the U.S. for France after her marriage to U.S. Congressman Adam Clayton Powell had fallen apart and appearances before the House Un-American Activities had derailed her career at home. With son in tow, she sailed for France joining the burgeoning American expatriate community in Paris. Her apartment on the Right Bank became a regular hangout for Americans in Paris such as James Baldwin, Lester Young, Dizzy Gillespie, Max Roach, and musicians from the Count Basie and Duke Ellington bands.

Scott began to appear in films, landing a memorable part as a nightclub manager and performer in *Le Désordre et la nuit* with Jean Gabin. A vocalist with awesome dexterity and expressiveness, she recorded an album in 1955 with Charles Mingus and Max Roach titled *Relaxed Piano Moods*. *Downbeat* magazine declared it one of the most important jazz recordings of the twentieth century and, in 2001, it was added to NPR's Basic Jazz Records Library. Scott returned to the U.S. in the late '60s, but the music scene had no place for her. She continued to play in smaller clubs to a devoted fan base until her death in 1981.

—*Gary Deane*

Club owner Dick (Roger Hanin) is about to break another heart—that of his bar manager—before breaking down a gun for his partner Tony (Pierre Vaneck with glasses)

Ironically, there's a case to be made that Michel Deville, while not really of the New Wave, was the first director to put some of the thinking of its theorists into action. Deville's precocious debut would be released the year before Claude Chabrol's *Le Beau Serge* (1958), a film held up as the movement's first born. By default, it can be argued that *Une balle dans le canon* also was the New Wave's first nod to film noir, later to be followed by Godard's *Breathless* and Truffaut's *Shoot the Piano Player*, both released in 1960. Deville would again succumb to the noir impulse with *Lucky Jo* (1964), starring Eddie Constantine as a hapless thief whose partners no longer want to work with him. The movie, though not without its fanciful mannerisms, is still a curiously effective film noir.

In time, Deville's films would take on a darker hue as he began exploring post-modernist tropes: the relationship between memory and the past, the boundaries between reality and fiction, and the transitory nature of love and attachment. His movies also continued to engage provocatively with genre conventions. *Dossier 51* (1978), a Kafkaesque police thriller, uses a subjective camera to create an aura of menace and paranoia (the film would win the French Syndicate of Cinema Critics award for Best Film, as well as a César Award for Best Screenplay). Other Deville films are assaults on bourgeois double standards and hypocrisy, more pointed than those of even Chabrol; among them: *Le mouton enragé* (1974) starring Jean-Louis Trintignant and Romy Schneider; *Eaux profondes* (1981) with Trintignant and Isabelle Huppert; and *Péril en la demeure* (1985), an emotionally layered thriller with Nicole Garcia, Richard Bohringer, and Michel Piccoli. These hand-signed noirs stand among the most popular and critically lauded of Deville's films. Henri Decoin likely would have been proud of his assistant—and probably more than a little envious. ∎

JASON PATRIC   RACHEL WARD   BRUCE DERN

PRIME CUTS

MY FAVORITE NEO-NOIR

All they risked
was everything.

**Rachel
Walther**

AFTER DARK MY SWEET

AVENUE PICTURES PRESENTS A FILM BY JAMES FOLEY

JASON PATRIC RACHEL WARD BRUCE DERN AFTER DARK, MY SWEET GEORGE DICKERSON MUSIC BY MAURICE JARRE DIRECTOR OF PHOTOGRAPHY MARK PLUMMER EDITED BY HOWARD SMITH BASED ON THE BOOK BY JIM THOMPSON

As Kid, Jason Patric hides his matinée idol looks under layers of manic awkwardness. As Fay, Rachel Ward is vulnerable, hard, and alluring

After Dark, My Sweet (1990) begins as many of the best noirs do: a handsome drifter arrives in town with dubious motives and immediately makes the acquaintance of a woman with sinister plans of her own. The twist in this story is that Fay (Rachel Ward) is a drunk and Kid Collins, the drifter "hero" of our tale (Jason Patric), may or may not be psychotic.

Having escaped a mental asylum, mostly because he couldn't stand the boredom, ex-boxer Kid Collins is wandering through one desert town after another making a nuisance of himself. Having run away from an unpleasant past, of which we learn steadily more through flashbacks, Kid is in no hurry to do anything or be anywhere. He has no responsibilities and no ties to anyone. When lovely local lush Fay picks him up during a bout of daytime drinking, Kid suspects her intentions are other than amorous. And he's right: Fay promptly puts him to work cleaning up her date farm—neglected since the death of her husband and parched by the summer heat. She also invites over a friend—Uncle Bud (Bruce Dern), a sketchy desert rat type full of smiles and promised profits, who claims to be an ex-cop. Bud quickly takes a shine to Kid, saying that he recognizes him from his boxing days. He welcomes him to town, assuming that Kid will be around a while, "to rest up a bit and keep Fay out of trouble." Kid senses something illicit brewing between Fay and Bud—he figures he's being sized up for a part in some conspiracy. As Fay admits to him cryptically his first night in town, "This little scheme's been cooking for months, and if you leave it'll go right on cooking till it boils away . . ."

Kid may appear to be a filthy, punch-drunk psycho, complete with the jerky movements of a musclebound boxer gone to seed, but he's intelligent and perceptive. As he warns Fay after she's insulted him, "I am not at all stupid. I may sound like I am, but I'm really not." So Kid isn't surprised when Bud and Fay's scheme turns out to be the kidnapping of a boy from a rich family. He plays along, knowing Bud has him pegged for the if-need-be fall guy. As Kid calmly states in voice-over, "You'd have to be blind not to see what was gonna happen—I was due to be killed."

Bruce Dern's Uncle Bud is pure Jim Thompson: a malicious character concerned only with himself

Kid is too scarred by the past he's outrunning to care much about what's ahead, and his growing concern about Fay's wellbeing overpowers any concern that remains for his own future. As he explains to us: "When a man stops caring what happens, all the strain is lifted from him. Suspicion and worry and fear, all things that twist his thinking out of focus are brushed aside, and he can see people exactly as they are at last."

The kidnapping goes off without a hitch, with Kid pulling a double-cross on Bud that keeps the scheme in motion but shields himself and the snatched boy from imminent danger. During the first evening at Fay's house, their young hostage falls ill and, as Kid and Fay scramble to restore his health, they grow closer. Fay seduces Kid in an apparent moment of weakness, but it's also a moment that conveniently gives her an alibi when the boy goes missing. Kid isn't sure Fay really cares for him, but he reminds us that in many ways it doesn't matter: "I saw Fay then weak and frightened but basically as good as a person could be . . . the only thing that mattered was that she live, it was the only way my having lived would make any sense."

Jason Patric plays Kid with an anxiety and grace that emphasizes his underrated abilities as a character actor; his matinée idol looks hidden behind layers of tics and manic awkwardness. His matter-of-fact narration and gentle manner with Fay belie his tendency toward explosive temper when his sanity or intelligence are called into question. It's after Fay and Bud learn about Kid's fatal moment of violence—the one that ended his boxing career and landed him in the asylum—that the power dynamics shift: now Kid is calling the shots regarding the boy's ransom.

The story plays out as well as one would expect in a hard-bitten thriller; the suspense is not in what's going to go wrong, but *how* it will go wrong. The big mystery of the film is finding out if Fay truly cares for Kid or if she's only using him to further Uncle Bud's grand plan. Rachel Ward plays Fay as a husky, broken women who has retained an inner grace but is emotionally flailing. One moment she's tender and concerned, the next oblivious and hard. It's this mystery about Fay's true nature that keeps us on the edge of our seats until the final scene, and it's what keeps Kid winding the noose tighter around his own neck.

Director Jim Foley's 1990 film is a faithful adaptation of Jim Thompson's 1955 novel *After Dark, My Sweet*, down to it using much of the same dialogue. Thompson's characters typically revel in their own sinister machinations, but in this story both Kid and Fay display moments of genuine sincerity and concern for one another, despite Fay's nasty streak and Kid's moments of blind rage. In the scenes where they're alone, when they're too tired or scared to think of a sharp reply, a stillness emerges between the couple that is balanced between tranquility and sexual combustion.

Bruce Dern's Uncle Bud, however, is pure Thompson: he's affable and fatherly when reassuring Kid that he's among friends, but when provoked Bud drops his grin to reveal a malicious character concerned with no one but himself. While Fay and Kid share grave doubts about the kidnapping and want to suspend the ransom demand after the boy falls ill, Bud has no qualms; to him the kidnapped child is a boy-shaped stack of bills, spent just as easily whether the kid is dead or alive.

The perversity of their crime is just how unnecessary it is: with a paid-for house that's too big as it is, what would Fay do with all this money Bud is intent on collecting? The characters in *After Dark, My Sweet* are not a flashy bunch: Kid and Fay wear their same grimy outfits day after day; Kid's white work shirt graying with grease and sweat and Fay's oversized blouse and cutoffs matching her bare face in a display of natural, if uncultivated, beauty. What both Fay and Kid need is a sense of meaning in their lives, which can't be found in the loot from a dozen kidnappings or, as Kid suspects, in this lifetime.

A gentle and atmospheric score by Maurice Jarre, combined with the present-day setting, undermines any possibility that this story will be played as noir caricature. Instead, Foley lingers on moments of longing and tenderness, showing just how close Fay and Kid come to a tangible contentment before their actions necessitate a fatal showdown.

After Dark, My Sweet plays into the California-noir mythos of strangers washed up in an arid alien terrain, anxious to outrun their past. Fay's British accent is never explained, and Kid's flashbacks to his boxing days, now "a thousand miles away," are vague and filled with terror. Bud is the only creature in complete harmony with the desert landscape; he has the inherent reptilian qualities needed to survive the town's hostile temperatures and temperament. The fourth protagonist of *After Dark, My Sweet* turns out to be the Indio desert itself, with its omnipresent blue skies and vacant dusty roads offering menace to rival any rain-soaked urban alley. This is the landscape from which Kid emerges with just the clothes on his back and to which, Thompson argues, we will all return once the last con has been played out. ∎

SILENT NOIR

Pandora's Box (1929)

Mira Gutoff

Louise Brooks as Lulu in
Pandora's Box (1929)

Lulu (Louise Brooks) embraces Alwa (Francis [Franz] Lederer), her true love

"The Greek gods created a woman—Pandora. She was beautiful and charming and versed in the art of flattery. But the gods also gave her a box containing all the evils of the world. The heedless woman opened the box, and all evil was loosed upon us."

Although the prosecuting attorney aims these words towards Lulu, played by Louise Brooks, a modern audience isn't likely to see her as a harbinger of mythological damnation. When they think of Lulu, they'll see her dancing with joy, her hair bobbed and her long sleeves flowing with her movement, her smile lighting up the screen almost unbearably cute. Such is the appeal of Lulu, the doomed—or damned to some perspectives—heroine of the 1929 German silent film *Pandora's Box*.

Directed by G.W. Pabst, *Pandora's Box* was based on the plays *Earth Spirit* and *Pandora's Box* by Frank Wedekind, who himself drew inspiration from the 1888 pantomime *Lulu* by Félicien Champsaur. The cabaret tune "I Am a Vamp" by Mischa Spoliansky contains the line "Like Lulu, I have bright red hair"—a reference to the movie's literary source, for Louise Brooks' short black hair was so iconic she was known as "the girl in the black helmet."

Pandora's Box tells a story that would become familiar in film noir—the rise and fall of a bad girl. But what does it mean to be a bad girl? In one reading, Lulu is a heartless seductress who cares only for money and sex, and who destroys everything she touches. In another reading, Lulu is more sinned against than sinner, being exploited and hurt by every man who desires her—her sugar daddy, her pimp, and finally (and fatally) a serial killer. This ambiguity positions her in the middle of a transition that was occurring across movie screens in both Germany and the United States during this time: the evolution of flapper into *femme fatale*.

The flapper, epitomized by Clara Bow and later on by Jean Harlow, was a girl out for a good time. She wanted to dance and drink, flirt with men, gossip with women, and maybe even land a nice millionaire to take care of her. In the roaring twenties, she was a scandalous but appealingly new kind of woman, and even into the thirties she retained her charm. With The Great Depression hovering over everyone, could anyone blame her for wanting to vamp her way to financial security?

Perhaps it was WWI, perhaps it was the Hays code: one way or another, the flapper turned into something much darker. 1930's *The Blue Angel*, the first feature-length talking picture from Germany, gave the world Marlene Dietrich in the persona of Lola Lola, a woman so callous she doesn't even intentionally lead her lover to destruction—she simply doesn't care. ("Men," she sings, "swarm around me like moths to a flame. If they get burned, how am I to blame?") In America, Barbara Stanwyck would play steely-eyed dames hungry for money and love in 1940s films such as *Double Indemnity* (1944) or *The Strange Love of Martha Ivers* (1946)—women who would have been heroines in her earlier pre-code films, such as *Night Nurse* (1931) and *Baby Face* (1933). Seducing men wasn't cute anymore. It was evil.

Lulu sits right in the middle of this divide. It's hard to pinpoint anything she does that is truly wicked—her worst crimes are refusing to step aside quietly for another woman, escaping an unjust sentence, and having embarrassing friends attend her wedding—but it is her carefree attitude that is portrayed as dangerous. In some ways, Lulu is less the *femme fatale* than the hapless noir hero, not quite brave or clean enough to walk down these mean streets without emerging tarnished and afraid. She makes her play for wealth. She makes her play for happiness. She makes her play to reach out and connect with another lost soul. All she gets for her efforts is death in a cheap hotel.

Intentionally or not, Lulu brings a father and son down with her, as well. Dr. Ludwig Schön (Fritz Kortner) keeps her as his mistress until she becomes too embarrassing. When he tries to throw her over, she tells him, "You'll have to kill me to get rid of me!" And she means it! Lulu has no intention of playing nice in front of his respectable fiancée, and when he brings the new woman to Lulu's cabaret show, the cast-off lover insists upon making a scene. Humiliated into marrying Lulu, Dr. Schön then throws another fit when he sees her pimp at the wedding party causing a fight that ends with him trying to force Lulu to shoot herself. She's genuinely terrified knowing with certainty that her lover isn't making idle threats—he wants to kill her, and he doesn't intend to go to jail for it. She struggles for her life as he tries to press the gun into her hand and against her body. The gun goes off, but Lulu still lives…

And Dr. Schön's son, Alwa (Francis [Franz] Lederer), still cares for her. He cares for her enough to battle his father, to become a fugitive from justice, and to sit starving in a London garrett waiting for her to return from walking the streets. Alwa and Lulu's affection for each other seems genuine enough, but with so much misery riding upon it, it too is doomed. *Pandora's Box* is not a movie of black-and-white dichotomies between good and evil. If the film's bad girl is ambiguous, so is its vision of the ultimate bad boy—Jack the Ripper himself, still prowling the slums in the 1920s. Like Peter Lorre's child murderer in Fritz Lang's *M*, released two years later, Jack the Ripper is a haggard man suffering mental illness. He actively tries to stop himself from killing, to cast away his blade, but there always is a new victim everywhere he turns. He tells Lulu he has no money, and she feels compassion for the poor soul and invites him up to her room. Perhaps this is meant to signal her wantonness, but Louise Brooks' charm turns the scene into poetic tragedy. Lulu finally offers her love to a man without asking anything in return, and for offering a genuine moment of human connection, she will meet her death.

Lulu and the Ripper's confrontation is perhaps "proto-noir," but it is surely one of the greatest sequences of the silent era. It's not the typical horror scene of a monster stalking the maiden, for we can tell there will be no heroic rescue. The tension builds toward a crime we know is inevitable, the camera cutting between the Ripper's tormented hesitation and Lulu's warm-hearted flirtation. He throws away his pocket knife, but sees that Lulu has one in her room. She sees what he intends and screams.

Lulu faces a confrontation with her ex-paramour, Alwa's own father Dr. Schön (Fritz Kortner)

Dr. Ludwig Schön (Fritz Kortner, center) dies in the arms of his son Alwa (Francis [Franz] Lederer) as the doctor's former mistress, Lulu (Louise Brooks), is left holding the gun

There is a struggle, and then the struggle abruptly ends. Alwa will never know what happened to his love for whom he threw his life away. The Ripper will never find peace, no matter how many times he kills. Lulu will never again dance for sheer joy, her smile lighting up the screen.

Like Lulu, Louise Brooks' career would not live to see the advent of noir. She retired in 1938, nine years after *Pandora's Box*. Some have attributed this to her acting in European films being too subtle and naturalistic for audiences at the time to appreciate, while others have suggested studios blacklisted her for having left the American studio system. By the time she turned down what would become Jean Harlow's role in *Public Enemy*, she was tired of Hollywood, and like Lulu, she took up a career as a dancer. But unlike her character in *Pandora's Box*, Brooks was clever, canny, and insightful; when reflecting upon her life more than a half century later, her memoir *Lulu in Hollywood* turned her from an artsy ingenue to a historian of Hollywood's Golden Age. She retained some aspects of Lulu in her recollections, though—"In writing the history of a life," she said, "I believe absolutely that the reader cannot understand the character and deeds of the subject unless he is given a basic understanding of that person's sexual loves and hates and conflicts. It is the only way the reader can make sense out of innumerable, apparently senseless, actions." As a film, *Pandora's Box* agrees with her. Lulu's sexual history is neither condemned nor celebrated; it is merely an important part of her story.

History was less kind to director Pabst than to Brooks. While she transitioned from actress to admired film historian, Pabst ended up mired in controversy after working under Joseph Goebbels. The question of the degree to which he was a willing Nazi collaborator will always hang over him—unlike many German film stars and directors who fled or the many who ended up in the camps. Pabst's legacy includes such classics as *Pandora's Box* and *The Threepenny Opera*, but it has not been enough to turn him into a revered figure among film buffs.

Pandora's Box is revered on its own, though, and it's easy to see why. After almost a century, it still has the power to entrance and titillate and even draw tears. Watching this film, it is easy to see the place where noir came from: a world where love is negotiable, heroes are few, bad girls still deserve to survive, and happy endings are few and far between. What could have been a simple morality play about the fate of loose women becomes a sad look at a life of exploitation and the society which let it happen. If Lulu doesn't escape judgement, neither do her gentleman callers.

When viewers reflect upon *Pandora's Box*, they most likely will think of one of two images: Lulu's desperate and doomed struggle with Jack the Ripper or her joyful smile at the very beginning as she embraces her latest lover; a helpless and ugly death or a fun-filled start to life, Thanatos or Eros. Such is the duality of Lulu's story, and such is the duality of noir. Perhaps Lulu would have said it was all worth it just for the chance—and that if she were to live again, she would do it all the same way. She's no villain and no traditional heroine, but down these mean streets she must go, nonetheless. ■

THE LOST

Vince Keenan

On the final pages of Charles Jackson's 1944 novel *The Lost Weekend*, Don Birnam ends his marathon drinking binge by preparing for his next one. He slinks home with six pints of rye. One he'll enjoy now. One will serve as a decoy for his brother to find. The other four he hides, hanging two outside the window of their shared apartment, a cord extending from the neck of each bottle "to a tiny cleat that was used for the awning in summer." Fortified for the future, he downs a slug, goes to his bed, "and crawled in, feeling like a million dollars."

WEEKEND

Adaptation is a ruthless art, screenwriters often performing radical surgery so a story can live in a new medium. Still, it's startling to see Jackson's closing image—a sign of how far Birnam has yet to fall before striking bottom—transformed into the opening shot of Charles Brackett and Billy Wilder's script as a camera pans across "the man-made mountain peaks of Manhattan." But then this storied partnership excelled at such deft cinematic shorthand.

More shocking is the entry from Brackett's diary of March 8, 1946, the day after *Weekend*'s triumph at the Academy Awards, where it claimed prizes for Best Picture, Director, Actor, and Adapted Script: he arrived to find the windows of the Paramount writers' building "garlanded ... delightfully with a row of whiskey bottles suspended from every one." A harbinger of doom becomes a slick character intro, then an elaborate joke. Such a strange journey befits *The Lost Weekend*. This trailblazing addiction drama may not seem like noir, but it looks and ultimately plays like one. And its production is as steeped in darkness as the cherry at the bottom of a rye Manhattan.

Wilder randomly picked up Jackson's book before a train trip to New York City. Choosing to make it the next Brackett/Wilder project was tempting fate, given the subject matter. Charles Brackett's wife Elizabeth was an alcoholic, her addiction and mental illness requiring frequent hospitalization before her death in 1948. But as his grandson Jim Moore notes in the foreword to Anthony Slide's compendium of Brackett's journals, *It's the Pictures That Got Small*, "Nowhere in the diaries is the word *alcoholism* used to describe her condition." Booze also affected the marriage of his eldest daughter, likely contributing to her death and her husband's in separate incidents. Throughout his life Brackett would provide comfort to many bibulous colleagues, offering emotional and financial support to the likes of F. Scott Fitzgerald, Dorothy Parker, and Dashiell Hammett.

As for Wilder, he had recently completed adapting James M. Cain's *Double Indemnity* with Raymond Chandler in a break from his partnership with Brackett, who looked down on Cain's novel. Ignore the Paramount-issued biography claiming "unlike his detective, Chandler rarely touches alcohol at any time, and never while working. When at his work, Chandler stimulates himself continually, and exclusively, with tea." The creator of Philip Marlowe arrived at the studio every day with a bottle of bourbon in his briefcase. Chandler's stealth imbibing irritated Wilder, much as Wilder's quirky mannerisms and chronic womanizing fueled Chandler's disdain. Wilder would later call his contribution to keeping Chandler off the wagon "the small revenge I had" for their stormy collaboration. His biographer Maurice Zolotow claimed Wilder made *The Lost Weekend* "to explain Raymond Chandler to himself."

Jackson's novel is largely autobiographical, including material about living as a closeted gay man that would, out of Production Code necessity, be stripped from the film. The author also omitted the most noir episode of his life: his role as a suspect in the 1936 murder of his friend, writer Nancy Titterton. Jackson's biographer Blake Bailey notes that Jackson's drinking didn't account for the brief period the NYPD viewed him askance—blame an affectionate dedication in a book Titterton gave to him at their last meeting—but that didn't stop the *Hollywood Reporter* from hyping the incident into the stuff of Cornell Woolrich nightmares, larding on erroneous lurid details and suggesting Jackson couldn't alibi himself because he was coming off a real-life lost weekend. What Jackson resented most about becoming gossip-column fodder, according to Brackett's diary, was the notion that this brush with the law scared him out of drinking: "I stopped because I made up my mind to. I hate that story. It's discreditable." Brackett and Jackson had a strained relationship, with Brackett at one point severing all contact with the novelist. When Wilder recounted Jackson's ensuing emotional turmoil, Brackett wrote in his diary that he felt "deep regret that I'd upset the nasty little neurotic so much, and a horrid smugness that I'd been able to do so."

In the novel, Jackson places the reader in uncomfortably close proximity to Don Birnam as he jettisons everyone close to him and debases himself to secure liquor as his sole companion for the title stretch. "It wasn't because he was thirsty that he drank, and he didn't drink because he liked the taste. ... He drank for what it did to him." What it chiefly does is ease Birnam's despair at his failure as a writer and so much else in life. ("All the things that had never happened yet were never going to happen after all. It was a mug's game and there ought to be a law.") Years of addiction have made Birnam skilled at deception. Upon receiving his first cocktail of the weekend, he doesn't down it right away. "Instead, he permitted himself the luxury of ignoring it for a while ... When he finally did get around to raising the glass to his lips, it was with an air of boredom that said, Oh well, I suppose I might as well drink it, now that I've ordered it." On another night in another bar, he relishes "a sense

There's no one in the place 'cept you and me: Birnam and the only company he wants to keep over the title stretch

The harrowing scene in which Birnam tries to hock his typewriter to buy booze would land Ray Milland in the gossip columns for all the wrong reasons

of elevation and excellence that was almost god-like" provided by his solitary drinking—then swipes a woman's handbag to pay for the cocktails that bestow this hollow confidence.

Ray Milland played Birnam after Paramount nixed Wilder's choice of Jose Ferrer and Cary Grant passed. In his memoir *Wide-Eyed in Babylon*, Milland blithely admits dozing off the first time he read the book. Upon finishing it, he pronounces it "beautifully written ... but depressing and unrelieved. Damned interesting, though." His biggest fear wasn't the depth the role demanded but the risk of appearing foolish in the drunk scenes: "I was afraid I would overdo them and be amateurish." The actor had starred in Wilder's 1942 directorial debut *The Major and the Minor* and that familiarity bred its standard ration of contempt; Brackett visited *Major*'s set and wrote in his diary that he found "Ray Milland giving a dry, wooden performance (his usual performance to speak the truth)," while Wilder churlishly told Cameron Crowe in *Conversations with Wilder* that Milland was "surely not an Academy Award–worthy actor. ... He's dead now, so I can say it," adding that Milland helped *The Lost Weekend* because "he had no comedy in him."

Other casting choices would have a more lasting impact on the director. Doris Dowling impresses as the hard-bitten "bar hostess" with a penchant for abbreviating words, punctuating her conversation with "natch" and "don't be ridick." She was also Wilder's mistress, cast over Brackett's objections, with Brackett certain this state of affairs would end Wilder's other key partnership with wife Judith. Instead, during filming of the scene when Birnam steals the handbag, Wilder found himself bewitched by the actress playing the woman who wordlessly hands Milland his hat before he's bounced from the joint. "I fell in love with her arm first," Wilder said. He and Audrey Young would be married from 1949 until his death in 2002.

Location shooting in New York provided its share of challenges. Wilder filmed Birnam's pitiful stagger along Third Avenue in search of an open pawn shop where he can hock his typewriter with cameras so discreetly placed that gossip columns reported actor Ray Milland was on an epic Big Apple bender. To prepare for a critical scene, Milland made a research trip to Bellevue Hospital. In a case of life mirroring art, bedlam broke out in the ward and a panicked Milland fled outside, where he was intercepted by a police officer who recognized the hospital's robe. Milland explained he was a movie star staying at the Waldorf Towers. The cop sure-buddied him and led him back inside. Filming then shifted to the Paramount lot, where the New York bar P.J. Clarke's was re-created so meticulously that, according to Milland, a man presented himself every afternoon at five o'clock and asked for a bourbon. A bottle of the hard stuff had been placed on set for verisimilitude and Howard Da Silva, in character as Nat the bartender, would pour one. The lone customer would quaff half of it "and with a long exhale of pleasure look around and make some inane remark about the weather." Then Robert Benchley, another of the dipsomaniacal writers in Brackett's care, would finish the drink, slap down fifty cents, and leave. Milland, ever oblivious, assumed he was homesick for New York.

For a film about the dangers of John Barleycorn, odd references to alcohol surround *The Lost Weekend*. After an early screening, Milland was so discomfited by his performance he fled to a nearby bar for "the largest Scotch and soda I could get," likely the last drink he would ever enjoy in peace. Brackett and Wilder distributed booze on set for crew Christmas gifts. Distilleries fearful the film would be "the *Uncle Tom's Cabin* of Prohibition" offered Paramount five million dollars to buy the negative, with gangster Frank Costello serving as go-between. Brackett cheerily responded that he and Wilder "are highly bribable persons who, if we receive a case of Scotch a week in perpetuity, will manage to make the spectators lick their lips."

The Lost Weekend may bear the trappings of an Oscar®-bait issue film, but Wilder, fresh off *Double Indemnity*, used much of the same production team, chiefly cinematographer John F. Seitz, to re-create its noir palette. Suspenseful moments abound, like Birnam's ill-advised foray into theft and his humiliating comeuppance, or his frantic flight from Bellevue, aided by slipping on a doctor's coat (which in actuality was Charles Brackett's). His desperate bid to chain his door before his girlfriend Helen (Jane Wyman) can gain entry with a pass key is as nerve-jangling as any heist sequence. ·

At least superficially, *The Lost Weekend* may not appear to be noir. There's no real crime to speak of, no *femme fatale* tempting our protagonist to ruin. But who needs a crime when there's a raw, insatiable thirst? Noir is fundamentally about the self-destructive impulse. *The Lost Weekend* strips that story down to the studs, doing away with external enticements in favor of an incessant internal one. Don Birnam doesn't require accomplices or enemies, not when with a few belts in him he's abundantly capable of playing those roles himself. He's a one-man show of obliteration, the only supporting players needed are a couple of bottles of rotgut—with a few prominently placed so they'll be easily discovered by those foolish souls looking to help, natch. ■

PRIME CUTS
MY FAVORITE NEO-NOIR

"And I don't want any more of these in-formal talks. I've nothing to say to you or the police and I'm tired of being called things by every crackpot on the city payroll. If you want to see me, pinch me or subpoena me or something and I'll come down with my lawyer.

—Sam Spade
The Maltese Falcon (1941)

"And no more of these informal chats, either. You got a discipline issue with me, write me up or suspend me, and I'll see you at the parent conference."

—Brendan Frye, *Brick* (2005)

BRICK

Brian Thornton

Student shamus Brendan Frye (Joseph Gordon-Levitt) has his own idea of extracurricular activities in Rian Johnson's acclaimed high school noir *Brick*

'll never forget the first time I encountered Dashiell Hammett. It was 1979. I was fourteen. On the "Favorites" table of the local B. Dalton Bookseller, I found a hardcover edition of Avenel Books' *Dashiell Hammett: Five Complete Novels*. After tearing through the first twenty pages while standing in the bookstore, I was hooked. Hammett was my introduction to crime fiction. In the nearly 100 years since his literary heyday in the 1920s, Hammett's work has inspired and influenced generations of writers and filmmakers, including me. And Rian Johnson.

Yep. *That* Rian Johnson. Of *Star Wars: The Last Jedi* (2017) and a few choice episodes of *Breaking Bad* fame.

Before he wrote and directed *Knives Out* (2019), before he became The Man Who Killed Luke Skywalker, before he gave us hit men hired to murder their time-traveling future selves in *Looper* (2012), Rian Johnson made his initial splash in fine indie auteur fashion with a quirky neo-noir gem called *Brick*.

And his major influence? Dashiell Hammett.

I rediscovered Hammett after I started writing my own stuff, and several authors whose work I respected steered me in the direction of Hammett's short stories. As a teenager I had focused solely on his novels, not realizing the short stories contained some of his best work. Not just the plots, or the characters. The *language*. Hammett had worked as a Pinkerton detective and was intimately familiar with the world of professional criminals: their habits, their methods, and their lingua franca, the literal thieves' cant with which they communicated.

This background knowledge helped inform Hammett's writing, lending it an authenticity many of his contemporaries in the pulps found difficult to match. His sales were good enough that traditional publishers came calling once his novels had been serialized in the likes of *Black Mask*, the magazine that more than any other helped make Hammett's reputation.

Close on the heels of said publishers came Hollywood. The movies have for the most part been kind to Hammett's work. He sure managed to live high on the proceeds from adaptations of his canon during the 1930s and 1940s.

Some of the films have been great, like John Huston's iconic 1941 version of *The Maltese Falcon*, Hollywood's third bite at that particular apple, which changed the career arc of longtime character actor Humphrey Bogart. Others, not so much (not even Bette Davis could save 1936's *Satan Met a Lady*, an earlier swing-and-miss at *Falcon*). Some have been straight adaptations, like the first *Thin Man* film and the Alan Ladd vehicle *The Glass Key* (1942). The Huston/Bogart *Falcon* practically transcribes whole swaths of Hammett's original (minus the overtly homoerotic subplot, including a shift in the perceived meaning of the word "gunsel"). Still others, such as Akira Kurosawa's *Yojimbo* (1961) and the Coen brothers' *Miller's Crossing* (1990) are more oblique, employing aspects of Hammett's plots while reinterpreting and reworking them.

Brick is one of the latter films. Johnson precisely employs Hammett's brand of now-anachronistic dialogue to advance his plot. In many ways *Brick* is a traditional noir film, honoring the tropes so beloved by devotees of the genre. What makes it different is that Johnson, as if taking his cue from modern-dress productions of Shakespeare, placed *Brick* in a contemporary high school and populated it with teenage characters. Instead of declaiming rhyming couplets and lines of iambic pentameter, these students spout lines like, "I didn't shake up the party to get your attention, and I'm not heeling you to hook you," and "Don't need no blades, shamus. I just gotta squawk."

It's a conceit that is both effective and ironic. I taught high school for a number of years and am here to tell you that "youth speak" is constantly evolving, ever-changing, always confounding to preceding generations. (I know. "Duh.") And like the ouroboros, the ancient symbol of the snake devouring its own tail, Johnson's youth speak doubles back on itself. The resulting dialogue hits all the harder, employing language that time and distance has rendered nearly as challenging to navigate as what is actually getting slung around high school hallways at this very moment.

Another constant of high school life is that its most vibrant moments tend to take place *in these very hallways*. Johnson embraces this and takes it one step further: there are scenes in the halls, in the parking lot, backstage in the school's theater, in the office, even in the library. But not one moment of *Brick*'s screen time is spent in anything resembling a classroom.

And it works. In no little part because Johnson—whose sole prior directorial credit was a short student film of the variety that garners course credit, not IMDb entries—is such a steady hand on the tiller. This was a guy with a clear vision of what he wanted to create, and when his chance came along, he made the most of it.

Influenced in equal parts by Japanese anime such as *Cowboy Bebop* (1998), at least visually, plus the aforementioned *Miller's Crossing* and that film's own source material—again, Hammett's *The Glass Key*—Johnson spent the first few years following his graduation from film school refining *Brick*'s script and pitching his idea all over Hollywood. After getting nowhere, he set about marshaling the resources to make the film himself.

Johnson's family, most of whom were involved in the construction business, put up the lion's

share of the seed money for the film's production costs (a modest half-million dollars). Johnson himself both wrote and directed. His cousin Nathan Johnson composed and performed the critically acclaimed soundtrack (long-distance from his home in England, no less). *Brick* was shot in a mere twenty days, almost exclusively on weekends, mostly at Johnson's alma mater, San Clemente High School. Once shooting wrapped, Johnson edited the entire film in his bedroom, on his MacBook Pro.

The result is a compelling mash-up of classic film noir and teen angst. This is definitely a film that wears its influences on its sleeve. The best noir is about character (or, just as often, the lack thereof), and the classic noir archetypes are all there in *Brick*.

The reluctant hero—in this case an intellectual loner named Brendan played to the twitchy hilt by

Femme fatale with a hall pass Laura Dannon (Nora Zehetner) attempts to wrap Brendan around her little finger

a young Joseph Gordon-Levitt— is pulled against his will into a conflict not of his making by forces beyond his control. Teen potheads standing in for street-level hustlers. An overbearing "assistant vice principal" (whatever *that* is—but, hey, the character is played by *Richard Roundtree*. So John Shaft is this "assistant vice principal? Damn right ...) playing the role usually reserved for corrupt law enforcement types. A spec-wearing nerd (dubbed "Brain" because, duh) filling the slot of the brilliant sidekick. Laura Dannon (Nora Zehetner), a beautiful and popular scenester, a member of what Brain labels "the upper crust," is the *femme fatale*, with a dumb, arrogant jock as her boyfriend/tool. A dope-smoking weightlifter with 'roid rage acts as the local drug lord's enforcer. Then there's the drug lord himself, underplayed by Lukas Haas: a twenty-six-year-old "gothed-up cripple" who runs his operation out of his mom's basement.

Johnson leverages plot devices from *The Glass Key* and Hammett's first novel, *Red Harvest*, as a means to toss all of the above characters into conflict with one another. Brendan is drawn into the action by a panicked ex-girlfriend named Emily. She may have moved on from Brendan, but Brendan has clearly not moved on from her. When said ex-girlfriend winds up dead in a culvert, Brendan commits to finding her killer by involving himself in whatever mess she had gotten herself into. As he tells his only friend, Brain, he intends to "make Em's troubles mine."

As Hammett's Continental Op did in *Red Harvest*, Brendan accomplishes this by infiltrating the criminal gang at least indirectly responsible for Emily's demise, and either causes or exacerbates a rift between the drug lord and his enforcer, bringing about a full-on gang war. Much like Ned Beaumont in *The Glass Key*, he finds himself largely unable to direct and control the ensuing conflict.

And of course there are call-backs to Hammett's work throughout the dialogue. At one point Brendan says to Laura, "Now you *are* dangerous." A direct cribbing of Spade's line in *The Maltese Falcon*. In the climactic scene when Brendan confronts his own *femme fatale* with what he knows and what he merely suspects, he says, "That was you, Angel." An echo of Spade's words at the end of *Falcon*: "But he would have gone up there with you, Angel. He was just dumb enough for that."

So if you like your neo-noir both traditional and original, Rian Johnson's *Brick* is definitely worth checking out (say, in advance of screening *Knives Out*). Just make sure to turn on the subtitles. Kids these days, it's like they speak a whole other language. ■

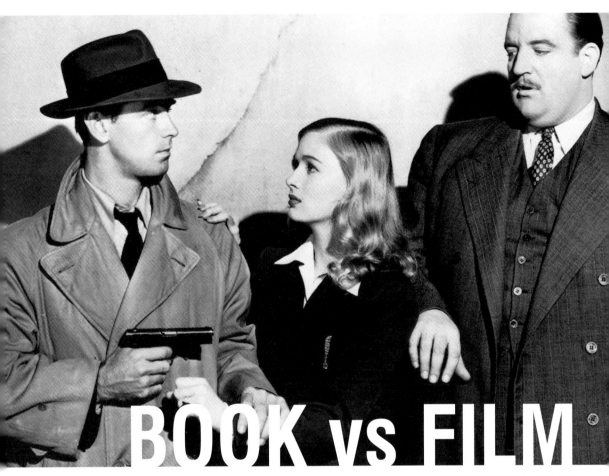

BOOK vs FILM

SECTION FIVE

Shamus Mike Hammer (Ralph Meeker) picks up hitchhiker Christina (Cloris Leachman) and plenty of trouble in the 1955 adaptation of Mickey Spillane's *Kiss Me Deadly*

Ben Terrall

Brooklyn-born Mickey Spillane was a wildly successful writer of detective fiction who inspired either fierce devotion or profound irritation.

Influential book critic Anthony Boucher called Spillane's 1947 debut novel, *I, the Jury*, which introduced detective Mike Hammer, "so vicious a glorification of force, cruelty, and extra-legal methods that the novel might be made required reading at the Gestapo training school." In 1966, Boucher amended his take slightly, saying that although he still didn't appreciate "Spillane's excesses of brutality and his outrageously anti-democratic doctrines," he also considered Spillane to be "one of the last of the great storytellers in the pulp tradition."

The right-leaning Spillane loved scenes where dirty communists were sent to the great beyond, making him a particular favorite of reactionary libertarian author Ayn Rand, and Spillane in turn admired Rand's über-right novels. The eye-for-an-eye vigilantism of his books also targeted drug dealers, double-crossing women, and anyone else who violated Hammer's rigid moral code, which centered mostly on loyalty to his friends and the USA.

Spillane started his career writing for comics, creating stories for the 1940s staples *Captain Marvel*, *Captain America*, *Batman*, and *Superman*. He served as a flight instructor during WWII, and, after the war, returned to a comic book industry in the doldrums. Spillane responded by turning a comic-book character he'd created named Mike Danger into private eye Mike Hammer and banging

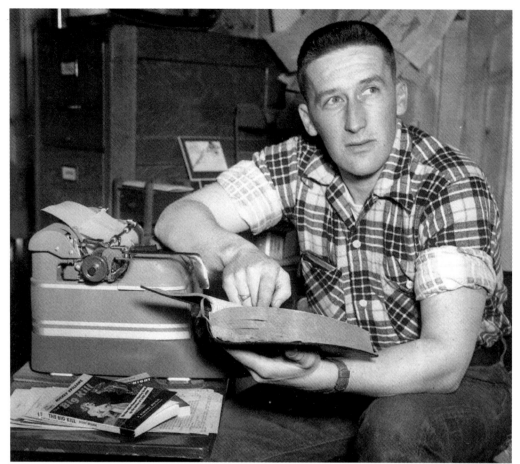

Writer Mickey Spillane looking ready for action as he leans against his typewriter. *Kiss Me, Deadly*, published in 1952, was the first private-eye novel to make the *New York Times* bestseller list

out a hard-hitting novel about him. *I, the Jury* would sell more than 8,000,000 copies in paperback.

Kiss Me, Deadly, published in 1952, was the sixth in the Hammer series, and the first private-eye novel to make the *New York Times* bestseller list. Though it had plenty of violence, *Kiss Me, Deadly* noticeably had less sex than previous Hammer books; Spillane's hero plants a few kisses between punches. but doesn't go much further than that. The shift may have been a result of Spillane's transition to life as a Jehovah's Witness, a conversion Anthony Boucher referred to as "probably the most widely publicized since St. Augustine's."

In *Kiss Me, Deadly*, Hammer narrates a one-man crusade (with some help from contacts in the police department) against the Mafia. The tale begins with Hammer driving somewhere near Albany, New York: "All I saw was the dame standing there in the glare of the headlights waving her arms like a huge puppet and the curse I spit out filled the car and my own ears." Hammer grudgingly agrees to give the woman the ride to Manhattan that she's begging for. But they're sandbagged by a car full of thugs who torture the girl to death, stuff the both of them into Hammer's car and push it over a cliff. Hammer wakes up in a hospital bed, his secretary Velda at his side. "Velda's mouth parted in a slow smile that had all the happiness in the world wrapped in it." Hammer's cop friend Pat enters to inform Mike that government men are investigating the case for unspecified reasons. With Velda's help, Mike learns that his mysterious pick-up had escaped from a sanitarium and was the mistress of a mobbed-up character named Carl Evello.

Director Robert Aldrich (right) discusses the penultimate scene of Bezzerides' crazed *Kiss Me Deadly* screenplay with Albert Dekker and Gaby Rodgers

Once he's in full-on vendetta mode, Hammer tells a low-level crook the score so word will pass up the underworld food chain to Evello and his associates: "They've killed hundreds of people, see, and they finally killed the wrong dame. They tried to kill me and they wrecked my car. That last part I especially didn't like. That car was hand-built and could do over a hundred. And for all of that a lot of those top dogs are paying through the keister starting now."

Hammer is as good as his word; much mayhem ensues.

Mickey Spillane sold the rights for four of his novels to British producer Victor Saville, who had mixed success with productions of *I, the Jury* (1953) and *The Long Wait* (1954). But Spillane did have the good sense to hire Robert Aldrich to produce and direct *Kiss Me Deadly* (1955). For some obscure reason, the film dropped the comma from the source novel's title.

Aldrich had cut his teeth in Hollywood as an assistant director to an illustrious array of filmmakers: Jean Renoir, *The Southerner* (1945); Abraham Polonsky, *Force of Evil* (1948); Joseph Losey, *The Prowler* and *M* (both 1951), and Charles Chaplin, *Limelight* (1952). Aldrich was to the left politically, but later noted, "I was either too dumb or too young to be a Communist."

Aldrich was not a fan of Spillane's novel; in 1968, he told an interviewer, "The book had nothing. We just took the title and threw the rest away. The scriptwriter, A.I. Bezzerides, did a marvelous job contributing a great deal of inventiveness to the picture."

Bezzerides was also a leftist, though, like Aldrich, he was never blacklisted. He was even more underwhelmed by Spillane's novel, later recalling, "I read the book and thought it was awful. But I could see what I could do to fix it. ... It had a pretty good structure but I didn't like the things it said." Bezzerides finished the script in about three weeks. For what Alfred Hitchcock would call the MacGuffin, Bezzerides switched Spillane's cache of heroin (which Bezzerides thought "stupid") to a case full of radioactive fissionable material.

Bezzerides told film historian Lee Server, "I wrote it fast because I had contempt for it. It was automatic writing. You get into a kind of stream and you can't stop ... People ask me—or they asked Aldrich—about the hidden meanings in the script about the A-bomb, about McCarthyism, what does the poetry [quoted throughout] mean, and so on. And I can only say that I didn't think about it when I wrote it. Those things were in the air at the time and I put them in there. There was a lot of talk about nuclear war at the time, and it was the foremost fear in people's minds. Well, I though that was more interesting than the dope thing in the book." The screenwriter said, "I was having fun with it. I wanted to make every scene, every character interesting."

Spillane hated the result, saying, "That script was so terrible! I got so mad I threw it away ... why did they mess up something so good?"

THE FILM OPENS with a young woman (Cloris Leachman, in her first role) running down the middle of a road wearing nothing but a trench coat. Hyperventilating, she throws herself into the path of an oncoming car, a Jaguar convertible driven by Mike Hammer (Ralph Meeker). He swerves off the road, and the camera follows Leachman as she walks toward the car. "You almost wrecked my car!" Hammer yells, before grudgingly barking, "Get in." As Nat King Cole croons "I'd Rather Have the Blues (Than What I've Got)" on the car radio, they drive off, credits rolling out backwards, following the flow of the road.

After Hammer determines that his passenger, Christina, is "a fugitive from the laughing house," she launches into a dissection of his character. "You only have one real lasting love," she surmises. "You—you're one of those self-indulgent males who think about nothing but his clothes, his car, himself." She continues on, "You're the kind of person who never gives in a relationship—you only take."

The off-the-cuff analysis proves to be dead on.

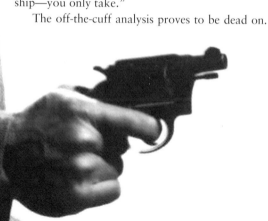

Above: Gaby Rodgers as *Kiss Me Deadly*'s Lily Carver shows how to be assertive while lounging in a bathrobe; Opposite: Ralph Meeker as private eye Mike Hammer in *Kiss Me Deadly*

While Velda (Maxine Cooper) is loyal to and romantically inclined toward her boss, Hammer pays little attention to her beyond their investigative work, which, given the nature of his specialty, gets pretty sleazy. Interrogators from the "Interstate Crime Commission" lay out Hammer's modus operandi: "He's a bedroom dick," one explains. Says another, "He gets information against the wife, then he makes a deal with the wife to get evidence against the husband ... thus playing both ends against the middle." Velda's job often involves seducing the husband of the wives in question. Adding insult to that injury, Hammer lewdly tells Velda that a tape he'd heard of her bedroom talk with one set-up spouse "sure was nice."

Mike's creepy behavior is entirely Bezzerides' creation. Spillane's dick doesn't do divorce work, he's just out for vengeance. The filmic Hammer may suffer a bit when his best pal is killed, but he's mostly a coldly calculating cat whose characteristic question is, "What's in it for me?" He's a malevolent bully when extracting information, as when he breaks an opera lover's prized Caruso record, or when he gleefully smashes another poor sap's fingers in a desk drawer.

Bezzerides appreciated Aldrich's work on the film, saying the director "Made some of the things I did even better." For his part, Aldrich "was very proud of the film. I think it represented a whole break for me. In terms of style, in terms of the way we tried to make it, it provided a marvelous showcase to display my own ideas of moviemaking." Aldrich uses a range of techniques to keep the story zipping along. It's hard to imagine more creative camera placements, with all sorts of low- and high-angle shots, dramatic views from the tops and bottoms of stairways, from inside bathroom cabinets, from a morgue slab's POV, canted shots of Hammer in a hospital bed, wild rides with the camera mounted on a speeding sports car.

Cinematographer Ernest Laszlo, who made 11 films with Aldrich, exploited natural light on locations that are landmarks of '50s L.A., including the Hollywood Athletic Club and the Third Street steps in Bunker Hill. Rickety tenement interiors contrast with the modernist trappings of Hammer's swank bachelor pad. The checkerboard linoleum floor and ballet barres in Velda's apartment make for more visual élan. Combine all this with Bezzerides' dialogue and you've got one wonderfully warped pack-

On the beach: Hammer and Velda (Maxine Cooper) face down atomic annihilation

age. As the always-astute critic J. Hoberman wrote, "Like one of *Mad*'s parodies, the movie unfolds in a deranged cubist space, amid the debris of Western civilization—shards of opera, deserted museums, molls who paraphrase Shakespeare, mad references to Greek mythology and the New Testament."

The actors are all fun to watch. The film's strongest women, Cooper, Leachman, and villainous pixie Gaby Rodgers, all stand up to Hammer and make an ass of him at various moments. Mercury Theatre veteran Paul Stewart (as Carl Evello) radiates suave menace, and Albert Dekker hams it up in grand style spouting Bezzerides' deranged mélange of classical and biblical allusions. Seasoned tough guys Jack Lambert and Jack Elam dish out convincing beatings before falling prey to Hammer's martial arts prowess (off screen). Percy Helton and Juano Hernandez are, as usual, great, and one-time Duke Ellington associate Madi Comfort acquits herself handily singing "I'd Rather Have the Blues" in an African-American joint (an actual bar called Club Pigale).

Like Mickey Spillane's novel, the Aldrich/Bezzerides film drew criticism in some quarters. Aldrich even made some minor cuts in response to demands for major changes from the Catholic National Legion of Decency, which ultimately gave the film a B rating (condemned in part). During the June 1955 Senate hearings on juvenile delinquency, Senator Estes Kefauver pointed to a poster for the movie and said, "These producers have told us that in all of the pictures, horror and crime and sex pictures, there is some moral they are trying to prove. I just wonder if you get the moral in this advertising up here. There is a '*Kiss Me Deadly*. White-Hot Thrills! Blood-Red Kisses!' That is all it says about it. What is moral?"

When later prompted, Aldrich said that *Kiss Me Deadly* "did have a basic significance in our political framework that we thought rather important in those McCarthy times. That the ends did not justify the means." Elsewhere, he explained that the film "at its depth, had to do with the McCarthy era ... and the kind of materialistic society that paid off in choice rewards, sometimes money, sometimes girls, sometimes other things." And in a 1955 defense of the film in the *New York Herald Tribune*, Aldrich wrote, "Just so long as the world contains two human beings who in the face of an emotional crisis desire to commit or actually resort to physical retaliation, we may expect to discover short stories, novels, plays, and movies that deal with similar experiences." He pointed out that his film's most brutal scene used screams and the suggestion of violence without actually showing the abuse on screen (a lesson for today's torture-friendly horror and action directors).

Not surprisingly for such a loopy, subversive, and frequently perverse movie, *Kiss Me Deadly* was not a big hit. The movie was shot in 22 days on a budget of $410,000. It grossed $952,000 worldwide. Perhaps in part due to its black characters not being presented as subservient to whites, theatres in many southern states refused to book it. *The New York Times* didn't deign to review it—but it was wildly popular in France where François Truffaut praised it extensively. "It was the first year of *Cahiers* [*du Cinéma*]," Aldrich recalled, "and those guys jumped on the picture like it was the second coming."

In 1999, the Library of Congress selected *Kiss Me Deadly* for preservation in the National Film Registry. It has been referenced in *Repo Man*, *Pulp Fiction*, *Southland Tales*, and many other movies. If you haven't seen it, you're in for a treat. If you have, trust me when I say that this amazing film bears multiple viewings. ■

Alan Ladd and Veronica Lake, paired for the first time in *This Gun for Hire*, would help power Paramount through the 1940s

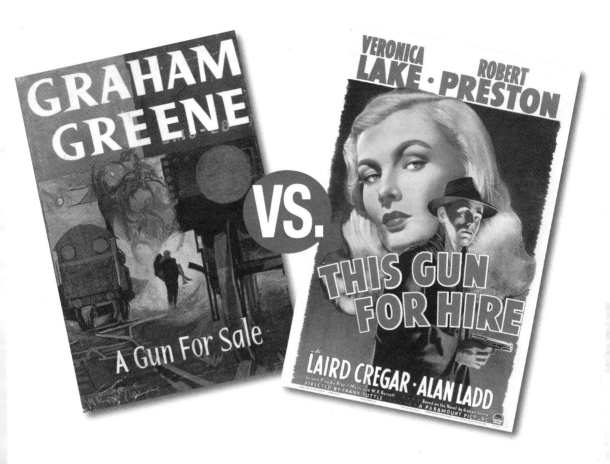

D.A. Kolodenko

In the 1936 British novel *A Gun for Sale* by celebrated writer Graham Greene, the alienated hitman Raven—whose hired assassination of a British government minister working in Eastern Europe triggers a march toward war—is haunted by his mother's having committed suicide; she slashed her throat, which he witnessed as a child.

"She didn't even lock the door," he reminds himself bitterly and constantly, even confessing it to the novel's female protagonist, Anne Crowder, as one more proof point among the many injustices and failures of humanity he catalogs to justify his murderous ways. Likewise, Raven's nemesis (and Crowder's fiancé), police detective Jimmy Mather, had similarly discovered in his childhood the body of his brother, also a suicide. The tragedy leads him to a life of order rather than crime.

These parallel deaths in the backstories of the main characters could feel like a too-obvious conceit to demonstrate how the trajectories of depressed people may be shaped differently by extreme poverty or class privilege. But consider that Greene had tried to kill himself several times when he was a young student at the boarding school in Hertfordshire, England, where his father was headmaster—once by Russian roulette; and on another occasion an attempted drowning in a swimming pool.

His lifetime of depression informs the way Greene underpins the contrived plot with deep character insights. Never mind that *A Gun for Sale* was one of the novels he categorized as an "enter-

Graham Greene separated his books into "literature" and "entertainments," although both varieties were avidly adapted to the movies

tainment" as opposed to his serious, literary novels like *The Power and the Glory* (1940), about the persecution of Catholicism in Mexico.

A Gun for Sale is entertaining enough—a suspenseful crime thriller that overcomes its reliance on Woolrichian coincidence and illogic through the sincerity of the author's compassionate investment in its characters; the quite real and serious political underpinnings; the novel's manic, dark energy, and a prose style that evokes Dostoevsky in its balance of storytelling force with social and philosophical investigation.

Greene deftly lays bare the in-the-moment minds of his characters, revealing their insecurities, desires, judgments, and self-justifications. It's breathtaking to read Greene because he deploys the third-person limited omniscient perspective so fluidly that his seamless shifts from character to character can leave you feeling you've been given a god's insight and empathy—tempered with a generous dose of cynicism.

Creating the Killer Raven

"Patriotism had lost its appeal," Greene is quoted as saying about his creation of Raven in W. J. West's biography, *A Quest for Graham Greene*. "It was difficult in the years of the depression to believe in the higher purposes of the city of London or the British Constitution." So it is that Raven, the working class antihero, is out to avenge the raw deal he's been handed by life, not to fight for his country. And, thus, the book's true villain, the greedy industrialist Sir Marcus, who betrays Raven, was based on real-life arms dealer Sir Basil Zaharoff, a "plausible villain for those days," Greene said.

The warning Greene implies—that war profiteers ought to be or are likely to be murdered by the common man—is hardly the stuff of light "entertainment." And even the machinations of the plot, according to West, were derived primarily from testimony Greene heard at a 1935 armaments conference where the question of whether to nationalize the manufacture of weapons led to the grilling of private gun manufacturers, whom Greene described as being unprepared and unforthcoming in the hearings.

One gets the feeling Greene could never have written anything as pure entertainment. After all, according to Michael G. Brennan's *Graham Greene: Political Writer*, in the year he began work on *A Gun for Sale* Greene told his brother, Hugh, that he would rather catch bubonic plague than write another novel.

Heroes and Villains

It's not just the motivation to take down the crooked munitions magnates that elevates *A Gun for Sale*. It would be one thing for the story to be an entertainment qualified with a critique of avaricious capitalism; it's not enough for Greene to show that the murder of the minister is the catalyst in Sir Marcus's plot to foment war to cash in on steel production. We need to feel the self-satisfaction and hedonism of Marcus and his lackey Willie Davis as desperate bulwarks to stave off rejection and death. We also need to experience Raven's rage at his awful upbringing and at his ugliness from a botched harelip operation, which has fostered in him a monstrous, festering resentment, leaving him a "sour, bitter, screwed-up figure." It's Greene's interest in the destructiveness of villainy to the psyche that anticipates the noir ethos.

By contrast, the courage and perseverance of the protagonist, nightclub performer Anne Crowder, and of her devoted detective boyfriend Jimmy Mather read as an unsurprising illustration of British middle-class resolve, and, as in many noirs, the heroes are more sympathetic but less interesting. But Greene sets them on different paths and exposes and thoroughly tests their doubts about each other, lending an extra layer of noir-like insecurity to the novel when they're apart. Greene shows us how easily anyone can die, how easily war can be fomented for sinister self-interest, and how easily we can lose faith in love, humanity—anything.

The Hollywood Version

A Gun for Sale might have been a different book had it been written a few years later, when post–World War I, Depression-era antiwar sentiment lost its appeal as the Nazis marched across Europe. The 1942 American movie *This Gun for Hire*, the most famous of several film adaptations of the book, illustrates not only the Hollywood-ification of the novel, but also this different "great war" context: the film transforms the industrialist into a California chemical manufacturer selling out to the imperial Japanese enemy, and Raven not only opens his heart a little to confess his mental anguish to the patriotic Anne Crowder (Ellen Graham in the film, portrayed by Veronica Lake), the only friend he ever had—he also forces confessions from the bad guys and redeems himself by helping the war effort.

The film preserves the architecture of the novel but lightens up the behavior—the backstory of his mother's suicide, for example, is replaced with an abusive aunt; Raven kills, but no longer sadistically finishes people off at point-blank range to watch their heads "shatter like a China doll." There's a greater emphasis on his redemptive behavior in the film. And Laird Cregar's Willard Gates is ridiculously weak and funny in the film, where Willie Davis in the book is a repulsive monster who tries (unsuccessfully) to murder Anne and stuff her in a fireplace. And of course, Raven's facial disfigurement in the novel is changed to a more innocuous deformity in the film to help preserve the compelling on-screen sex appeal of Alan Ladd. He and the similarly featured Veronica Lake went on to appear in six other films together.

The movie is the entertainment that the book claimed to be. The book is as serious, dark, despairing, and brilliantly written as anything of the era. And in spite of Greene's blatant anti-Semitism—Zaharoff was Greek, but his fictionalized counterpart Sir Marcus must be made Jewish—and some period-typical and equally cringe-worthy racism toward Chinese people, Greene's novel, now overshadowed by its 1942 adaptation, is better than the movie. ■